To Rachel ~
my memoir is truly a
God's love story.
Enjoy!
Cecily

Becoming the Admiral's Wife

Cecily Watson Kelln

Buy Cecily & Al's books at:
www.cecilywatsonkelln.com

Becoming
the
Admiral's Wife

A Dual Memoir of a Called Pair

Cecily Watson Kelln

XULON PRESS ELITE

Xulon Press Elite
2301 Lucien Way #415
Maitland, FL 32751
407.339.4217
www.xulonpress.com

Unless otherwise indicated, scripture quotations taken from the King
James Version (KJV)–*public domain*.

Printed in the United States of America.

PAPERBACK ISBN-13: 978-1-6305-0297-3

EBOOK ISBN-13: 978-1-6305-0298-0

A Word from the Author

❧

This book is dedicated to all my readers, especially Shirley. She got me started on writing the book and continued to be a helper and encourager over the years. She told me, "Yours is the most interesting story of somebody's life that I have ever heard. I do read a lot and listen to others tell me of their lives. I'm in my 60s! I have some stories of my own, but nothing like yours."

Shirley's reactions at an early reading.

And, to my husband, Al, who shared my vision, and whose love and patience never waned.

Note to the reader: There are no fictitious characters in my memoir, only real ones. Some, however, have been given pseudonyms.

Why am I writing this? Because I have had a complicated, blessed life that leads me to trusting God. In spite of rejection, poor choice, heartbreak, divorces, I have a victory to share that may be an encouragement to others.

I want the reader to travel the road with me. I want the reader to see how Jesus impacted my life. With Jesus, I overcame: fear, boredom, pride, self-pity, anger, betrayal, ignorance, jealousy, despair, disappointment, and confusion. I received forgiveness and forgave others.

The reader will see that it is possible to hope, love, and trust once again. I want the reader to think about dying to self, putting on "the new man" (Ephesians 4:24) in Jesus, and finding an identity based on how God sees them, which is not of this world.

Table of Contents

Prologue

My husband, Admiral Al Kelln, has played the exemplary role of Jesus to me. He has held nothing from my past against me. He has told me every day that he loves me, and, even when I have just woken up all puffy-faced, he has said I am beautiful. If I put on ten pounds, I am still beautiful. He urged me to keep going with my book and encouraged me throughout the process. I decided he was my life's prize. I felt honored to call my book "Becoming the Admiral's Wife."

Quietly, Al turned to his laptop computer and tapped out his own life story. His book was born before mine. He called it "Living the MIRACLES: a Sailor's Life in the Nuclear Power Age." I was proud to put my writing on a back burner to become his editor, to get his book published by Xulon Press, and make sure it was available online.

Excerpts of his book are sprinkled throughout the pages of this memoir.

Al's story and mine are totally different. He was a first generation offspring from Okie German-Russian immigrant farmers. Then he stayed the patriotic, unwavering military course for all his adult life. He earned his medals of merit for bravery and accomplishments. He deserved to be honored at the 2018 Naval Submarine League Symposium when he spoke as their founder.

I never knew him when he went off for months on a stealthy, untraceable submarine. I wasn't the wife who stayed behind to take care of the children and wonder how he was doing. However, years later, both of us had become single, and our two lives collided on a square dance floor in 1999 when an improbable love began.

But let me start at the beginning.

Part 1
Cackleberry Farm

Plásticos de México, Incorporado

A year and a month before I was born in January of 1943, Japanese bombers surprise attacked the United States naval base at Pearl Harbor. Multiple unsuspecting ships and aircraft were destroyed. Over two thousand Americans were killed. It was this act that drove the United States into World War II. A wave of patriotism spread across the country. Men and women left their jobs and signed up for the military in droves.

Dad was among the fervent volunteers. He had been an organizer of a small glass factory that made mirrors. Samples of his wares were all over our house. Big square mirrors covered the folding doors that divided the dining room from the front hall. A huge etched mirror faced the front stairs. In the powder room, a circular window was tiled with one-inch square mirror pieces. When I leaned my head into the circle, I could see hundreds and hundreds of images of my own face. It was magical and my sisters and I spent many childhood hours entertaining ourselves there.

For now, Dad would set the mirror work aside to join in the war effort. He appeared at the naval recruiting center in Philadelphia and returned home with a white uniform, which he proudly modeled in the back yard. Someone snapped a photo. I saw it in a family album when I was older. He was mighty handsome. "You look like Humphrey Bogart," friends had told him.

That photo, however, was as far as he got in the Navy. He received a most disappointing letter. The Navy had to reject him because he was color blind. It was true. He could not differentiate red from green. To him, both colors looked brown. The way he knew whether to stop or go at traffic lights was to decide which one was shining brighter. In his rebuttal letter, he cajoled with, "I can see things under water that others can't. I will be a benefit to the Navy." The Navy disagreed.

Nurse Peggie with baby Cecily Clay Watson.

I was a baby then but I heard these stories later in my life at cocktail time—which was after five o'clock coffee (which we affectionately called "fivesies") and before supper.

Since I was the fourth child, Dad hired a live-in nursemaid to change and rock me after Mom finished nursing me. That freed Mom up to follow after the other three in our very big house, especially Marion, who was only two. The boys were five and seven. They were a handful too but they already went to school. Mom, in her own humility, attributed my "good-natured character" to nursemaid Peggie's divine touch.

In my first two years, Dad's business circles led him to play around with a budding new product called *plastic*. It was a chemically concocted material that would hold his fascination and engineering ingenuity for many years of his working life. Whether creating flat or corrugated sheets, molded forms, or reinforcing the plastic resins with woven fiberglass, Dad's wings as an inventor and industrial designer took flight.

Things had ramped up overseas and the horrors of war filled the pages of the *Philadelphia Inquirer* and the *Evening Bulletin*. Dad and Mom noticed new commodities were continually added to the list of rationing. Dad seized an opportunity to escape all the belt-tightening and teeth clenching of the War and move the family to Mexico City to start a company called Plásticos de México, Incorporado.

Dad went to Mexico City first and found us a nice house in the suburbs, near a deep ravine (where my brothers later told me the robbers who had stolen Dad's clarinet lived). Mom booked several connecting puddle-jumper flights and bravely flew down to Mexico with four little children. My parents had rented out our house.

Upon arrival in Mexico, Mom surprised Dad with the news that baby number five was on its way. In March of 1946, we kids were blessed with a baby sister.

"¿Cómo se llama la bebita?" the curious neighbors asked.

"Dorothy," Mom told them. She was named after Mom.

"¡Ah, Dorotea!" they said in translation. Already they were expressing endearment towards the little black-haired baby. Then the beloved little Dorothy became known as "Dorita." Back in the States, the family settled with the final diminutive name of Dita, which she kept.

My brothers, Bruce and Bob, learned Spanish by total immersion in the local Mexican elementary school. They made close, lasting friendships with neighborhood kids. I had my third birthday there, and as young as I was, I returned with memory flashes of things like getting lost under my covers, of watching our maid Eusabia walk on her bare heels across the wet kitchen floor, and of collecting snails from deep within the yucca plants with Marion.

I had a close call with death when my fever raged out of control with a serious case of pneumonia. Mom recalled that when she placed me next to her in bed, I felt like hot bricks. My breathing was labored. She feared I was dying. "No wonder," she would recount. "God was coming for His little angel." Fortunately for me, (and maybe this is why we were there) Mexican doctors were experimenting with a new medicine that was not yet accepted in the States. It was called penicillin. And it worked.

In the year we were away, the War had ended. Dad brought all of us back to the big house on Roberts Road in Bryn Mawr. Apparently, Mexico was not ready for Dad's avant-garde product. Plásticos de México ceased to exist after we left. The word "sabotage" floated through dinnertime conversation, and I never caught the details on that particular piece of Dad's string of business disappointments.

Chef Boyardee Bonks the Cozy Club President

Childhood began full swing in the early 1950s once I turned seven and we were all old enough to scatter and play independently of Mom or Dad. With very few rules, we explored all the nooks and crannies of our house, finding the most fascinating places to disappear during hide-and-seek. There was always someone to play with. At times we were daring. We climbed high in the crab apple tree. We hung from the second floor bannisters. We straddled the joists in the high attic, even in the darkened wings, where a misstep onto the open insulation could cause our foot to appear in the room below.

One time, we even climbed onto the roof of a high dormer. Now, there wasn't much that shocked Dad but when he heard of this, he clearly was not happy. He met us face on with a firm, soft-spoken though emphatic disapproval. That, accompanied by his good reasons why we were to stay off the high roof, created a "rule" within us—*Do NOT climb on the high roofs*—a directive we respected from then on. The truth for me was that I liked <u>finally</u> getting a boundary. And I liked that it was from Dad.

It is not that I was always a tomboy. My favorite past-time was playing with baby dolls. Part of the high attic had floorboards where we positioned several years of birthday and Christmas gifts, such as dolls and dolly clothes, cribs and cradles, miniature kitchen, the whole works. Dita and our neighbor girlfriend Beau were just as enthusiastic to play dolls as I was. Our cousin Nancy, who lived up the hill, joined us too. Whenever

5

we pulled on the rope of the trap door on the upstairs hall ceiling and let down the stairs to the high attic, we were gone into the blissful world of make believe. For hours on end, we were serious mothers taking good care of our babies.

"Hey, let's go out to Dad's work shop and have a meeting of the Cozy Club," I suggested when it was time for a change of scene. The Cozy Club for girls met fairly often for a few years. It sprang from our imaginations, and acquired its own form of government. We took turns holding the various positions of President, Vice-President, Best Boy, and Messenger, though since I was the oldest in the Club, I usually played President. The Best Boy got to sit up high in the most comfortable seat, like on a stack of tires. The Messenger ran to the house for scissors and scotch tape. The Vice-President got to choose when we would sing "Lily Pads in the Water—Splash, Splash, Splash." The President decided the agenda for each meeting. I didn't always know what we should do but someone always came up with a good idea.

Sometimes we would meet in the old wartime chicken coop up the hill at Uncle Ross's. This weathered fifty-foot structure no longer had chickens. One half was now used for lawn mowers and tools, and the fenced area had become a kennel for Uncle Ross's duck hunting dogs.

The Watson properties sat on the red clay soil of the geological Radnor Fault. The soil was a frustration to persistent gardeners like Mom, who described the outcomes of her growing season as "pitiful." But, to the Cozy Club, the soil produced a most valuable asset called mica, little thumb-sized mineral flakes that glittered. We collected mica and stored it in piles in the egg laying bins, which we called our bank. It was our medium of exchange. The more we had, the wealthier we became as members of the Club. We never did find a market to exchange goods and services with it, so the piles sat there and got dusty.

Nearby, was the fabulous mud ball place. It was a burrow into the hill along Roberts Road under the protruding root entanglement of a black walnut tree. A couple of us were able to fit into this dirt cave. One of the roots was horizontal with a natural trough the length of it—perfect for lining up the mud balls side by side. The question presented was, should we wait half an hour for the next car to drive down the road so we could throw a mud ball at it, or were we actually running a bakery and creating a supply of little cupcakes?

The meeting had been long and fun. The sun was casting longer shadows from the trees. Soon Mom would be out on the circular driveway at the sycamore tree sounding the loud clang of the "time-to-come-home" bell. The Cozy Club formed a circle and held hands to sing its end of session song, which I had made up: "Now we close our meeting, our meeting, our meeting. Now we close our meeting. Good bye, good bye to all." Then we ended in unison with a cheer, raising our hands and saying happily, "Good bye, Cozy Club!"

Filled with the pomp of leadership all afternoon, I was about to be put in my place.

It happened to be Mom and Dad's night out to rehearse for the Parent/Teachers' Association annual show called the Rosemont Rollicks. Dad was directing a skit he had written, and Mom was dancing the can-can in a chorus line. The creamed chicken, rice, and green peas were all steaming nicely in their various pots and pans. Bobby, hovering over the stove with a serving spoon, had been assigned the job of dishing up supper for the five of us kids.

"I'm not eating that!" I announced emphatically, as I dragged a chair to the high food shelf, climbed up, and pulled down a can of Chef Boyardee ravioli. "I'm having ravioli."

"Oh no you're not!" Bobby said with fury, his steely blue eyes glaring at me. No insolent little sister was going to destroy the success of his honored kitchen duty.

"Yes, I am! I don't want..." And before I could finish my sentence, we struggled and Bobby got hold of the can. Still, I was determined a hundred percent that I would eat ravioli. It was my favorite in those days, and I figured since Mom was out, I could choose whatever I wanted to eat. But it was obviously a no-win situation for me. I just couldn't get the can away from him. We both grunted and turned red-faced, bending towards the floor like two wrestlers. Before I could resort to biting or scratching, Bobby raised his arm and used the can for a crowning blow to my head.

This was a blow that continued to hurt at the very thought of it. Yes. Once I had stopped crying, with sad and pitiful eyes and a stomach all in knots, I ate what Bobby served me, the dinner that Mom had so lovingly fixed. The egg on my head was so large it startled even Bobby. From that day on, the only physical inflictions I got from him were occasional knuckle noogies to my upper arm.

*M*y name is Albert Kelln. I was born in the small town of Shattuck, Oklahoma, on 17 December 1929. That area of the United States was buffalo grass country and the area where the real Indians lived. I was the youngest of my father's five children. A few months before I was born, the United States economy was devastated and suddenly most jobs disappeared. My father David, who was a very successful rancher raising cattle, was unable to pay the land mortgage payments and was only allowed to keep his house in Shattuck. We and most other families were utterly broke and poor.

Concurrently, with the demise of the U.S. economy, a terrible severe years-long drought occurred in the Midwest. No crops could be grown. The wind kicked up "dust storms" which lasted for several days at a time. We couldn't go outside of our homes, as the air was filled with unhealthy dust and the visibility was zero. The people provided some food by raising chickens in their backyards and growing vegetables in small gardens, if they had water.

Al and his Father in Oklahoma.

The International Harvester

My dad had an affinity for unusual cars. To him, they were like borrowed pets. He never discussed his thoughts or plans. He would just appear at the driveway with his next trophy. They would leave as suddenly as they came. Boom. Here was a horse drawn fire engine with a brass smokestack. We were allowed to climb on it and play fireman. He got us old firemen's hats. We took photos. Neighborhood children stopped by to climb on it. Then, poof. It was gone. In its place was a genuine Conestoga wagon with its sloped wooden sides and drab canvas covering. It was parked near the crab apple tree, which was bearing rock-hard little apples. Once the word got out, the boy cousins up the hill, and the neighbors down the hill joined Bobby and Bruce for a knock-down, drag-out cowboy shoot out. The boys jumped in and out of the wagon. Crab apples flew everywhere and hurt when they hit. I ducked into the tool shed and watched from a distance. It was a good thing they enjoyed it while they could, because the next thing we knew, the wagon was gone.

A shiny black 1930s Pierce Arrow limousine took its place. Dad built a special carport where it could sit protected from the weather. He never drove it. We were never invited to sit in it. Dad's buddies came over to gawk at it and remark on the abundance of chrome and the leather seats. Mom seemed detached about it. Pretty soon, a dealer man came by, talked to Dad, then it disappeared. A beautiful forest green Jaguar touring car took its place. This time, Dad did take it out for spins but again a dealer took it off Dad's hands.

The one purchase that came and stayed was a 1910 International Harvester farm wagon with huge wooden-spoked wheels with non-inflated rubber tread. It was the original pick up truck. Dad poured his heart into knowing and fixing everything that made this baby go. He took his time, and we all got to see the innards when he had it apart. We saw the big chain and gears that caused the wheels to turn. Dad twiddled this and toggled that. When all was reassembled, he filled it with gas, went around to the front, stuck a big crank into the base of the radiator, and flexed his muscles hard as he turned the crank with both arms.

The "International," as we called it, came to life with the rhythmic sputter of its early combustion engine, emitting a sound that would come to be a clarion call to anyone nearby. It meant that Bob Watson was going out for a spin, and you'd better run and hop on if you wanted to go along. Dad had fashioned two bench seats for the truck bed, creating the rider capacity of an open station wagon. He shined up the brass transmission rod by the driver's left hip and the brass gas and choke levers under the wooden steering wheel. He bought handsome kerosene lanterns for the buckboard and painted the seats bright red. Mom wore a big straw hat secured with a flowered scarf to protect herself from the windy, sunny rides along Darby-Paoli Road. There were outings to Skunk Hollow to collect acorns, to Veldes Store in Newtown Square for thick ice cream sandwiches, and to Ardrossan Dairy Farm to see their Guernsey cows and their kennels of beagle dogs.

Coming back home up steep Roberts Road to our house, the International strained almost to a halt. At the perfect moment, Dad would tell me to step on the "Go-Getter," an iron spike that protruded from the wooden floorboard near his right foot. Amazing to me, the engine would receive a new burst of louder power and get us up the hill to our driveway. The final touch was a genius inspiration on Dad's part. He took out a fine paint brush and wrote in block letters "CACKLEBERRY FARM" on the outsides of the middle seat. All at once, our family of seven had a name for our seven-acres homestead.

The Watson family in the Cackleberry Farm International Harvester.

The name "Cackleberry" caught on instantly and became synonymous with endearment, family, love, and security—not just to the seven of us, but scores of people for whom the mere mention of Cackleberry would continue to bring warmth to their souls.

At Cackleberry, I raised a Woolworth's 5-&-10 Easter chick until she became a genuine egg-laying hen. She was my pride and joy for years. Her coop was up in the drying yard, yet mostly she roamed free around our seven acres. I named her Angostina. For some reason I called her Nocken. Dad loved her too. At Christmastime, he tied a red ribbon around her neck and let her loose in the house. He built a shelf on the sill outside our kitchen window. On frigid winter mornings, he pushed puffed wheat cereal, one at a time, through a hole he had drilled in the window frame. Nocken gobbled each one up appreciatively. I loved Dad for doing that.

Thanksgiving at Granny's

We never ate out in restaurants. Eating out as a family happened on the holidays at another home. There were Easter dinners at Aunt Nornie's and Halloween cookouts at the Treats' barn nearby. Granny always had us to her house for Thanksgiving dinner. We piled in the car and sang, "Over the river and through the woods to Grandmother's house we go. The horse knows the way to carry the sleigh through white and drifting snow-oh!" And Mom finished the song with, "Hurrah for the fun. Is the pudding done? Hoorah for the pumpkin pie!" The gleeful three-mile drive took us over sloping hills, past grey-walled estates and under tall bare-limbed trees.

Ellie always met us warmly at the door by the kitchen, drying her hands on her apron. She greeted us by name in her Irish accent and was obviously glad to see us. Her eyes sparkled. Her smile was catching. She had worked for Granny for years, even cooking and cleaning for her at the "Sand Box" beach house in Stone Harbor, New Jersey, every summer.

Granny once told me she needed Ellie because she had never learned to cook, not even so much as to boil an egg. The Irish maids of her childhood bore all housekeeping responsibilities without imparting any skills to the budding socialite. When we visited Granny at the shore, Ellie's soup and grilled cheese sandwiches provided a nourishing respite after spending hours on the hot sand and in the pounding waves two blocks away. At the "Sand Box," Ellie washed Granny's nylon panties by hand and emptied her nighttime chamber pot. She rested in her own upstairs bedroom while

Granny played Scrabble with us in the screened porch with its delicious salt air and sea breezes.

This Thanksgiving evening, Granny hobbled with sore knees to her accustomed arm chair where she would cheerily receive all the arriving Watson family: her two sons Ross and Bob, their wives Ann and Dottie, and their combined nine children, including the five of us, and my four cousins Ross, Rowley, George and Nancy.

Granny was a generous and regal woman. Her father was the founder and first Director of the Philadelphia Museum of Art, and helped fund the start of Philadelphia's Public Library. She grew up in the city with her parents and two sisters. Her hand-written journals bespoke a carefree young life of social teas, plays, balls, church, ice skating for miles on the frozen Schuylkill River, and interim days of sleeping in. Despite an embarrassing divorce from a philandering first husband (my grandfather Watson), then a remarriage, and widowhood, Granny could throw her head back and laugh with the best of them at her own self-amusing jokes.

On scheduled weekdays, Mr. Watkins chauffeured her from Bryn Mawr to the Acorn Club where she had dinner, then to the Academy of Music, for her season seat at the opera or the symphony with Eugene Ormandy conducting the Philadelphia Orchestra. On two separate occasions, Granny invited me to come along. Even though my evening gown was zipped too tight, I sank back into my cherry velvet box seat by the brass rail. Every penetrating note and chord touched my soul. To think I was the one chosen out of all nine of her grandchildren to sit next to my venerable Granny at the opera.

I found it fascinating that Granny still volunteered for the hospital thrift shop and had once worn pants and tall leather boots on big game hunting trips with each of her husbands.

Granny dinged her knife against her glass making a ringing sound once we were all seated. She invited us to bow our heads while she blessed the meal with the traditional Episcopalian prayer: "Bless, O Lord, this food to our use, and us to thy loving service. And make us ever mindful of the needs of others, in Jesus' Name."

"Amen," some of us chimed.

Mr. Watkins, with his high cheekbones and balding black head, was dressed in his finest Thanksgiving blue suit and bow tie, grateful for his annual butler job for Mrs. George H. Stuart 3rd. He cleared off the mahogany lowboy to make space for the twenty-pound roasted turkey he would be carving there. Highly polished silver serving sets shone. Flowered porcelain dishes sat ready to be laden with peas, mashed or sweet potatoes, and giblet gravy. He leaned down respectfully to serve each of us sitting side by side at the lace-covered table.

Uncle Ross addressed him as merely "Watkins." I couldn't understand that. It sounded rude to me. I was embarrassed.

"*He's MISTER Watkins, Uncle Ross!*" I would think. After all, he was Teddy's father and we went to school together.

George dropped peas into my crystal stemmed goblet of milk.

"Georrrge!" I whined in a singsong way, inwardly pleased with his attention. His nostrils flared as he chuckled with mischievous delight. I loved his dimples. We were only four weeks apart and he was like a brother to me. The evening was now complete.

The nine Watson cousins with Granny at Thanksgiving.

Mrs. Stradley's Carol Sing

At Christmastime, our neighbor, Mrs. Stradley, Mom's best friend, invited several families in the community to gather at her family's colonial farmhouse for a sumptuous buffet, followed by her annual Christmas carol sing. Our uphill cousins were there, as were many other neighbors. Everyone was dressed in their Sunday best, the little girls with patent leather Mary Jane shoes and red or black velvet skirts. Everyone crowded into the living room with its low beamed ceiling, and sat on sofas, chairs, or on the floor in front of the walk-in cooking fireplace.

Accompanied by piano, we sang all the familiar carols. The young men with singing voices (Bruce, or my cousins Rowley, Ross, or George) vied for who would be chosen to sing the roles of the three kings, the ones who were "bearing gifts" and had "traversed afar."

"Bruce, you lead off as the wise man who brings gold," Mrs. Stradley directed. Her sister's hands were perched on the keys ready to begin. Bruce's verse said the gold was for a crown for the baby Jesus, who would become the King to reign over us forever. "Gold I bring to crown Him again. King forever, ceasing never, Over us all to reign." *Beautiful and regal!* I thought. Just like my picture books where the wise man walked straight-backed, holding the gold outstretched as he approached the manger. My Sunday school teacher had explained they were guided by a prophetic star. And Bruce sang it in perfect pitch and rhythm! No wonder. He was in school chorus.

Rowley was assigned the verse about the wise man who brought frankincense. *What is frankincense?* I wondered. The verse explained it as an incense for all mankind to raise up the deity of Jesus. "Incense owns a deity nigh." So maybe the frankincense was symbolic that God was nearby. The carol continued to describe that the traveling wise men prayed and "worshipped Him" as "God on high." My young girl heart was in awe. This indeed was something greater than Rudolph the Red-nosed Reindeer.

George had to ruin things by singing about the wise man bringing myrrh, a "bitter perfume" that "breathes a life of gathering gloom." "Sorrowing, sighing, bleeding, dying—sealed in the stone-cold tomb," he sang. It made me feel sad. Here we were celebrating the birth of the baby Jesus with such love and joy and cuteness, then we had to go and be reminded of how Jesus died on the cross and was placed in a tomb.

I didn't hold it against George. His voice carried the tune just fine and it sure sounded impressive. I was proud of him. But why did Jesus, my beloved Jesus, the one whose name I counted over and over in the pages of the Episcopalian Book of Common Prayer, have to go through such sorrow and agony?

My young mind cycled quickly to remember that Easter was coming again, as it did every year, and we would be rejoicing with Aunt Nornie and my other cousins that Jesus rose from the dead, so I shouldn't worry. I was being groomed to understand and conclude that this life has its highs and lows, its victories and defeats, its beginnings and its ends. And its surprises. Death was not the end for Jesus.

One Christmas

Christmas Day was coming soon and I would be getting lots of presents wrapped by Mom. Our tradition was to all gather at the top of the stairs to wait for Mom. When she was ready, we sang "Happy Birthday" to Jesus, then went downstairs in our PJs to the living room by the Christmas tree to open our gifts. Afterwards, we had a big breakfast.

One year when I was eight, Dad had an unusual surprise for us. He had closed the folding mirrored doors to the dining room, which in itself was a new sight. When we three girls were at a peak of curiosity as to what he was hiding, he opened the doors to reveal a bright red playground slide. It stood where the dining room table normally was and towered to the ceiling. It had a steep, stainless steel surface, and sturdy handles for climbing up the ladder. We were astounded at the great surprise. How was it that Mom would agree to the disruption of the formal dining room, and that Dad could fit that huge apparatus inside the house, and furthermore, that they pulled it off without any of us knowing?

Dad was visibly proud of himself. He looked out the window and pointed his finger towards the bleak frosted reaches of the back yard. "That's where we'll put it," he said.

Later that morning, when all the other gifts had been opened and our parents were lingering over coffee in the kitchen, Marion and I got permission to try out the sliding board. By now we were in our play clothes. We started out gingerly, not wanting to create a full-fledged indoor playground. Our neighbor, Marcy, had stopped by with her parents and decided to join us. After three turns each, we wondered if we would descend faster if we only had underpants on, so we took off our outer pants. It didn't help because our skin stuck to the metal and slowed us down even more.

"Oh, I have an idea," I offered, as I eyed the back yard hose, and pictured us running under the sprinkler on a summer day. "Let's pour water down the slide and we won't stick anymore." Loving the suggestion, Marion returned with a bucket from the tool shed and we filled it with water from the spigot in the garage.

"We're gonna get our shirts wet," Marcy warned. "Let's take them off." So we did, flinging them carelessly onto the heirloom chairs that were lining the room on this different kind of Christmas morning. Totally eager, I climbed up the ladder and sat at the top of the slide. Marion followed me up and poured water under me. I took off. It worked! I went down like a bullet. What a thrill!

"I want to try it," Marion shrieked, sharing my excitement. So I poured water for her and she, too, shot down the slide.

"Whoa!" Marcy said, pointing to the puddle on the Persian rug at the foot of the slide. "Look what we did!"

"We need towels!" I pronounced. I took off for the upstairs linen closet and grabbed a pile of the neatly folded towels that our maid Doris had expertly stowed. No problem, I thought as I stacked towels on the soaked carpet. Marcy took other towels and spread them out to catch any water that might slosh off the sides. Marion refilled the bucket.

Marcy was now ready for her turn. I tipped the bucket for her and the water was so heavy that it all came out at once. She squealed with delight as she sped down the incline. Yes! The more water, the faster the ride.

Just when we were catching the hang of true fun, the door opened from the kitchen. Mom came first, and her mouth opened wide while her hand muffled whatever sound she was able to emit. Dad and Mr. and Mrs. Rymer piled behind her, peering into the dining room to see what was going on.

Instantly, our childhood spree with its delightful recklessness came to a screeching halt. We looked at the adults, and then at our half-naked eight- and ten-year-old bodies, racing to put on our shirts. Only then did we notice the disarray around us and how we had sopped the Persian rug of the formal dining room.

Mr. Rymer ordered Marcy to put her trousers on over her wet underpants. I watched as they grabbed her coat, yanked her by the arm, and fled out the front door. Mrs. Rymer poked her head back in to shout, "I'm so sorry, Dottie Dear!" I could tell that Marcy was going to get a severe comeuppance. Maybe even a whipping! After all, she deserved it.

Come to think of it, so did I!

Guilt! I didn't know how to express it, nor how to get rid of it. It was rightfully there, welling up inside me and wanting to bubble over. Dad had given me a good gift and I had misused it. I didn't know how to tell him or Mom I was sorry. I, too, wanted to be yanked by my arm somewhere to be scolded and spanked. Whop! Another whop. Those wordless whacks of understanding, of recognition, of correction. A wrong act was now in the past. A fresh start was being ushered in.

I wanted to be able to look my parents in the eye and cry and acknowledge that I had been careless and thoughtless at their expense, just so I could have fun. I knew they loved me but I wanted to hear if they STILL loved me. And I wanted them to know that I still loved them. I needed to be hugged and to give them hugs. I guess if I really wanted a spanking, I would have to go see Mr. Rymer. Mom and Dad were not the spanking type.

Instead, Mom internalized any disapproval of us. She seemed more upset about her abused room and towels than her unruly children. She kind of scolded Dad whose idea it was to place the slide in the dining room in the first place, and set about gathering up the towels.

She had him and my brothers take the heavy new toy out in the cold. There it was to sit until the change of seasons brought the warmer weather, and my heart was ready to climb up again, which I did, though never with that former abandon, and always with my shirt on.

*T*he Kelln early history starts with the mention of a royal Knight Collinge, who lived in the northwest portion of Germany. We have his coat of arms dated way back to the early year of 1259. That is a long time ago. These people lived by the North Sea and were farmers, hunters, and fishermen. They were very hardy people as they lived in a cold part of Germany.

In the late 1700s, there was a Queen of Russia, Catherine, who was of German royal birth. In Russia there was much land that needed development near the Volga River. She invited her German countrymen to move many hundreds of miles to the Volga, to settle there and raise food and build cities and roads in exchange for the settlers having autonomy in their villages. They would not have to pay taxes nor be drafted into the army for 100 years.

But, around 1880, there was a change of leadership in Russia and the rebels attacked the German villages. Consequently, many families left and moved to the United States, Canada, Argentina and Australia. My father's parents moved to the raw grasslands of Kansas and again became wheat farmers. My father became a cowboy and worked as far south as Mexico. Around 1900, there were several land openings in the Indian Territory of Oklahoma. Most of the Kelln immigrants moved to Oklahoma and claimed their homesteads. They sometimes lived in dirt houses dug into the side of a hill, which is how my mother lived as a child. Times were hard. But they never gave up, and they were able to break up the grasslands to create farms and raise families.

"The Japs are Coming!"

The school bus stopped for us way down the long hill at the south end of our seven acres, on Darby-Paoli Road. Invariably, we (the Robert Watsons) and the four Ross Watson cousins up the hill were late for the bus. So our driver, who we affectionately called "Sam, Sam, the Bus Driver Man," would lay on his horn as he barreled down Bryn Mawr Avenue to give us a heads-up that he was on his way. At Christmas, Mom had each of us wrap a gift for Sam, as a token of our appreciation for his concern for us.

In kindergarten, in 1947, I learned the unpleasant truth that enemies in a faraway war had the potential to bomb even the sanctuary of my classroom inside a sturdy brick building. Miss Biddle taught our class to hide under our desks for what she called an air raid drill. When we got older, we went to the basement of the school and stood flat against the wall. An ominous warning horn suddenly protruded from the telephone pole at the top of Roberts Road. For several years, whenever I or my friends heard a siren we would flinch and warn, "The Japs are coming!" as we covered our heads in our arms and listened for the droning sound of airplanes approaching, which we never did hear.

The fear such exercises engendered was counter-balanced by the patriotic Pledge of Allegiance to the flag of the United States of America, and by carefree songs Mrs. Duffy led at school assembly, like "Finiculi-Finicula" and "Welcome Sweet Springtime," and the daily comfort of a classmate reading from the Bible in homeroom. We also took solace that our country's military force was strong and ready to protect us.

At outdoor recess, Susan, Bette, Lynn and I galloped freely down the hill tethered to one another with a string of jump ropes as if we were wild horses escaping potential captivity.

*I*n spite of the inferior World War II high school education I received—all of our good teachers were in the war effort and only aged retired teachers were left for us—I excelled at the Naval Academy, except in foreign language. I had no high school language training but I was placed in a German class where I learned to read and write German from a dictionary. I only knew the spoken language up to the age of five, when my parents stopped speaking German at home. While my classmates were enjoying weekend social life, I had to study on Saturdays to keep up and make good grades. Since my pay as a Midshipman started at three dollars and grew to nine dollars a month as a senior, I had no money for a social life anyway, and probably attended only six to ten social events in four years. I never regretted a minute of the effort I had to expend. All was repaid to me later on in my career.

And I remember getting five demerits in Plebe summer, during our indoctrination period. So I decided that I had enough of that, and worked hard so that I received no demerits for the next four years. Consequently, I graduated first in my class in CONDUCT, which made me feel real good, as I was competing against many prep school and fleet-input Midshipmen. This attitude of discipline was to be a hallmark of my career, as you will see in later chapters.

Al as a midshipman at the US Naval Academy.

Hurl down the Hall

One day in second grade, I was afraid to tell my teacher that I was feeling sick to my stomach. The class was focused on a reading session and I didn't want to interrupt. The teacher had an enlarged poster version of our Dick and Jane reading book propped up on an easel and was leading us through the story. Recess was coming up in five minutes. But, vomit doesn't wait for anybody, not even shy little Cecily.

What happened next was literally an out-of-the-body experience. It wasn't ME running alone down the hall, around the corner past the front office, heaving splats of white vomit every twenty feet till I got to the girls' room. Out of breath, I looked in the mirror, surprised to see that the reflection was actually me, little Cecily Clay Watson. My red plaid dress was wet. I was stinky. *What should I do? No one should see me. No one could possibly love me.* My life was over.

The next thing I knew, my teacher, Mrs. Letzkus, was in the bathroom, helping me wash my hands. She dried them lovingly with a paper towel and dabbed my dress. She took me to the office. With comforting words she told me they had called for a ride and I would be going home. A nice secretary gave me a chair to sit on while I waited.

To my horror, it was not Mom pulling up to the front of the school, but our longtime cleaning lady, Doris, in her own grey Desoto, the one she always parked at the far side of the driveway circle out of obstruction's way for the milk or bread delivery truck or the bevy of ladies' cars from Mom's weekly prayer group. Never had I entered Doris's personal life. Even though she was like family in our home, she was not the comfort of

Mom that I needed. Having her as another person to know about my most embarrassing performance only added to my humiliation.

I sat in the back seat. As we rode home, I realized I now felt fine. In fact, the purge caused me to feel even better than usual. Maybe I should have just changed my clothes and stayed in school. But no. Doris made me take a bath, change into my pajamas, and take to bed! Inside, I was fuming. *She's going way overboard*, I thought.

"But, Doris," I pleaded, "I feel fine! I don't need to go to bed!"

"You've been sick, Cecily. Your body needs to rest now. You can talk to your mother about it when she gets home."

When Mom did get home and Doris had left for the day, I felt released from prison. I was allowed to get up and put on play clothes. Mom wrapped her arms around me and held me close. I melted into the comfort of her touch and told her about how it all happened and how Doris had overreacted.

"She was mean to me," I complained.

"I'm sorry you had such a horrid time at school today, my Cecy," she said. "And I'm sorry I wasn't home to get the school's phone call. You know I would have picked you up right away. But I'm glad Doris was there to get you. She wanted to take good care of you."

"But she made me go to bed in pajamas," I reiterated.

"Don't think Doris was being mean to you, Cecy. She did the best she knew how. You see, her husband died a long time ago and she never had children of her own. She did me a big favor to pick you up in her own car."

Wow. I had never known that about Doris. I hadn't even thanked her for the ride home. Slowly, the humiliation I felt was turning to gratitude for the love and care I had gotten, not only from Mom and Doris, but also from my teacher, Mrs. Letzkus, and the office secretary. My life was not over after all. I was able to carry on. I skipped off to play, loving my Mom and feeling very loved.

Mrs. Duffy's Scarf

In third grade, Mom showed me how to knit. We went upstairs to the wool closet where she kept her fur coats, mink stoles, and woolens in moth balls. She opened a leather trunk containing leftover yarns of various colors. I chose yellow. We sat down on the top step. She held a set of knitting needles and cast a row of stitches on one of them. Following her instruction, I was able to maneuver the second needle into each stitch, one at a time. Slowly I knitted my way across the row. She turned the needles and got me going back the other way for the second row.

"You can make a winter scarf," she suggested. "You're well on your way."

Immediately, I knew the scarf would be for Mrs. Duffy, my third grade teacher, who had also taught Bruce, Bobby, and Marion when they were in third grade, although Bobby's year was interrupted when we left for Mexico. Bobby had brought back a brightly painted piggy bank for her and it still stood proudly on her file cabinet in the classroom. It was apparent she had a special affection for the Watson family.

I liked how Mrs. Duffy's gold wrist bangles jangled with glee when she waved her right hand in the air to the beat of the music while leading the whole student body in song. She was going to be so happy with the scarf I was making her. I could just see her coming proudly into the front door of the school on a cold winter's morning with the scarf wrapped around her neck and tucked into her coat lapel.

Winter weather arrived quickly. Snow came and I dared toboggan down our steep hill, though I thought the sleds were more fun. Earles Lake froze up and so did Darby Creek. Mom fitted us all with ice skates.

Neighbors came out to the ice too. We each learned to skate in our unique ways.

Back in the house, I came across my knitting project. I had run out of yellow yarn when the so-called scarf was only five inches long. Having been discouraged, I had put it away. Now I took it downstairs to show Mom.

"Can you help me take this off the needle, Mom?" I asked. Then I explained, "There wasn't enough yarn for Mrs. Duffy's scarf. So instead, I'll give it to you, if you need a tiny potholder."

"Oh, Sweetheart!" she responded. "You poor thing. You didn't have to stop there. You can continue with a different color and make it a beautiful striped scarf. Go on up to the wool closet and choose another yarn. I'll show you how to tie it onto the yellow so you can keep going."

"Okay!" I said, as I ran fast up the stairs. A clump of rainbow yarn caught my eye. It was made with all the primary colors dyed one after the other with no knots in between.

Knitting with that yarn was great fun. My project grew at least twelve inches before that whole clump had been used. Mom helped me attach a thicker wine-colored woolen yarn which was a little harder to work with, until I changed to smaller needles. Next I chose a vivid fuchsia, followed by lime green, mustard and turquoise.

Several weeks had gone by. The snows had melted and Earles Lake was no longer frozen.

Mom put our skates away. Mittens went back into the mitten drawers above each of our lockers that Daddy had built in the powder room. Marion made a comment that I probably would have Mrs. Edwards in fourth grade, like she had that year.

Uh-oh! I thought. *Winter is almost over. I need to finish the scarf and give it to Mrs. Duffy.* I pulled it out of my bottom bureau drawer and held it up. It was still attached to a knitting needle. It was about three and a half feet long.

I was startled. It was atrocious. The colors didn't match. The edges were curvy where I had either added or subtracted stitches. There were two holes where I had dropped a stitch without realizing it. The thick wine-colored stripe felt itchy. Some sections were knitted so tight, it was hard to wrap around my neck.

I felt ashamed of my work. As much as I wanted to surprise my special teacher, I just couldn't bring myself to offer her something so unattractive. I put it back in my bottom drawer and forgot about it for years. Mom must have forgotten about it too because she never mentioned it.

Then one day in seventh grade, when I had moved to the high school building, I got word that Mrs. Duffy was retiring from teaching. This was her last year in that same third grade classroom. Winter was coming. She had taught all five of us Watsons and we all loved her. She deserved a special retirement gift.

Without skipping a beat, I thought of Mrs. Duffy's scarf. I pulled it out and performed the finishing stitch that released it from the needle. I was old enough to see it as laughable, perhaps something made for a clown. But I was also mature enough to recognize that every single stitch was made with loving, sincere, and innocent hands. She should have this scarf as a token of her decades of dedication to children like me. She could keep it in her bureau drawer and pull it out from time to time to have a good laugh with her friends.

I wrapped it up with pretty gift paper.

Mom gave me a ride to Rosemont Elementary School and waited in the car while I went into the third grade classroom. Mrs. Duffy was energetically erasing spelling words from the charcoal grey chalkboard. She saw me and gave me a warm hug, remarking about how grown up I looked. I handed her the gift box and she opened it in front of me. Tears welled in her eyes as she pulled out the scarf from the tissue paper. She hugged me again, hard. It felt funny to be as tall as she was.

"I started making it for you back when I was in third grade," I explained. "I'm sorry it took me until seventh grade to finish it. I'm still not very good at knitting."

"Don't you worry, Little Miss Watson," she said. "You made it with love. All I can say is thank you. I will always treasure this scarf."

I left her, still embarrassed, thinking she was just being polite.

Years later, I was driving down Lancaster Avenue when I spotted an aged Mrs. Duffy in a winter coat heading into the Acme grocery store. Around her neck was something multi-colored and very familiar to me. She was wearing the one-and-only Mrs. Duffy's Scarf.

It had taken me five years to gain the confidence to finish and deliver what I considered an inferior object. Seeing her now taught me that I could make someone happy with efforts motivated by love, even if the result seemed imperfect. It came to her at the perfect timing, the winter of her life. She wore a tapestry of color as diverse as the children she taught. The scarf boasted of the continuity of her teaching career. She was like the thread that endured in the hearts and minds of the ones, like me, whom she had touched.

Cecily skating at Earles Lake.

Fourth through Sixth

In the fourth grade, I started ballet class at Miss Baynor's studio in Garrett Hill across the road from school. A nine-year-old can feel so very grown up dressed in black ballet shoes and a brightly colored skirt, striking a tambourine and twirling in a gypsy number in the recital. Oh, and then the pink shoes, tights, and tutu for the "Waltz of the Flowers"! I learned first position, second, and third, with my arms so graceful and my feet placed just so. That wasn't all. We also donned patent leather tap shoes for the shuffle-hop-step rhythmic routine to "Way Down Upon the Swanee River." My cousin George's taunting epithet calling me "Cess Pool" instead of Cecily had always annoyed me but I knew better. If he could only see me now. I was too girly to be a cess pool.

In fifth grade, pretty Mrs. Greeley had us stand in rows to recite the times table out loud, in unison, as we faced the impressive, bold-printed memory charts in front of us on the wall. Then, we had to turn around and run through the drill again, without any visual aids. She also used flash cards. Even though we groaned every time, the good part was that we learned our multiplication. Thank you, Mrs. Greeley!

I continued ballet lessons with the hope that I could advance to toe shoes, like Joan Kinder. But, to my chagrin, Miss Baynor explained to Mom that I was a little too chubby to go up on my toes. Deflated, I stopped dance lessons that year. Maybe I really was a cess pool.

Sixth grade's high point was having a male teacher, Mr. Daiutolo. His voice comforted me. He looked professional in his white shirt and necktie. Besides that, he was handsome like Perry Como. He always looked like he had just showered, and smelled like good cologne. He seemed to know so very much and taught us about the nine planets and how they orbited around the earth. Mercury, Venus, Earth, Mars, Jupiter, Saturn, Uranus, Neptune and the farthest one, Pluto, all triggered awe in me as I imagined their orbiting continually and faithfully in their set patterns. We also learned about the forty-eight states and memorized their capitals. I had a bit of a head start from Daddy's painted states that decorated our kitchen.

*A*s I neared graduation, I became an avid student of Admiral Nimitz of World War II fame. He also was of German speaking origin and we shared many common experiences early in life which culminated in attending the Naval Academy. What is even more of a coincidence was that, many years later, my retirement home was Llano, Texas, a small town forty miles north of Fredericksburg, Texas, the Admiral's birth and retirement home.

I graduated from the Naval Academy on 6 June 1952. The Korean War had begun before I graduated. I was selected to enter the Naval Aviation branch of the Navy. But before starting flight training, we all had to first acquire the Officer of the Deck qualification on a surface ship. I chose to serve on a Destroyer involved in the Korean War. With my high class standing, 105 out of 750, I was assigned to a fast Navy Destroyer, the USS BLUE (DD-744). I was elated and ready to serve my country in combat. After four years of school, I was eager to apply my skills.

Bras and Stuff

I had to leave Mr. D's class mid-year. A brand new elementary school was opened after Christmas vacation. There were only four of us from that class being transferred. One of them was George. He insisted that I be the first to enter the unfamiliar room filled with a whole new group of kids.

"Ladies before gentlemen," George told me. He moved aside to let me lead. I bit the bullet and led the four of us into the room. It turned out not to be so bad. I started making new friends. We went as a class to an overnight camp, and a girl named Lucy J. stuffed Kleenex into her bathing suit to make herself look big-breasted at the pool. After swimming, she created a shower room scandal when all the wet tissues ended up in gloppy piles strewn across the cement floor.

"Oh, Lucy! What a mess you made," several girls scolded. Lucy just laughed and seemed proud of herself.

The next year, Lucy's form filled out quickly and there was no longer a need for tissue inserts. I wondered why she would want to rush things along like that. But when I suddenly realized in seventh grade that Brenda Stewart and I were the only ones who still wore undershirts, I asked Mom to take me shopping for a bra, even though I didn't need one yet.

"Are you sure you really want to start wearing a bra?" Mom asked me. We looked through the selection on the rack. None of them was designed with flat cups. I was caught between three embarrassments: one at school for not wearing a bra, one at home for having to broach the subject with Mom, and now one in front of the saleslady who was surely judging this flat-chested seventh grader. Growing into womanhood had its awkward moments.

But the hormones started to activate in all of us. Seven of us girls formed a friendship group called the Seven-Ups: Bette Raezer, Joan Kinder, Judy Hahn, Katy Krieger, Judy Smith, Susie Moyer, and there were others. Some of us had boyfriends. We had spin-the-bottle kissing parties. And the girls circulated a blank notebook called a "slam book" in which we revealed private information about ourselves, like favorite color, favorite movie star, most handsome seventh grader, ever been kissed?

We wore mid-calf length skirts to school, and knee socks to keep our legs warm, and penny loafers. There was comfort in conformity.

I arrived in Japan in August 1952 and soon was onboard the USS BLUE (DD- 744). I was the most junior officer aboard and was assigned to Damage Control Officer duties while I undertook completing the Officer of the Deck (OOD) qualification, comparable to a Bridge Officer on a civilian ship. The BLUE also carried a Destroyer Squadron Commander aboard. He was a respected World War II destroyer hero and had written a book on naval ship handling. Our Commanding Officer was a USNA graduate, as were the Commodore and myself. The rest of the Wardroom officers were war experienced reserve officers, plus some more recent graduates from NROTC college sources. So off to the Korean War we went.

Our national policy, at that time, was to try and starve their people by cutting off their primary food supply, and thus hurt their war effort. After four months, I understood my ship's capabilities and I had qualified early as an OOD. I was ready to leave the ship for pilot's training, or so I thought. My skipper had other plans.

Destroyer USS *BLUE* (DD-744) underway.

It disturbed me that I still did not have orders to Pilot Training. So one calm day, I confronted the Captain and asked if he knew what happened to my orders. He replied rather off-handedly, "Oh yes, they came while you were on Christmas leave but the Commodore and I decided that you were more valuable on this ship during the war."

I tried desperately to stay calm and told him that I had passed five aviation physicals and all the other tests one needs to be a pilot. He saw my distress, and told me that when we returned to Japan for some repairs the following week, I should consider doing something just to humor him. There was a small ship there that could give me a pressure test and a physical exam necessary for submarine training. If I passed both, he would give me a positive recommendation for submarine training at Groton, Connecticut. Later, I found out that both of his roommates at the Naval Academy had been aviators and were killed while flying combat missions during World War II.

Green

Bobby's old Austin-Healey convertible was a garish green. All the more visible for the flocks of girls to notice him as he pulled into the high school parking lot. He was handsome, like Paul Newman, and he knew it. Add to that, he was captain of the varsity football team.

I didn't spend a lot of time in his room but one time he let me in, and even showed me his scrapbook of photographs. They were all of girls! Pretty ones too. And I knew their names. All of them were gaga over Bobby. Most of them were cheerleaders.

To me, though, he was an enigma. I couldn't understand why he made me take the bus when I could easily ride to school with him in his green car. Marion was excluded too.

Finally, one morning he said yes. He had put the top down and we were to ride in the back, sitting up on the top of the seat with our feet on the leather upholstery. Marion and I were beside ourselves. We quickly stashed our books in the car and started to climb in.

"Now, wait a minute!" Bobby said, standing by his car. His blue eyes gave each of us a visual once-over as he scanned us up and down. He continued, "You can't ride in my car unless you're wearing argyle knee socks."

I looked at Marion and she looked at me. *Argyle socks! What does that have to do with riding in a car?*

"We don't have any," we blurted simultaneously. We sounded whiny and annoyed.

Without saying anything else, Bobby removed our books from the green Austin-Healey and returned them to us. He jumped into the driver's seat, turned the key, and revved the engine.

"Too bad!" he called out as Mr. Big Shot sped down the gravel driveway, leaving two miffed and baffled sisters in the dust.

I don't know about Marion but I never did get a ride in that car. It didn't stay long with him. "Bobby stripped the gears too often," brother Bruce told me.

I made it to Connecticut and found the Submarine Base. I was eager to start my new Submarine career. I had written my senior thesis at the Naval Academy on the exploits of the CSS HUNLEY. During the Civil War, this hand cranked submarine had attacked and sunk a Northern Navy ship, a first in naval history. I began to read about the successes that U.S. Submarines had during World War II. This is really where I wanted to be. All thoughts of becoming a Naval Aviator were soon forgotten.

Submarine school was exciting. A complete new lexicon to learn, but I was very much at home when it became apparent that the submarine was just a bunch of valves, motors, engines, wheels and mechanical stuff. Just like driving a tractor or combine during wheat harvest season at my sister Wilma and her husband Wes's farm. Also, just as on the farm, one had to be careful around machinery, as one mis-step could result in an injury.

Another benefit of Submarine School was that Connecticut College for Women was just across the river. Special dances were provided so that the submarine students could meet the pretty girls, in many cases from wealthy families. I tried dating them, but could see that we had different values. Finally, on a blind date, I met a pretty college student. She was a local girl from a friendly family. They were interesting and fun folks. Soon I was engaged to Prudence, and, a few months later, after Submarine School graduation, we were married.

I ranked number two in the final class standing and thus was able to choose my next duty station. I graduated second in my class, after Carl Trost, later a Navy CNO, and chose a submarine that was thick in the action of the Korean War. So off I went with a new wife, new car, and a new ship on which to report for duty. Life was great.

"Push 'Em Back!"

A couple years later, I had my unexpected day in the sun. Bobby had already left for Dartmouth. I was still taking the bus as a ninth-grader to Radnor High School. Mom was the bookkeeper full time at Dad's business, Sealview Plastics (which had not yet burned to the ground). The chance to stay after school for an activity or merely on whim was rare.

Cheerleading try-outs were coming up. You couldn't NOT know about them because the girls practiced cheer chants and moves in the halls and at lunchtime. I watched them, aloof. Cheerleaders were known to be bouncy, popular, and full of school spirit, like Bobby's girlfriends had been. But I was still in the little-sister-who-takes-the-bus mentality. Why would I get caught up in the hubbub?

On the day of try-outs, a friend pestered me enough to stay. I called Mom at work and she agreed to pick me up. There were at least fifty excited girls clustered on the bleachers. They listened to the instructions from the varsity cheerleader captain. Five of her seasoned cheerleaders faced the crowd. I was there to watch.

"I want all of you to line up behind one of these girls," she told us. "Don't worry. I don't expect you to know the cheers. We'll teach you one right now."

I was the only girl who did not leave the bleachers. I was still in school clothes with my homework books on my lap. The other girls had all changed to gym shorts. Two friends coaxed me with great kindness to go out on the floor.

"C'mon, Cecily!" they entreated. "We're all going to try out. You should too." It worked. I awoke from my "not me" stupor. At this point, I had no choice. Being the sole person to not participate would have been too uncomfortable.

It turned out this was a pivotal moment for me.

I followed all the instructions and discovered my new skill was cheer-leading. In a flurry of procedure, they narrowed the group down to twenty. I was not eliminated. They taught us more cheers. The final group of eleven girls became the new squad. Everybody clapped. There I was, selected again! Still in my own dream world, they told us to huddle and choose our captain. Before my mind and spirit had caught up with the moment, they were all turned towards me as their new Captain of the Radnor Junior High Cheerleaders.

Slowly, I fell into my new role. At games, the squad wore maroon sweaters with white below-knee skirts, whereas my uniform was opposite in color. I stood out, and that helped me realize that I needed to lead. My problem was that I didn't know the games of either basketball or football. So what cheer should I call, "Push 'Em Back, Shove 'Em Back" or "Get That Ball"? Thankfully, my squad kept me alerted, and we all had a good, peppy time. Being a leader was kind of fun.

So many times I watched life happen, as if from the bleachers, just as I was literally going to do that day. Other people fully engaged in new activities, whereas I would be reticent. Because of my wait-and-see tendency, I missed out on great opportunities. I held back for time to search my soul and formulate my own values. Learning to make good choices was a difficult dance and I wasn't so adept at it. My life was to be peppered with a potpourri of poor, impulsive decisions that got me in lots of trouble. Other times I had great blessing and favor.

Cecily as Captain of the Radnor Junior High cheerleaders.

*A*fter a safe, uneventful car trip across the U.S., Prudy and I arrived in San Diego, California, and searched for an affordable apartment. We found a small one over a garage on North Island.

The diesel submarine USS RONQUIL SS-396 was moored alongside a submarine tender (mother ship) in the midst of San Diego Harbor. To get to the RONQUILeach day for duty, I had to catch a Navy motor launch bright and early. My primary duty upon reporting aboard was to complete a rigorous training program called "Qualification in Submarines." We were given a year to complete all of the requirements and then tested at sea and in port by another submarine's Commanding Officer. Upon satisfactory completion, one was awarded and presented his first Gold Dolphins, the badge signifying acceptance into the select community and "band of brothers" who lived and operated covertly in the ocean depths. Submariners are known for their skill as stealthy hunters, who stalk their prey and kill the enemy without notice.

During the next six months, the RONQUIL conducted several training exercises in preparation for overseas deployment to Russian waters to monitor the Russian Navy's activity during the Korean War. One exercise that we practiced was a night surfaced approach into an American merchant ship convoy to find and make mock torpedo attacks on a certain prime target. Running on the surface and in the dark of night, Captain Medley maneuvered the RONQUIL expertly into the convoy midst, just as he had done during World War II. Little did I know how dangerous submarine life could be, and that is why we received extra salary, just like our aviator friends.

Shortly after reaching Japan, the RONQUIL was assigned a special mission to land North Korean defectors, who now were trained as saboteurs and spies for duties inside of North Korea. One person's mission was to become employed in a North Korean explosive factory, blow it up and find his way back to safety using a special route formed by resistance supporters. This reminded me of the "underground railroad" used by escaping slaves during the Civil War.

Landing spies is always a thriller. We found a coastal area with deep water near the prescribed North Korea drop-off point. The Captain slowly maneuvered our sub within about one-half mile (1000 yards) of the coast, and slowly surfaced the ship. The coastal mountains of Korea loomed right next to the shore and we could hear voices and animals in the distance. Silently, with no fanfare, we inflated a rubber raft, loaded the passengers and their tools, along with two strong Navy sailors, and off they went. From the submarine's bridge we could see the raft slowly approach the shore, unload the passengers, and soon our sailors were back on board the ship. Whew! Everyone used the hand signals that we had been taught for this operation.

We never learned how successful the saboteurs had been.

Diesel submarine USS Ronquil (SS-396).

A.I.S. (and Norway)

One afternoon back when I was in elementary school, I was with Mom in her room. I watched as she made her and Daddy's four-poster bed. The white sheets were fresh from the clothes line and brought sunshine into the room. Mom pointed to her antique writing desk in the corner as if it held the information she wanted to tell me.

"You should know, Cecy, that from the time you were born, I have signed you up to go to a school called Agnes Irwin, starting in tenth grade."

"Why, Mom?" I asked her.

"Because that's where I went. We called it Miss Irwin's. I took a train to Philadelphia to get there. But now the school is closer—in Wynnewood. I'd like to send you sooner but private school is expensive for three daughters, so at least you can each have three years there."

I tucked that information deep inside me and almost forgot about it as the years in public school went by. The time had come. I needed to let go of the Seven-Ups and transition to private school. Tenth grade meant the fulfillment of Mom's plan for me go to her Alma Mater, Agnes Irwin School. Granny quietly paid the tuition behind the scenes.

I joined the class of 1960, a small group of thirty-six girls. Most of them had been classmates since kindergarten. We met in a stone castle-like building with creaky wooden floors. We carried navy blue canvas book bags and dressed in uniforms of blue and yellow. Intellectuality filled the halls. I tried to catch up with girls who had already studied Latin.

"What books did you read over the summer?" Miss Lent asked me privately at her desk, peering over her lowered glasses. The summer's Required

Reading list had been mailed out, and I was sure it was somewhere in one of the rooms of Cackleberry but I hadn't taken the list seriously. I still couldn't read the Dick Tracy cartoons in Dad's morning paper. At some point, that story had started, probably before I was born. I didn't know the characters nor the plot, so I couldn't jump in. That's the way I felt about life. There was too much water over the dam. Where did I fit in to the bigger, grown up picture? There was no pivot point, so I just felt carried along in the sea of humanity.

Sheepishly, I told her, "Nancy Drew and some magazine articles." Miss Lent gasped. She proceeded to hand out copies of *Macbeth* and a syllabus that showed when our assignments were due. The dreaded blank blue book that I scribbled stuff in at exam time came back to me with a red "F" above my vague paragraphs. The same thing happened in Mrs. Neel's history class. I wasn't ready to track Assyrians and other ancient Mesopotamian civilizations in the Tigris and Euphrates river basin, and my second semester grades proved it.

I did well in Latin, though, and French and geometry. My very favorite class was art history where our eyes feasted on rich, colorful slides of works by famous painters like Monet, Degas, Renoir, Van Gogh. By the end of that year, I could enter an art museum and eagerly seek out and identify the artists I now felt I knew.

One day, at assembly, a buxom, grey-haired lady in a grey suit came as a guest speaker to tell us about her girls' camp in Horten, Norway. Each girl would be hosted by a Norwegian family in Oslo. She would travel to that family's summer place, then spend a week with her Norwegian "sister" at Camp Eiken on the shoreline of the Oslofjord. Captivated by the idea of this experience, I took the brochure home. Dad put on his reading glasses and pored over the fine print. He handed it to Mom.

She caught the vision for the trip and even shared the idea with her best neighbor friend, Catherine. Granny agreed to pay the $900 fee, not only for me, but for Marion too. Before I knew it, on June 28th, 1958, Marion, neighbor Judy, and I set sail across the Atlantic Ocean with other girls on the Norwegian cruise ship *MS Oslofjord*. I was fifteen years old.

We hit a storm in the North Sea. I saw the results of the angry sea out the dining room port holes as we pitched. Out one side there was sky, while at the same time all I saw out the other port hole was just dark green water. Then we would roll to see the opposite shocking views. Our waiter pretended to puke on me with his hand pressed on puffed out cheeks. Thankfully, the return crossing two months later on the *Stavangerfjord* had much calmer weather.

I stayed with the Tenden family in Oslo. Their daughter, Anne, and I bonded quickly. She seemed happy to be my host sister. We took the tram to the city where we stopped in a small grocery store. Anne pointed to a nice-looking young woman down the aisle.

"That's Princess Astrid," Anne told me. "She's Norway's First Lady."

"She pushes her own cart?" I asked incredulously. "I can't believe that."

"Of course," Anne replied. "Ve always see that. Ve think nothing about that."

The family car was packed with our suitcases. We drove past green countryside for hours to their summer cabin on the side of a mountain in Telemark. Anne and I swam in the icy pond below. We watched goats appear at the trail clearings above us. A young girl with a stick herded them to their mountaintop farm. Their collar bells jangled at each switchback.

The next day, I felt like the storybook Heidi as Anne and I hiked up there for a visit to buy goat cheese. She carried a fistful of Norwegian kroner. It happened to be cheese-making day in the weathered wooden barn. The farmer spoke no English. What a once-in-a-lifetime experience. We bought a wheel of the orange-colored curds. I tried to disregard its pungent smell, like aged urine, and ate it at breakfast, along with breads and the fish that Mr. Tenden had caught in his gill net down at the pond. After the meal, all of a sudden, "Heidi" erupted her innards into the adjacent outhouse, and a lifetime aversion to goat cheese began.

The Norwegian girls' camp was more like a casual get together compared to my experience as a girl at New Hampshire's Singing Eagle Lodge. I found myself restless as I wished for the next structured activity. Even with such freedom, the girls preferred languid sun bathing over diving off the dock into the breathtaking fjord water. I saw bikini bathing suits for the first time.

At the noon meal in the main lodge, I caused the staff to scurry when I requested a napkin. They ran to the Director, who came up with a folded cloth that became my personalized place setting for the remainder of the week. Though glad to have a way to wipe my mouth, there was the flashback memory of embarrassment from Mrs. Rawle's nursery school where I was assigned to a chair much higher than all the other children's. I stuck out. This time, I felt like a spoiled American. I looked over at Marion and Judy who were using their shirts and shorts for napkins like the rest.

There had been no talk of God or church on this trip. Except once, when we passed by an historical stave church built way back in medieval days with its steep-roofed timber structure that was now a relic museum, the Tenden family shared that they did not participate with the predominant Lutheran faith. At Camp Eiken's dinnertimes when we sang a plaintive song in Norwegian, I was fed with a familiar comfort as if I had been to church. The girls sang it with sincerity and a sweet unity. I memorized it. It sounded like a hymn. However, the translation talked about the stress of getting through another cold winter. Nothing about Jesus.

Once we said goodbyes and thanks to our Norwegian families, the American girls finished up the summer with a scenic boat trip up a fjord. We also trekked up Galdhøpiggen, the highest mountain in Norway, and were roped together to cross a large glacier along the way.

The trip to Norway, where I met so many new people, helped me make social headway once I returned to eleventh grade at Agnes Irwin.

*A*fter completing several missions near Russian waters, the RONQUIL returned to Yokosuka, Japan, for a normal upkeep period.

I applied for a call for volunteers for Nuclear Propulsion training. I was informed that Captain Hyman Rickover was in charge of a new program of designing reactors that could fit into a submarine, and that, if the program was successful, the submarine could operate for many months without a need for fuel replacement. That appeared neat and I would be delighted if I could be selected. The skipper of the RONQUIL forwarded my request with a strong endorsement. All I had to do now was wait.

Finally, the day came for the big interview with Captain Rickover. He looked at my interview sheet, asked me what year Oklahoma had been admitted to the union, which I answered almost correctly. He then asked me who was the current Senator from Oklahoma and I answered, "Bob Kerr." He retorted by asking me if I knew him on a first name basis. My reply was, "No, but everyone calls him Bob." He then grumbled and commented that he would guess that I was "Okay," and curtly dismissed me.

The next day I and eight others of the group were notified that we would be attending the next Nuclear Power School course at New London, Connecticut. That class would be the second class for Nuclear Propulsion Operators and, if completed, we would be a group of less that 200 people in the world that would be qualified to both train on and operate this amazing new source of energy, never before harnessed.

The academic program at Nuclear Power School at Groton, Connecticut, was best described as intense. The six months of courses centered around higher Math and the new field of Nuclear Physics, accompanied with nuclear power plant piping arrangements and an understanding of radiological effects on man and machine.

After academic training, the students were transferred to Idaho for six months of operator study. In Idaho, we had a fifty-mile bus ride to get into the National Reactor Testing Site. Life in Idaho was at a more relaxed pace and our days were consumed with qualifications at the various engineering watch stations.

This program consumed another six months and was topped off with qualification as the Engineer Officer of the Watch. When we were qualified as Reactor Watch Officers, we were told that we were in a group of less than fifty people worldwide authorized to operate and supervise a Navy nuclear reactor. As a qualified team, we felt that our efforts had not been in vain. We were ready to be assigned to any one of the initial nuclear powered submarines being constructed. It was time to put the pedal to the metal.

At this time, several nuclear powered submarines were being constructed at four different shipyards. I was assigned to the USS SKATE SSN-578 being assembled at Electric Boat Shipyard in Groton, Connecticut.

The SKATE was the first of a series of four submarines designed to be swift Attack Submarines. The Cold War in 1957 was heating up, and Russia was flexing her political dominance over much of the world. Russia was constructing the first of a huge nuclear powered submarine fleet and her navies were intimidating. The US attack submarines would be our answer to this world wide threat to peace and freedom.

When SKATE's initial underway training was completed, the senior planners of the Navy decided it was time to stake a United States National Presence to the ice-covered Arctic Ocean. The submarine NAUTILUS had made an attempt to transverse the Arctic Ocean before, but was not adequately prepared and outfitted for the mission. So, with great secrecy and many meetings under the cover of night, both SKATE and NAUTILUS were given anew this significant mission. We were assigned to the Electric Boat Shipyard, and many new innovative types of equipment were installed.

The SKATE's officers were reading and cramming over every book that involved the history of previous explorers to the Arctic Ocean. One question that no one could answer was, "What is the density of natural openings in the Arctic ice cap caused by wind or currents for the August period?" This information and answers to many other questions were just not available in that era.

The solution was simple. Send Lt. Kelln, loaded down with multiple cameras, in an airplane over the SKATE's intended track in the Arctic. The Navy assigned a P2V aircraft to the task.

This flight was uneventful. I took hundreds of photographs, counted the density of openings, called "polynyas" in Russian, and filled my log books with data. When we flew over the North Pole, the aircraft crew who had brought an American flag tied to a steel pipe dropped it at the North Pole.

I was also responsible for much of the special equipment being installed for this journey. There were newly designed underwater TV cameras, upward-beamed high frequency ranging sonars, and mine detection sonar installed on the sub's deck to look for polynyas. But most fascinating to me was the inertial navigation system.

SKATE's mission was vital. We were ready to take this tremendous knowledge leap for our country.

"Best Mixer" and Bleeding Finger Tips

I saw that my classmates at Agnes Irwin tended to cluster in cliques where they felt most comfortable. My advantage as a newcomer was to avoid that trap and try to be friendly with all my classmates. At lunch, I scanned the room and took my tray to a new group each day. In spite of occasional rolled eyes from certain tight clusters, I plunked myself down in their midst like I belonged. I wasn't trying to win any favors. This was just my personality. The girls seemed to like and trust me. They elected me as their class Vice-President.

How beautiful, then, that at year-end assembly, I was awarded a similar citizen prize that Mom got thirty years earlier. It was the 1932 Cup for *"The girl in the Junior Class who by quiet loyalty and unobtrusive cooperation does most for the unity and spirit of her class."* I considered it a great honor to be recognized by the school that way, and to be like my Mom.

The momentum continued in senior year. The yearbook committee named me "Best Mixer" in the Class Poll. Also, I was elected President of the Senior Class, which was amazing for someone who had been in the school for only two years. Mrs. Bartol, the headmistress, invited me into her office where I sat in a wing chair, the same place I was to sit later when she suggested I apply to Lake Erie College (which I did). She recognized I needed guidance for my new leadership position. She told me to keep track of important dates and issues that would affect the senior class. I bought a pocket-sized notepad and stuck it in my blazer pocket where it was handy to jot down worthy concerns. As agenda items were addressed,

I crossed them out, and then dog-eared the completed page to expose the next clean sheet.

The most pressing and controversial issue emerged towards the end of the year. Because we were a class of thirty-six students graduating, we were told our number exceeded the protocol for single file procession at the graduation ceremony to be held at the famed Goodhart Hall on the Bryn Mawr College campus. We must break tradition and walk down the aisle two by two.

"Okay. No problem," I would have answered the administration. But when I told the class at the next meeting, there was a sudden uproar of "No way!" from half of the girls. It caught me off guard. We had gotten through the selection of our look-alike white dresses and flowers with great unity. To these girls, though, this was like asking the bride to walk with the bridesmaids. I could see their point. They were adamant. Others, like me, didn't care one way or the other. So I chose one girl from each persuasion and brought them to the front of the room. I stepped aside and told them to work it out. They bickered back and forth until I felt they were done. I called for a vote. Single file won.

I took the wish of the resistance group to Mrs. Bartol and told her I was sorry that the senior class disagreed with the administration's directive. The good-hearted headmistress patted me on the back in an understanding way and said, "That's alright. Your class is over the limit by only two ladies, so we'll work out the timing of the processional hymn *Gaudeamus Igitur* and let you walk in one by one."

A.I.S. had competitive sports teams for all athletic levels, whether intramural or against other schools. We were all encouraged to try out for a team. I played on the varsity softball team. I was center fielder with a limited territory. A gigantic oak tree crowded my turf and I had to work around it. Susie Clattenburg's parents were the only parents who came to watch our games and cheer us on. Mom and Dad never came, and I actually hadn't thought to invite them. They were overworked at Sealview Plastics. Dad came home with underarm sweat stains that almost reached his belt. He had underbid on a government contract for fiberglass radar domes and the stress was immense. Anyway, I kind of felt sorry for anyone who had to just watch and not play. It must be a bore for them, I thought. But not for us. Playing on a team was a fun time of bonding and challenge and good exercise.

All the sports were new to me when I had arrived as a tenth grader. I was excited that Mrs. Laskey saw fit to place me on the junior varsity basketball team. We wore canary yellow pleated tunics and high top basketball sneakers.

"Lace up those shoes and tie them tight!" Mrs. Laskey warned us before the game. "I want you to be able to pivot on the spot and not break your ankles." I played guard. We couldn't cross the center line into the offensive end where the forwards made baskets and scored. We were allowed three steps as long as we dribbled the ball. I hated being confined to just one half of the court. I'd no sooner start a dribble when my turn was up and I had to get rid of the ball. There was no one in the clear to receive it. I held it too long. A shrill whistle blew.

"Pivot!" Coach bellowed. She dropped her whistle to her chest. "You missed Patsy right behind you!" With both hands on her hips, she leaned toward me and yelled with perfect enunciation, "When you're out of options, pivot!"

Good advice. I tucked the idea of pivoting into my heart. Years later, I would advise my own children to pivot with life's circumstances. My own life required many serious pivots.

Oh. There was so much to remember, like that my nails had to stay trimmed. Mrs. Laskey had inspections of our fingernails and decided mine were too long.

"If you can see them from the palm side, they're too long." She held my hand up and, sure enough, my nails showed. "I don't want you clawing the ball," she added, loud enough for all the other girls to hear.

"But I just cut them last night," I answered truthfully. "If I cut them any shorter, my fingers will bleed."

She dismissed my protest. "Go home tonight and cut them again," she said rather coldly as she moved to the next set of basketball hands. I walked to the other side of the gym and cried quietly. My feelings were hurt because I really had tried to comply and she didn't recognize that. Nor did she care if my fingers bled.

And besides, that weekend I was supposed to get dressed up to go to a special debutante dinner party, which you don't do with open wounds on your fingertips.

*T*he SKATE's journey to the North Pole was busy with both safety and surfacing-in-ice drills. As we proceeded north we found that the ice canopy averaged about fourteen feet thick, with upended ice projecting down about thirty to forty-five feet in spots. We learned that the ice canopy was affected not only by the predictable water currents, but also by the wind.

It was Sunday, and during the afternoon worship services we read from the 139th Psalm, which said in part that God was there in the uttermost parts of the sea and His hand was leading us. We were entering an unknown world and we all knew that the sea was the enemy and was not forgiving if we made any mistakes.

Then at 0147 GMT on 12 August 1958, we passed directly under the solid ice canopy at the North Pole. The ice hummocks were too deep to safely try to force our way through the canopy. So we circled the North Pole at a few yards distance, and, IN LESS THAN A FEW MINUTES, WE HAD GONE AROUND THE WORLD!

On the evening of the nineteenth of August 1958, we surfaced for the ninth time in ten days in the ice pack. By now our well-honed team worked smoothly and almost effortlessly as we conducted our last in-ice surfacing.

Soon after, Washington sent us a message, **"Proceed to Boston to receive a ticker-tape parade and the gratitude of a grateful nation."** Our reply was, **"AYE AYE, SIR."** The Captain ordered, "Ahead Full. Navigator, Set course for Boston."

The SKATE was again assigned the task of exploring the Arctic Ice Cap—this time in the dead of winter to demonstrate that it was feasible to operate in the Arctic in the unforgiving winter months. Our intended track to explore was classified and to my knowledge has never been released by the Navy.

We set sail on the third day of March, 1959. It was a cold, still, dark day en route to the North Pole of the Arctic Ocean. On the 17th of March, we had arrived in the North Pole area. After several attempts to match our ice drift opening with our geographical position, we were blessed with a perfect match. Even if the submarine was mostly underwater, we had our sail exposed. We slowly emptied our ballast tanks to secure our mooring.

WE HAD ARRIVED AND SURFACED AT NINTY DEGREES NORTH LATITUDE—*a feat never done before in history. The crew was elated. They all had labored so long and faithfully with complete confidence in their Captain.*

We had finally surfaced at the North Pole.

Nuclear submarine USS SKATE (SSN-578) surfaced through the ice in the Arctic Ocean near the North Pole.

The Debutante

D ebutante season was an important part of the private school experience. There were going to be festive gatherings from luncheons, to dances, to balls.

"Families are going to have coming out parties for their daughters," Mom explained. "You may be invited to parties given for girls you don't even know." She pulled out the black *Philadelphia Social Register* from the phonebook shelf in the kitchen and opened to the printed page showing that she, *Dorothy Clay*, was *married to Robert Campbell Watson, Jr.* It listed their five children, *Bruce, Robert Jr., Marion, Cecily, and Dorothy Jr.* "See?" Mom continued, "So when you get an invitation, we can look up the name of the family to help decide if you should go to that party."

It sounded like fun. I had learned ballroom dancing at Mrs. Hill's Dance Class, though I never learned to waltz. I knew enough to know that if my partner could dance it, I could follow. Mom and Dad sometimes waltzed together in the kitchen after a couple of cocktails. But not one boy in the class could catch on to the one-two-three rhythm to lead me. How nice it would be to find a mate someday who could lead me and turn my world into a veritable ballroom.

One invitation was to a fancy school dance at Episcopal Academy. Unlike the debutante parties where I would just show up, for this one I was to be personally escorted by a tall friend named Dave. Mom took me to buy a formal gown at Mrs. Brownback's dress shop in Ardmore. Betty, as Mom called her, was determined to put me in the latest style—a strapless dress with metal stays sewn into the side seams to keep the bodice stiff, and a full crinoline that puffed out the canary yellow skirt.

"Do you really think I could wear a strapless gown?" I asked buxom Mrs. Brownback, needing reassurance. Mom seemed just as unsure. All Mom's gowns had sleeves. But we were open to hearing from the expert.

"Try it on, Sugar Darling. It's all the rage and the girls are buying them from me this year."

Sure enough, it looked very pretty and we bought it. But at the dance, a most embarrassing thing happened that kept me from ever wearing a strapless dress again. The band played a rousing version of the "Mexican Hat Dance." Dave and I linked arms for the spinning part of the song. But, because of our exuberance, we whirled around so fast that my high heels couldn't keep up and my feet shot out in the air until I was horizontal, dangling from his arm. My beautiful yellow dress with the metal stays did not stretch like my body did. By the time I crashed to the floor (with all eyes on me, of course), I realized that my little right breast was no longer secretly hidden behind daffodil lace.

Fortunately, either no one actually saw my predicament, or else they saw it and were discreet enough not to say anything. So, after that, I determined to clothe myself with small-breasted modesty, annoyed that God had not seen fit to endow me more fully. I even had Mom take me to see Dr. Aldrich to ask for hormones. He was a wise old southern gentleman who had watched me grow up and had been at my bedside many times to stick me in the fanny with a needle when I had a fever. Now at his office, with Mom in the room, I stripped to show the doctor what I thought I didn't have. His reaction surprised me and his words supplied a profound comfort.

"You're a fortunate young lady," he told me, as I put my blouse back on. "The good Lord has made you just right. Don't let's mess around with hormones." He went on to describe the medicinal reasons why not. Then he switched subjects, "You want to marry, don't you?"

"Yes," I answered.

"Well, your breasts will go through natural changes as you marry and start having babies. Be thankful for your size. Large-breasted women have to carry a great weight all day. Their shoulders get deep gouges from bra straps. Sometimes they even get a rash underneath."

"But Dr. Aldrich," I asked shyly, "will I be big enough to nurse my babies?"

"Oh, by all means yes, Miss Cecily. The good Lord will see to that. He'll give you all the milk you'll need."

I left the doctor's office feeling good about God after all, and much better about myself.

At the height of the season was the oldest ball in the United States, the Philadelphia Assembly. It began in the mid-1700s as a social gathering for early Philadelphia families who were privileged to subscribe. Our family subscription trickled down from Granny's paternal ancestors. Her father William Platt Pepper was one of the managers of the 1866 ball, according to historical archives.

Dad was especially excited to be presenting me at the Assembly Ball. He still fit in his wedding tuxedo, which he was wearing when I came down the Cackleberry stairs dressed in a blue satin gown. Upstairs, Mom had just taken me to her dressing table where she opened a drawer and pulled out her diamond and sapphire teardrop wedding pendant. "You should wear this," she said, putting the sparkling necklace on me. It matched my elegant dress. She opened her glove drawer and offered me a long white pair that reached above my elbows. I could tell she was having vicarious fun reliving her own debutante years. She looked gorgeous too in her bright cherry-colored dress. We both added the final touch, dabbing Arpège Lanvin perfume behind our ears and in the crease of our elbows. Her room was filled with "fragrance like a thousand flowers." I twirled in front of the mirror and admired the transformation of an erstwhile schoolgirl, now a beautiful young woman.

Uncle Ross had wandered down the hill to have a cocktail with his brother and to help see us off. "Let me take a photograph of this moment," he suggested. I gave him my Brownie Hawkeye camera which had two pictures remaining on the roll of film. The flash went off as I posed with Mom and Dad in the first, then by myself for the other. I loved being the center of attention.

Off we went to Philadelphia's historic Bellevue-Stratford Hotel. All the young debutantes proceeded single file down a grand spiral staircase. My gloved hand slid along the ornamental brass railing as I descended the marble stairs, full of anticipation for the evening ahead.

Mom hadn't told me there would be a receiving line of formidable social matrons at the bottom to greet us before we entered the ballroom. I hadn't practiced a curtsey but my full-length gown hid what were actually awkward squats as I passed from woman to woman, extending my right hand to touch gloves while trying to give each one eye contact and a sincere smile. They were all strangers to me. I figured there must have been the likes of a Mrs. Biddle, a Mrs. Geyelin, or a Mrs. Morris in the lineup.

I had a sudden realization that I was not like them, that I was not going to become one of them. I didn't know why, but just knew that I would be headed in a different direction.

I swished my way past more tuxedos and gowns until I found my parents. Dad had saved me a place at the table and offered the glass of champagne he had waiting for me. He presented it in such a way as to say, "You're a young woman now, so let's drink a special toast to celebrate." Mom's cheeks were already rosy from her first drink.

The dance floor was filling up due to the live music of Lester Lanin and his band. A straight-backed young man invited me to dance. I had barely caught his name before another man cut in, and then a few bars later, a sweating man took me to the end of the seemingly endless medley. It was foxtrot all the way from "You're Dee-lightful" to "My Heart Belongs To Daddy." My feet were pinched in the blue satin shoes that had been dyed to match my dress. The bubbly was giving me such bad heartburn that I thought I would burst.

"Dad," I whispered loud in his ear so as to be heard above the hoopla. "I need an Alka Seltzer." There was urgency in my voice.

"Can't you wait till we get home?"

"No. I need one now. I'm bursting."

"But, Cecy, I don't have one." He looked at me and saw the misery on my face. "Okay. Come with me and I'll try to find you one."

"Thanks, Dad. Let's hurry before someone else asks me to dance."

The rest of my evening was the fiasco of hobbling through the back rooms of the servants' stations, following Dad, who had no idea where to find my Alka Seltzer.

So ended the ballroom dancing. For days, months and years, Dad recounted that fateful night of Cecily's heartburn at the Philadelphia Assembly Ball. For me, getting dressed had been lots more fun than the actual event. I took my roll of film to be developed at Allen's Photo Shop in Bryn Mawr, excited to have at least the memory of the glamor of it all in the two pictures Uncle Ross had taken. But even that was to be a disappointment. The film had not advanced inside the camera and all I had was a tantalizing double exposure that resembled a Picasso painting.

In spite of my heritage, I was not cut out to be a garter-belted society belle. It wasn't just because of heartburn in a tight fitting dress. There was something different for me. What that was, I had no idea.

*A*fter surfacing at the North Pole, the crew then affixed the American Flag into the ice. They attached a waterproof cairn containing the written description of the day's events of 17 March, 1959. The crew and officers were sober with all that had occurred this day.

That evening, the Captain called me to his stateroom, his office, which was an unusual event. He shut the cabin door. He addressed me formally, which he seldom ever did, and said, "Lieutenant Kelln, you were detailed to fly over the North Pole in 1958 to ascertain certain Arctic Ocean features on the intended voyage of the SKATE to the North Pole. Also in 1958, you were a crewman aboard the SKATE which, while submerged, passed under the ice at the North Pole. Today, on the 17th of March, 1959, you physically stood on the Arctic Ice at the geographic North Pole."

The Captain continued, "In view of these three remarkable feats, **you are the first and only person who has flown over the North Pole, gone under the North Pole, and stood upon the North Pole.** I desire to know if you would like to be detailed and honored as an explorer with this extraordinary accomplishment. Or would you rather continue on being a Navy submarine officer and serve the Submarine Service?"

Without hesitation, I replied, "Sir, I desire to be the best Navy Submarine Officer that I can be."

Ogden and a Close Call

Shortly before high school graduation, an engraved invitation showed up in the Cackleberry mailbox. The year was 1960. A classmate's cousin was holding a debutante dinner at one of the famous boathouses on the Schuylkill River. I had seen Boathouse Row many times off in the distance while whizzing along the expressway. Once I even saw a rowing race in progress. I couldn't see detail but I got an impressionist's snapshot like that of a Thomas Eakins painting.

This particular evening, Dad dropped me off in the parking lot of one of the boathouses. The old wooden structure was not as romantic as I had imagined from afar. Long sculls were set on brackets along the walls. There were spider webs.

I wore a new summer dress which fit in well among the girls. The guys wore ties and short haircuts. We were seated at a long table which was set in simple elegance for the occasion. The girls bubbled over with excited chatter as the caterers hovered about. It seemed as though the girls all knew each other from their many years of private school parties and sports events.

As I scanned the guests, my eyes suddenly beheld the most handsome man I had ever seen. He was a younger version of the actor Steve McQueen. He was sitting at the head of the table far to my left and out of earshot. What with his khaki dress suit, blond wavy hair, blue eyes and full (kissable!) lips, I decided I MUST meet this man.

Sally, my classmate at Agnes Irwin, sat across from me. I motioned to Sally and got her attention then mouthed the question, "Who is that guy down there?"

"Cecily! You don't know him?" she shot back incredulously. "That's Ogden. EVERYONE knows Ogden! He's going to be a sophomore in college."

Hmm. Ogden. I watched Ogden often with furtive glances for the rest of the dinner and realized that, no matter what social hurdles were involved to make it happen, I wanted to meet him and see his blue eyes up close. I decided he was mine.

Meanwhile, life needed to go on. Marion had a baby boy, the first grandchild for our parents. Graduation came and went. Mom and Dad gave me a portable Smith-Corona typewriter to take to Lake Erie College where I was to be an English Literature major. We took a family vacation to "Clay Cottage," our ancestral lake house in Eagles Mere, Pennsylvania. I visited Granny at the "Sand Box" and let the delicious ocean waves pummel me with their undying strength. There was still time to accept a four-week babysitting job at the beach.

And, then it came. Ogden called to ask me out. The grapevine rumor that Cecily wanted to meet Ogden actually made its way to him and he responded. Both of us were leaving home for college, so we had only a few dates to meet each other's families, go to the movies, and talk together about our lives. He was still so knock-out handsome. I couldn't believe his eyes were on me.

After that, we communicated mostly by letters. Ogden had become my heart flame whom I rarely saw. Our schools were far apart and our semester breaks didn't coincide. He lived in a fraternity house while I lived in a dormitory. We were not likely to get ahold of one another on the in-coming-only single hall phones available. Nevertheless, absence made my heart grow fonder—and fonder. My roommate, Barbee, was a great listener to my rambling words about how much I liked Ogden, and how I couldn't wait to see him again. I tried hard to focus on my classes.

One morning in Anthropology 101, I heard a new word—*evolution*. The professor was lecturing about how science has a theory that man evolved from another species, that we all developed into our physical form by adapting to our environment, and that only the fittest survived. This was absolutely astonishing to me. He went on about a man named Charles Darwin and the 1925 Scopes Monkey Trial.

I raised my hand high. He called for my question. "But, Dr. Williams," I started. My voice cracked as seventeen years of Sunday school teaching reverberated through my every cell. "I thought God created the world in six days; and that He created man as man, and each animal separately."

I looked around the classroom. Every girl sat still. In fact, it felt like the earth had stopped spinning and the whole universe was still. I couldn't swallow.

Perched high on a stool, Dr. Williams stroked his black mustache. His bald head glistened in the sunlight coming through the classroom window. Behind him was the blackboard with its important chalk timelines. He looked straight to my face and said in measured tone, "Welcome to the world, Miss Watson."

The bell rang for the end of the period. I gathered my books and moved on to Spanish class, feeling utterly dejected and betrayed. This was much worse than finding out there was no Santa Claus. If Barbee or another friend had tried to tell me about Darwin, I could have just discarded the notion as false. But this was a college professor with a PhD. *And he should know!* I was now under the tutelage of an institution of higher education. Anything I learned here at Lake Erie College trumped my home learning, where Mom didn't even go to college. *And the Episcopal church sure is lagging behind*, I concluded to myself. *They insist on teaching about God's creation from the book of Genesis.*

I ran to the basement of the library at my first free moment where I pulled out books on evolution. Sure enough, Dr. Williams was right. It was all there in writing. The world was taking that theory seriously.

My conclusion? The Bible, Mom, and the church had all duped me. After that, I stopped going to church and tried to be a better student, even though I personally didn't feel as though I had evolved from a sea creature.

There was one episode which engendered a close call to getting me back into church. It was shortly before sophomore year began, and after

I returned from a summer job in Long Island working as a nanny to four little girls. Billy Graham was coming to Philadelphia for a crusade. Normally, I would not have considered going but Marion and her husband, Richie, knew of a church bus with extra seats and invited me and Ogden to join them. He and I both agreed it would be a lark. He was a non-practicing Quaker, and I figured we would be surrounded by southern-style holy rollers who were used to the words *gospel* and *preacher*.

The stadium was packed that warm summer night. It was 1961. Billy appeared as a small speck in the distance but still his southern drawl projected loud and clear over the loudspeakers. I was so excited to be sitting next to Ogden that I neglected to pay attention to the sermon. Things changed, however, when the choir began singing "Just As I Am Without One Plea" and people stood up all over the stadium and started filing down to the center field in front of the platform. In typical fashion, as had been my mindset back in tenth grade at the cheerleading tryouts, I remained seated with no intention of participating. To my complete shock, Marion and Richie rose from their seats and took to the stairs. What were they doing? Why were they going? I listened as Billy repeated an invitation to come forward and give our hearts to Jesus. *No way*, I thought. *I'm not going to do that.*

Then Billy continued as the bleachers became noticeably emptier. "If you're still sitting there, you're sitting in a pool of your own pride. You're making a statement to the world that you don't need a savior. You don't need Jesus in your life." Okay. This time Billy hit me—Cecily—with a conviction of pride. *If Marion can go forward, then so can I.* Forgetting Ogden was even there, I stood to my feet and headed down to the field. To my great surprise, Ogden got up too and followed me.

We stood side by side in the swell of people as night fell and the stadium lights went on. Somehow, though, when we were asked to bow our heads and follow a spoken prayer, the magic of the moment lifted. After the "Amen," crusade workers circulated with printed forms and pens, asking for our names and addresses. A woman approached us.

Ogden spoke first saying, "Put me on your atheist list." *What? Did Ogden just say that?* I couldn't believe he had that thought, or even the guts to verbalize such a horrid thing. For that moment, I felt an alienation from him. He was like a sour note in a symphony, like a pop in an ethereal bubble. But even so, we gave her our names and addresses, then returned to the bus.

Later, back at school, classes and routines resumed. I received some pamphlets from the Billy Graham Crusade. On one of our rare phone calls, Ogden told me, "I got that envelope too. I just tossed mine in the trash."

Cool, I thought. *I'll do that too*. And I did. Billy Graham, God, and Jesus all went in the trash. *That was a close call. I almost became a Christian*.

My eyes were fixed only on Ogden. We saw each other on weekends when we could. I told him how I wished we could get married and what names I liked for our children. He was still the most handsome man and took my breath away every time I saw him or his photo.

Though Ogden and I continued to call and write into my junior year at Lake Erie, with time and distance, the ardor was missing, especially on his part. Our conversations were stilted.

It took him a few months to explain to me what he needed to say. It boiled down to something like this, "Our relationship has gotten too serious. It seems like you are ready to get married. I'm not. I need to meet more girls, have more life experiences, graduate from college and get a career going. I want to travel and sail. One day, I'll marry, and the wife I want will be someone like you."

His penetrating words sent me reeling totally off-kilter. I had assumed too much—that he was as crazy about me as I was for him. *Oh, Ogden*, I thought. *We met too soon!* I didn't know what to say. After all, truth be told, he was right. In the light of his ambitions, it was almost debasing for me to admit that I could easily have left college and gotten married and embraced motherhood. I could only internalize my disappointment, because we obviously didn't share the same dream. I had to respect that he was on a determined path. It was clear he needed to break away from me. But, oh, how it hurt.

At least he left me with a hope that I would measure up to be the wife he wanted, perhaps, in the future. This was a hope I was to hold onto for the next few years, silently and painfully. There was no one I felt comfortable to confide in, not my roommate, not even my parents. I was on my own to harbor my dashed dreams about being Mrs. Ogden.

Dad noticed I was different and commented on how I had lost my sense of humor since going to college. Come to think of it, I could see how he would say that. "I've moved on to more serious study," I told him.

In the meantime, college held a much anticipated distraction with its upcoming Winter Term Abroad program. Tuition covered the expenses for all of us junior women to travel to Europe and study in the country of the language classes we were taking. This meant that in January of 1963, I was headed for Spain. My Spanish professor ramped up our classes to include advanced grammar, literature, Spanish history and culture. We spent hours of repetitive listening and speaking under headphones in the language laboratory. In Spain, all our classes would be taught solely in Spanish.

With this new direction and intense preparation, there was not much time to think about Ogden nor grieve over him.

*F*ollowing my tour aboard SKATE, I was assigned to USS SHARK, under construction at Newport News, Virginia. Once USS SHARK SSN 591was commissioned in 1961, one of its early assigned missions was to be the first USA nuclear attack submarine to operate in the Mediterranean Sea, as soon our Navy Fleet Ballistic Missile submarines would be assigned there. The SHARK's preparations for operations in the Mediterranean were a matter of concern to the wardroom officers, so we had special operational reviews and drills in addition to our current activities.

The Sixth Fleet naval training exercises with a NUKE submarine were their first exposure to future at-sea warfare tactics. Admiral Rickover's dream of the naval application of nuclear propulsion would soon be applied and installed in Aircraft Carriers.

The first was to be the USS ENTERPRISE. Was I to play a role aboard in his quest?

Frog Legs, Spain, and a Rocking Horse

O n the afternoon of November 22, 1963, friend and classmate Sara burst into my dorm room. "Did you hear the news?" she asked out of breath.

"What news?" I asked her.

"JFK was shot and killed today in Dallas. He was riding in a motorcade with Jackie and someone shot him. It's on the TV!"

I gasped with disbelief. "No! It can't be!"

Kennedy was my hero. I was proud of him. Besides, he was handsome. And Jackie was like a model. And their two little children were so cute. So now he was dead! Kennedy had been our President since my freshman year. I idolized him. In my sophomore year, he had negotiated with Russia's President Khrushchev to remove their missiles from Cuba, the ones which were pointing menacingly at our mainland. He also faced up to our enemy, Cuba's Marxist dictator Fidel Castro, who had asked for the missiles. Our Air Force was on alert, including Bruce, who piloted a B-47 bomber. There was talk of imminent nuclear war! I was so afraid Bruce would die. In fact, we all could die. It was a scary couple of weeks.

Several of us rushed to the campus television in the basement of the Commons. We huddled around and tried to hear the live broadcast. Feelings of grief and shock united us as reality set in. We were witnessing extraordinary world events which entered our psyches and added topics of conversation for our classes and lunch table gatherings.

In a matter of weeks, I was having frog legs in a French restaurant in New York with Mom and Dad. They had taken me to board the regal *RMS*

Queen Mary, along with the rest of the Lake Erie College junior class. We were headed to Paris, where we would all disperse to our European country of study. I was to spend my winter term living with a family in the city of Valencia near the Mediterranean coast and attending the University of Valencia for two months.

Dad wrote me a letter saying: "I got choked up when the ship sounded its horn and the grand *Queen* started backing away from the pier. You looked so grown up as you waved from the bow in your homemade plaid overcoat. I kept waving back until you were out of sight. I watched her pull clear of the pier as she headed east through the tremendous ice chunks in the river. Then all three of the gigantic red smoke stacks were gone from view."

I wrote back: "I know, Dad. It was super exciting to be on board. I kept waving at you too. And guess what. We went right past the Statue of Liberty! I waved at her too. I feel so lucky."

We anchored offshore at Le Havre, France. A shuttle boat brought us to the pier where a train took us to Paris. We had a couple cold days there, then I peeled off with several other classmates on a train to Valencia.

I stayed with a middle-aged Spanish couple and their teen daughter, Maria, in a high-rise apartment building in the downtown area. They had a TV but no heat, so we wore our coats inside. In the dining room was a circular table with a heat lamp underneath and a shelf to put our feet on. We pulled the long tablecloth over our laps and warmed our bodies while we ate and talked. On Saturdays, "Papa" would plug in the on-demand water heater so we could take showers. Other days, we could straddle a cold water bidet to wash our private parts.

"Mama" prepared *paella* with all the fixings, including mussels and squid. She held the large pan up for me to see and posed ever so proudly while I took her photo. At dinner, I had to pretend that eating squid was a delight and not a dread. But every morning, she served me a delicious breakfast of espresso coffee with condensed milk in a parfait glass, and a sweet cookie. Mama always shook my fluffy duvet out our eight-story window and laid it on the sill to get air and sun after I went off to class at the university.

My family didn't know any English, so, if we wanted to learn about each other, it was up to me to crank out the best of my three years of Spanish training. I was thankful for the language lab hours of verbal parroting into a microphone that had forced me to actually speak. I was doing pretty well, though it was mentally draining to communicate entirely in Spanish. At this overseas school, I probably understood only fifty percent of my literature and history classes. The professors didn't slow down for us Americans. Thankfully, we were not subjected to exams.

I had no idea that soon I would be immersed in a Spanish-speaking culture for two whole years, becoming fluent in the language.

Papa drove a motorbike to the car repair garage where he worked. A long siesta hour brought him home for lunch and later he returned home again in time for the nine o'clock evening meal. Maria had a boyfriend but she saw him only in daylight. The two talked and giggled in the rarely used living room.

"We never hold hands," she told me, "or walk arm-in-arm in the street. That would mean we are engaged." She blushed. She was describing their provincial culture. After supper, no one in this family left the house.

For two months, I had no problem fitting in with their routine, until the final week. I suddenly broke away from my role as their "daughter" and didn't come home for supper. The temptation came up after I realized there was a night life in Valencia and I was missing out. Two classmates, including Dodie, who would become my roommate senior year, and I went to a restaurant/bar. We met three ensigns from the U.S. Navy's Sixth Fleet, who looked handsome in their winter blues, and spoke blessed English. The fun hours flew by.

Suddenly it occurred to me that my family might be worried. Also, I didn't have a key to the elevator cage in the lobby of my apartment building. I became as urgent as Cinderella racing home before the stroke of midnight. There was no chance of sneaking in unnoticed. I had to call Papa, wake him up, make him come down to the lobby, and not only face him head on, but ride up eight stories with him (probably dressed in his pajamas) while two cultures, two generations, and two sets of responsibilities clashed.

And that's just what happened. One of the guys escorted me home in a taxi. His ship was sailing off into the Mediterranean the next day, so I would never see him again. Too bad. He was a good-looking sailor and a proper gentleman. But I didn't have time to worry about him. I was too busy apologizing to Papa for behaving as a shameful, inconsiderate, turncoat, ugly American who had let down a host family in a lasting way. For a minute, I tried to explain that an evening out like that for a girl my age in America was not unusual. But in light of Papa's hurt, anger, and expressed disapproval, I dropped that idea.

Note to self: *In the future, I need to be sensitive to the mores that others hold dear, especially when I am their guest.*

What a contrast it was, after we said goodbye, to leave the confines of my Spanish family and be released to travel by train north to Zurich, Switzerland, alone. There I met classmate, Sara, to travel further north to Sweden to track down some of her relatives, then to Oslo to say hello to the Tenden family I had stayed with five years earlier. From Oslo, we flew to London where we met the entire Lake Erie College junior class at a certain hotel.

We almost didn't make it, though. While flying in a twin engine plane over the North Sea, I looked out my window and, to my horror, the propeller just stopped spinning. I didn't even nudge Sara to show her. I just thought we were going to go down. I figured there were a few more minutes before we would plunge into the water and all die. I bowed my head, braced myself, and spoke an expletive. No prayer. No seeking God. Just a cuss word that was not even in my vocabulary. Only one ugly word. Was that all my life was worth? I guessed so. You live. You plunge into the sea and die. And, poof. That's it. What else could there be?

Well, happily, airplanes can fly with only one engine. We returned to the nearest airport, back to Oslo, transferred to a different plane, then made a successful flight to London. The next day, the class took busses to Southampton, where we boarded the luxury liner *SS United States* and made a speed run home, full of endless chatter about our various European experiences.

While in Valencia, I chose to do my semester thesis on the treatment of the blind in Spain, even traveling alone three hours to visit an Institute for the Blind in the beautiful sea town of Alicante as part of my research. For years, I had thought I wanted to become a teacher of the blind. Mom had taken me to a local school for the blind to visit and talk to the students. My Girl Scout troop had shared a Christmas celebration with the blind students there, exchanging songs and homemade gifts. In my freshman year of college, I ordered a slate and stylus kit to learn how to write in Braille. However, I couldn't memorize the six-cell raised alphabet and subsequently gave up the idea of teaching the blind.

Still, the fascination was alive. I found Camp Wapanacki for the Blind in Hardwick, Vermont, and got accepted as a counselor there for the summer before my senior year. Granny had gifted me a royal blue VW Bug, which I drove to camp.

After two wonderful months, which included taking blind children mountain climbing, I set out to drive back to Cackleberry Farm. Going through a Vermont village, I passed a shop of rustic handcrafted items. A wooden rocking horse caught my eye. My heart leapt. "That's for my own baby," I declared to myself. I made a U-turn and bought the rocking horse with my newly received wages.

My future family had begun, though I didn't know who they were or when they would appear.

*A*ny sailor always welcomes a sudden unannounced visit to a new port. SHARK received such message orders while operating in the Mediterranean—to proceed to Piraeus, Greece, to host a State Visit for the Royal Family. Quick research identified them to be King Paul and Queen Frederica. The 1MC beckoned, "ALL HANDS TURN TO for FIELD DAY for the ROYALS." Every crew member got into the cleanup mode. Even the CPO Quarters' lights were turned on.

We anchored a mile offshore on the appointed day. The Royal Yacht was in sight at its moorings. We waited. Promptly at 0900 hours, we sighted smoke from the yacht and waited for the guests to arrive. The royal party consisted of the King and Queen, their two daughters, Sofia and Irene, and Sofia's fiancé, the King Pretender Juan Carlos of Spain.

After a tour of the ship, the Queen informed me that she had recently visited with Admiral Rickover, and he had informed her that he had completed the first commercial nuclear powered electrical generation plant and that it had been a success. He had also stated that Greece should likewise gather her countrymen to train engineers and construct such a plant. In addition, if she wanted to get more information, she should interview Lieutenant Kelln, the Chief Engineer of SHARK, who had progressed through all of the learning steps. And also, the ship he was on was present in her area and that he, Rickover, would arrange that the ship would visit Greece, and that she should get an independent opinion of the feasibility of constructing a nuclear plant. And, the Queen of Greece continued, she should inquire about the safety of nuclear technology and what it can provide, just like the safety SKATE felt as it operated on the trips to the Arctic Ocean and the North Pole, and how that experience proved the practicality of widely understanding and utilizing nuclear power.

I recommended that she pursue a country-to-country agreement for design and training matters. Above all, I recommended a system leader who would be an unbending professional and take no shortcuts. I sensed my part was done.

76

After my tour on *SHARK* was completed, in early 1963, I received orders to form a pre-commissioning detail named USS *JOHN C. CALHOUN* under construction at Newport News, Virginia. I was to be the Executive Officer (Blue Crew) and serve as Senior Officer until later in the construction period when both the Blue and Gold Crew prospective commanding officers would arrive.

All seemed well. The training programs I nurtured had progressed well, and it was near time for the initial pure water filling of the Reactor systems.

However, after being aboard a few weeks, the Skipper, Captain Dean Axene, received a phone call about 1900 hours in his office. It was Admiral Rickover. We were startled. In a very few words the Admiral stated, *"HAVE KELLN RELIEVED FROM CALHOUN AND HAVE HIM REPORT TO ENTERPRISE MONDAY AS CHIEF ENGINEER."* And then CLICK, the phone was dead.

So in December 1963, wearing a salty (well worn) uniform, I reported to the Quarter Deck of the largest Navy ship afloat, the USS *ENTERPRISE (CVAN-65)*.

I immediately sensed that the Navy was depending on me to pre-pare *ENTERPRISE* for an imminent Mediterranean deployment and, more important, the ship's first overhaul and eight-reactor refueling. That meant I had to learn all facets of the *ENTERPRISE* that reside with the Engineering Department, but also get smart about the other Departments so I could process their overhaul job orders with due diligence. I saw eighteen-hour days coming. The die was cast and it was only up to me to make every hour, every day count with my learning process. For some reason, I felt up to the challenge, not for me but for Admiral Rickover (known as the KOG—Kindly Old Gentleman) and the Navy.

Lift Off to San Diego

Two years before he was killed by an assassin in my junior year, President JFK had made a clear and jolting statement at his inauguration that reached the ears and hearts of the nation. "Ask not what your country can do for you, ask what you can do for your country." The message seemed elusive to me but it caused me to think when I took it personally. What my country had done for me was to merely exist as a free nation, as a land of opportunity, a home place of beauty and protection. To me, the country was established, complex, and grand, a winner of wars. The United States was greater than its succession of presidents, who surfaced, served their terms, and moved on. But with such a rich history; with an enduring God-inspired Constitution; with a focused Congress; how could I, as a twenty-one-year-old English major, do any one thing that could help my country?

In my senior year, my new roommate, Dodie, and I got wind that some Lake Erie College graduates had actually joined Kennedy's new program called the Peace Corps and had gone overseas for two years. *What? Liberal Arts women were eligible to be selected as Volunteers?* A circulating pamphlet confirmed the hunch and provided the contact information. We would go through a selection process, take an entrance exam, and be swept into a twenty-seven month sanctioned program where the government would train, oversee, and pay us a monthly stipend to help other developing countries.

According to the official legislation, the Peace Corps would "promote world peace and friendship" through three goals: One, to help the peoples of interested countries in meeting their need for trained men and women; Two, to help promote a better understanding of Americans on the part of the peoples served; and Three, to help promote a better understanding of other peoples on the part of Americans [Wikipedia]. I could do that! I was proud of my nation and I liked helping others and meeting new peoples. Maybe I would be sent to a Latin country where I could use my three years of college Spanish.

The Peace Corps entrance exam was being administered thirty miles away in downtown Cleveland at 8:30 am. Dodie and I took a bus the day before and checked into a hotel with twin beds. We unpacked our overnight bags, putting our toothbrushes on the sink and our pajamas under our pillows. We set out on foot to find a restaurant.

"What do you want to do tonight?" Dodie asked.

"I don't know," I replied, my mind blank for any other options than to eat and get a good night's sleep. I hadn't told Dodie but I was transforming into Miss America with this whole Peace Corps idea. I really wanted to excel at representing my country.

"I have some friends at Case Western," Dodie remembered. She slipped into a pay phone booth and came out with the news that there was a party just a taxi ride away and they would have food. That sounded good to me to save the cost of eating out. Pretty soon we were captive in an overcrowded apartment of people I didn't know. They were nursing bottles of beer and talking loud. I had tried to like beer, but just didn't. Lake Erie College girls would frequent a bar in Painesville that kindly served three-point-two beer which met the state restrictions for patrons under twenty-one. I went a couple of times and decided the long walk and silly conversations were not worth it.

Dodie, however, had developed a taste and enjoyment of beer. Already, she had one in her hand and a lit cigarette in the other. She mingled comfortably with the city students. The "food" was a picked-over table of cold pizza and chips. Someone handed me a beer, so I decided to force it down. The music got louder and so did the voices and laughter. The seductive beats of "Up On The Roof," "Surfin' USA," and "Deep Purple" put me in the mood for another beer.

The time flew by. I went to use the bathroom and beheld a guy draped over the toilet, passed out, having vomited first. *Disgusting! Oh, my gosh! Where is Dodie? What time is it? We are supposed to be at the hotel sleeping. How could I have forgotten our mission in Cleveland?* I found her with her new friends. The two of us got a cab, then made our way, laughing, to the silent fifth floor hall. Dodie pulled out her key and opened the door. I switched on the lights and we both were shocked to see a man sleeping in each of our beds! Giggling and reeling, grabbing each other for balance, we went to the front desk. I felt like Goldilocks as I reported our intrusion. With great apology, the clerk assigned us to a new room.

"But, we have to get our belongings out of the old room," I told him. He took us back to the fifth floor where we had to barge in on the sleepers, turn on the lights, and gather our toothbrushes from the bathroom and our overnight bags. On the way out, I remembered our pajamas were under their pillows.

"Excuse me," I said quietly to the man in my bed, as I reached under his head and pulled out my PJs. Without the beer in me, I wouldn't have been so bold and mellow. I actually don't know how I would have reacted— probably rant. *How dumb of the two men not to notice the room was already taken! How dumb of the hotel to double book!* I probably would have insisted the men be moved and not us. At any rate, it was in the middle of the night that Dodie and I crashed, exhausted, the new room spinning.

We never did make the Peace Corps entrance exam in the morning. Both of us overslept and woke up with headaches. With our tails between our legs, we caught a bus back to Painesville, accepting our defeat. Miss America would have to wait. There would be another opportunity to take the exam.

Undaunted, we both forged ahead with our applications, returned to Cleveland, and took the exam. We both felt confident that we were headed in the right direction and that the Peace Corps would include us in their next set of Volunteers.

Sure enough, our selection letters arrived. Both of us were assigned to Peru. I raced to the library's atlas to find Peru and get my bearings as to where I would be spending the next two years. It was directly south of me, but way down there! *How will Mom and Dad feel about me going so far away for so long?* Whatever, it couldn't matter. After two months in Norway with a Norwegian "sister," and three months in Spain as a student, I figured that, by now, they should know of my curiosity about living in faraway places.

This time, the travel was an opportunity to be useful, and I would be getting <u>paid</u> to live in the exotic place called Peru! Besides, if Ogden really meant that I was the kind of woman he wanted to marry, maybe, after two years, he will have sown enough oats and established himself in a job and want to snatch me up as his bride. I hoped he got wind that I was now a Peace Corps Volunteer and that he would be proud of me. He would see that I was good for something besides wanting to be a devoted wife and happy mother.

And Betty Friedan would be proud of me too! She had just written *The Feminine Mystique*, a groundbreaking thesis that women can (and should?) find their fulfillment outside of their traditional roles. The pressure was on, especially when my sociology professor, Dr. Lucy Huang, was making me read Friedan's book, which I tried, but hated, and told her so. Dr. Huang— "Please call me Lucy"—wanted me to change my major from English Literature to sociology. And because she had been personable enough to invite me and a couple girls over to her apartment for cheese and crackers, and had shown us her jar with a genuine one-hundred-year-old pickled egg from China, and even offered to let us <u>taste</u> it—"No thank you!"—I acquiesced to declare sociology as a minor.

Although I whizzed through the courses, to me sociology was an enigma the way it constantly viewed humanity in "people groups," like separate glops of cookie dough on a baking sheet. I much preferred to take each person one at a time, without pre-branding them according to their color, nationality, social class, or the current trends of either stigma or favor—or race or sex, for that matter.

What was so wrong about being a woman, anyway? We had God-given curves and anatomy just perfect for having children. We watched our own breasts grow and could dream about how they would fill with milk at the proper time to feed our babies. Even though we were athletic and strong

81

in our own right, there was a reason we were competing on separate sports teams from the guys. They were inherently stronger. MY guy would be the stronger one and protect me. He would take care of me financially, too, by "bringing home the bacon" to feed me and our children. I looked forward to cooking for him and putting a smile on his face. I wanted to create a place of peace for him to come home to. I wanted to please him. What was wrong with that?

Back in high school, at Agnes Irwin, our chorus sang two catchy songs which I crooned from my heart. "I Enjoy Being a Girl" was from Rodgers and Hammerstein's new Broadway hit *Flower Drum Song*. Its refrain was my innermost theme song:

> I'm strictly a female female
> And my future I hope will be
> In the home of a brave and free male
> Who'll enjoy being a guy having a girl... like... me.

The other song so pleased my parents who had come to the concert. Dad delighted that all forty of the swaying girls who were lined up on the bleachers declared such a cheerful, confident stance. It was called "I Feel Pretty" from another new musical called *West Side Story*, by Leonard Bernstein and Stephen Sondheim:

> I feel pretty
> Oh, so pretty
> I feel pretty and witty and bright!
> And I pity
> Any girl who isn't me tonight.
> I feel charming
> Oh, so charming
> It's alarming how charming I feel!
> And so pretty
> That I hardly can believe I'm real.
> See the pretty girl in that mirror there!

Who can that attractive girl be?
Such a pretty face
Such a pretty dress
Such a pretty smile
Such a pretty me!

Sadly, this play depicted a brutal gang war between the Jets and the Sharks, two "people groups" as I now understood from a sociological point of view. *Bummer*. But sadly it was real life from what I heard and read. I identified with the protagonist Maria, however, who didn't let her heart take sides. I did feel pretty and hopefully so did all my singing schoolmates surrounding me. It wasn't in a stuck up way, but more like an inner beauty that I hoped to carry with me always. I called it my Cecilyness. Back then, in high school, I was happy with the way God made me. I still was—in spite of my years in college. My studies were not going to steal that happiness from me. I was not going to succumb to survival of the fittest, nor view my ancestor as an ape. Nor was Ogden's rejection going to derail me.

Dr. William Hickerson showed beauty of character of another kind—wisdom. He was my college advisor and head of the English department. There were only five of us in his Creative Writing class. We gathered around a large table in his office, a windowless basement sanctum, surrounded by crowded bookshelves. He tilted the shade on the sole floor lamp so we could see our notebook scribbles and try to make sense of what we were writing. The springs on his desk chair squeaked as he tilted back and took a prolonged puff on his pipe. He exhaled words to inspire our young minds and to have us reach into nooks of creativity we had never pondered. I wrote something about a reverie during a minister's sermon wherein my spirit rose out of my body and up so high, to "where time didn't matter, and thought didn't matter, and stripes went with plaid."

Dr. Hickerson was the voice of wisdom I sought out during my sophomore year when I was so lovesick over Ogden that I wanted to quit college altogether. I had no other plan, but just to quit. He switched from professor role to the grandfather I didn't have. In just a few wise words, he convinced me to drop such a thought and keep going towards my college degree. That goal, which I achieved, combined with the excitement of Peace Corps plans, caused Ogden to fade from my conscious thoughts for the time being.

Well, now I was sitting alone on an airplane taking off from Philadelphia airport and heading to San Diego for three months of Peace Corps training. There I would meet a whole new group of people, all of us generalists, being trained in Community Development before the big catapult into Peru. Saying goodbye to Mom and Dad was a blur. What they saw was a focused, excited, determined college graduate who couldn't wait to get started on the new journey called the Peace Corps. "I'll write you often," I promised.

The plane roared fast down the runway, then lifted off the ground, and the things out my window shriveled in size. I looked over at the middle-aged woman next to me, a stranger. From somewhere deep inside or on the surface, I couldn't tell, sobs and tears overtook me as the realization of two full years away from home suddenly hit me. Thankfully, the woman didn't try to console me. I needed this moment to grow up.

*T*he days went by fast aboard the Aircraft Carrier, ENTERPRISE. First, I needed to get a good feeling and observe the larger divisions of the Engineering Department in order to validate that the training these officers received as a by-product of Admiral Rickover's training standards was up to par with what he had instilled early on in the introduction of Nuclear Physics and Power production to the Navy.

My engineers of all skills had firm refresher training every week before initial criticality was resumed. The inspecting teams were very pleased with the status of training my men had routinely achieved and they were rewarded by superior marks and certifications. I know that our Skipper, Captain Michaelis, was elated. My submarine training experience was smoothly introduced as a standard for surface ship engineering training. Perhaps that might have been on Admiral Rickover's mind when he detailed me to ENTERPRISE.

The ENTERPRISE under way periods were intense and multi-faceted before our February 1964 departure for a six-month operational deployment in the Mediterranean.

Part 2
Miss America Goes to Peru

Peace Corps Training

It was the summer of 1964 and we were the second wave of Volunteers being trained by the newly established Peace Corps. It didn't take long for us to become like family. We stayed in dorms on the University of California-San Diego campus and walked to a classroom building for the expected lessons of speaking the Spanish language and understanding Peruvian culture and history. At the helm in Washington was Sargent Shriver, former President JFK's brother-in-law. Although I didn't get to meet him, he and his huge planning team continued to impress me with their vision and attention to detail. They weren't winging it. The whole program proceeded with a confidence which rubbed off on me. Before long, I was learning to speak some Quechua, a mountain language still spoken by ancestors of the Incas. Our trainers flew one of these Indian women up from Peru to San Diego to meet us. She had brown skin and thick, straight black hair which she wore in two braids. Her constant smile and the warmth of her dark eyes drew me in and caused me to yearn for a country I had never seen.

One day, our director told us to wear old clothes. "You're each going to build a brick wall," he announced. Really? I had never seen Dad, nor my brothers, nor anyone I knew do that. But the next morning, I was wielding a mason's trowel and turning a pile of bricks into a three-foot wall. I returned to the dorm with a sense of great accomplishment. Even if this labor did not mimic our work in Peru, I saw the wisdom in having us conquer such a task.

On another day, we were told to wear sneakers and meet at the sports field in the bottom of a canyon that was part of the campus. Long stairs led down the sides of the cliff from the mesa above, where our classes were, to the huge grassy expanse below. We were all there, guys and girls. No sporting equipment was in view except for a white leather ball. "We're going to expose you to a game that's not common in the USA. It's called soccer. In Latin America it's all the rage. They are wild about it, so you need to be familiar with it," our leader explained. "They call it *fútbol*." In moments, we were running freely across the grass trying to kick the white ball and score a goal. The guys seemed kind of rough, so I held back, reminiscent of fifth grade dodge ball in the basement of Rosemont Elementary School.

The highlight and most challenging aspect of Peace Corps training was a ten-day period of cultural immersion. We were taken across the border to Tijuana, Mexico, and dispersed individually to live with impoverished families. My family had a faded-blue square home with a dusty brown yard. A sulky, sunken dog barely looked up from his tether as I was dropped off.

The woman of the house came out to greet me, followed by a girl about eight. They smiled and invited me inside. Both wore dresses. An unfamiliar cooking odor permeated the air. It was offensive and alluring at the same time. The tiny home had four rooms of equal size. Each room had an interior doorway a foot away from where the rooms intersected. Faded curtains served as doors. If you wanted to, you could make a small circle by walking from room to room. My room had a narrow cot and a chair. It belonged to the teenaged son, who graciously took to sleeping out front in the grey car that was propped up on cinder blocks. I figured the Peace Corps was paying the family to have me, so the son didn't mind the temporary inconvenience.

The other three rooms were the living room with a small couch and TV, the kitchen with dangling fly paper and a table bearing open pans of fly-covered rice and refried beans (which I had to eat), and a second bedroom with two single beds, each piled high with clothes, for the mother and young daughter. There was no bathroom. We brought water to the kitchen sink from a tap outside. I quickly realized I would be using an outhouse for a toilet. Somehow, this seemed harder than the time I used an outhouse in Norway. This one existed because of basic necessity. The one in the mountains of Telemark, with its view of the sparkling spring-fed lake below, was by vacationers' choice.

I found myself pretending I was poor. The little house was on a slope outside Tijuana on the unpaved road to the city's bullring. On fight days, cars carrying aficionados kicked up swirls of dust as they passed by, bumper to bumper, to go see the show. I put on my simplest dress and walked outside to the picket fence by the road. No one in these cars knew me. Cecily Watson was incognito. To play the role, I put my hands on the gate and looked longingly at each carload. What would they think of this *gringa* in a trashy yard like this one? *This is fun*, I thought. On and on they came. They all looked jovial and ready for a good night out, barely noticing me. They were the haves. I was the have-not. Wait. I wasn't going anywhere. I couldn't go anywhere even if I wanted to. *What's a bullfight like anyway?* For a minute I felt truly stuck. I had no car, no phone, no idea of my address, no friend, no driver's license, no money. Essentially, I was a hopeless, dust-covered waif.

Whew! That was a successful role-play, I thought to myself as I walked back to the house to eat reheated rice and beans and watch TV with the little girl and her mamá. They both called me *Señorita Cecilia*. It sounded so pretty. The little girl wanted to show me her bracelet. I held her wrist to get a good look and told her it was *bonito*. She moved closer to me on the sofa. I put my arm around her as she melted against me. Later, I wrote about this exercise in my training journal, happy to have regained my equilibrium. *But*, I also wondered to myself, *will the dichotomy of being a Miss America in a Peruvian slum for two years create in me an overwhelming I-want-to-go-home explosion?*

*S*oon after ENTERPRISE entered the Navy's 6th Fleet area of operations, we were joined by our Destroyer (DD) escorts and were thrilled to see that two of the ships were also Nuclear Powered. What a heartwarming sight. The USA had constructed only three nuclear powered surface ships to exploit and quantify the significant capabilities needed for the future. And here they were, operating as a team. We pushed the learning curve to identify and document all new operational needs for future ship designs.

In fact, ENTERPRISE, LONG BEACH, and BAINBRIDGE would, on departure from our deployment, be reassigned to Nuclear Powered Task Force One to conduct Operation Sea Orbit. It was a great patriotic sight to see ENTERPRISE and her escorts transit through the Straits of Gibraltar on 31 August 1964. The Helmsman rang the annunciator signal to the Engineers to proceed at average twenty-five knots, regardless of the weather conditions.

Our intended track was 30,565 miles in length. We were orbiting through "inner space" of the world's oceans, entirely without refueling on power derived from the largest complex of nuclear reactors anywhere in the world. This meant that we would be steaming farther and faster than ever has been done. We required no logistic support or replenishment of supplies of any kind. Our goal with this sixty-five day world cruise, Operation Sea Orbit, was to demonstrate that the United States had international peace-keeping capabilities for the world.

The route chosen by the Task Force Commander led through the crossroads of the equator at zero degrees latitude and zero degrees longitude, a point under the West African bulge in the Gulf of Guinea. This point "zero-zero" is less often visited by mariners but Sea Orbit was On-Point for performance of an ancient nautical tradition few others ever experience.

Operation Sea Orbit underway.

Year One-Lima

"Welcome to Peru."

With a renewed sense of purpose at the completion of the training, I flew to Lima by myself, where a Peace Corps Representative greeted me at the airport at daybreak. The airplane had just left behind a glorious sunny blue sky and descended through a thick covering of clouds to the pervasive grayness of a Peruvian coastal winter. Knowing that yellow sun was always up there above the clouds consoled me many a day to come.

"Stand here," the Rep said with a smile, pointing to a sign that said *"Bienvenido a Lima–Perú."* He held up his camera and took a photo of me. "Welcome to Peru," he reiterated, as his flash went off. "We're glad you made it." I had posed with the bleary eyes of an all-night traveler, wearing my trench coat and carrying Mom's old straw shopping bag. The photo, however, revealed the sparkle of a young woman ready to take on the world. Truly, I was honored to be entering this new challenge of my own choosing.

My trunk of supplies had been shipped separately, and all I had to claim was one suitcase. We proceeded to the hotel in center city where fellow Peace Corps Volunteers (PCVs) were greeting one another with great excitement as we congregated from various parts of the States. Dodie had trained with a different group learning how to start up and establish rural business cooperatives. She had already been transported up to the high Andes mountains, where the women still wore the colorful woolen skirts and carried their babies in shawls and spoke Quechua. I would later have a hair-raising trip up the precipitous roads to visit her but, other than that, we didn't see much of each other and had to settle for letter writing.

My assignment was to work in a suburb of Lima, in a huge *barriada*, or squatters' settlement, called San Martín de Porres. Several other PCVs were assigned there but this was a sprawling place about six miles long, and we soon lost track of one another, at least I lost track of them. The community was built on a dry river bed. Not one street was paved, nor were there any sidewalks. We walked on layers of small round rocks that had been smoothed by the passing waters of days gone by—ankle twisters for sure.

Unlike many other urban *barriadas*, this one was organized into square blocks, thanks to the city's intervention. Typically, families fled the mountains overnight, claimed their piece of land, marked it with powdered lime, and squatted, resulting in a hodgepodge of crooked, narrow streets. I was to spend my second year in a community such as this. But San Martín sat between Lima and its airport, and the city wisely planned for a wide thoroughfare to run the entire length. They called it Avenue Peru. The daily back and forth parade of old cars and buses had pressed the river rocks into the ground, creating smooth tracks. The plan was to pave the Avenue, which was started in 1965 while I was still living there. Sidewalks had not yet materialized.

Several shops were strung along the Avenue. The local Peace Corps director said I would be living above one of these. We stopped at the right block and entered the store. It sold bulk corn, rice, and beans, all from burlap sacks, plus candy, shelved soda pop, and sundries like lye soap and wooden clothes pins. A Peace Corps Volunteer named Sylvia lived in two rooms behind the store. She had already fulfilled her two year commitment, but had "upped" for another term. The couple who owned the store and his elderly parents lived upstairs. Their dog Laika was named after the Russian dog that had orbited the Earth seven years earlier in the Sputnik II space capsule. Was the world so small that a poor Peruvian couple would know and revere a Russian space dog?

Sylvia and the owners greeted me warmly as I was shown to my $7.40 a month rooftop quarters on the partially built second floor. I had a bedroom, bathroom, and cinderblock space to use as a kitchen. This was a perfect setup for my first independent housekeeping. All I needed was a broom to sweep the concrete floors. A simple cot and bed linens from the supply room at Peace Corps headquarters created both a place to sleep and a day sofa. A table, chair, orange crate for a bedside table, and shelves made with cinderblocks and boards completed my room's furnishings. I even had my own rooftop patio with potted plants that I promised to water. Off the patio were outside stairs that led down to the side street. I was given a key to the ornamental iron gate at the bottom. I felt safe and free to come and go at will.

I was grateful that my director had the wisdom to place me under the wing of an older woman. Sylvia, whose blue eyes sparkled with her ready smile, was probably forty. She had never been married and had left her career with the Girl Scouts to serve in Peru. Her experience and generous counsel helped ease me into my new surroundings. She never complained about not having hot water and said we were lucky to have flushing toilets and a cold shower. She pointed out that most of the San Martin residents had no connection to water or sewage yet. I watched from our flat rooftop as neighbors lined up at the community well in the middle of the Avenue to fill their buckets with water. Who knows how many blocks they walked on the riverbed rocks as they returned home with their heavy load. I decided I would not complain about cold showers and no toilet seat.

I watched with fascination as Sylvia used her mid-westernized Spanish unselfconsciously to communicate with our landlord family and neighbors, or buy groceries in the marketplace. The people understood her, so they would surely understand me too. She helped me identify popular Peruvian foods and taught me some rudiments of cooking, though she was not such a good cook herself.

Best of all, Sylvia taught me how to take the bus to Lima. For the next year, while I was in Lima, I was to take the bus regularly to various job sites, to the Peace Corps office, or to Miraflores where there was an American-style grocery store. The buses looked like pint-sized school buses painted in blues and reds. The front and rear doors were removed for easy access. The ceilings were so low I almost had to duck my head. Although I was only five foot six, I was taller than most of the Peruvians. A man with a leather money bag strapped to him passed through the crowd to take the passengers' *céntimos*. It was customary to enter by the front and exit by the front or the back. To signal the driver to stop at your block, one pulled a cord by the windows.

I noticed that many men rode in the doorway on the lower step. They held onto the rail and leaned out. When their stop came, they jumped off the bus while it was still slowing down. It was a very macho thing to do.

Thinking that was cool, one day I decided to try it on my way home. I pulled the cord for the bus to stop. As we slowed down, I got down on the step and leapt straight out onto the street. Trouble was, I ended up sprawled on the ground. The street had swept out from under me as the momentum threw me forcefully to one side. My pocketbook had spilled its contents around me. Thankfully, the bus continued on its route so that I could regain my composure in private. I brushed the dust from my skirt. At home, as I washed the scrapes on my knee and arm, I scolded myself in the mirror. *That's not how you do it!* I thought to myself. *You are supposed to step off running in the direction the bus is going.* Even with this realization, I decided that jumping off the bus was for the men. I would not try that again.

Another day, I had a different embarrassing experience on the bus. As there were no seats available at that time of day, I stood and held onto the ceiling bar. The bus was packed and we were all bunched together. I wore a pleated pink summer dress. As we lurched along, I began to feel air on my legs. I looked down and realized with shock that the three men pressing against me were slowly lifting up my skirt.

Horrified, I pushed my way up front to the driver. I leaned down and told him, *"Estos hombres me están molestando."* ("These men are bothering me.") The driver immediately understood and gave me sanctuary. He allowed me to stand next to him with my back against the windshield.

That day, I had donated to a cause on the street in Lima and had a paper "thank-you" badge attached to my collar with a straight pin. In anger, I saw the smug faces of the molesters. With a stroke of impulsive revenge, I pulled out the pin. As each man exited the bus, I pricked him hard on the behind with that pin. The bus moved along so quickly that there was no chance for the men to retaliate. When I got off at my stop, I walked to the welcoming iron gate of home. It was my turn now to be smug.

There was another memorable bus episode that had to do with the driver. For some reason, he pulled off the route and stopped the bus. With the engine still idling, he left his driver's seat and exited to the street. I watched as he argued with another man. Apparently, they needed time to iron out their differences. The passengers on the bus began to yell out the windows and cajole him to return to his duty of taking us all to our destinations. But he wouldn't return.

Suddenly, an impatient man in the back walked up to the driver's seat, plopped himself down, put the bus into gear, and took off as if he drove that bus every day. The other passengers rewarded him with cheers and applause. He succeeded in getting each of us safely to our respective bus stops. Meanwhile, the real driver had been left behind in the dust with his hands in the air, cussing in Spanish words I didn't care to know.

I spent a year in Lima working at a variety of jobs that my Director assigned to me. At first, I helped Sylvia with a key fundraising event for the Grand Opening of a daycare center she and a committee of Peruvian women had initiated. It involved soliciting the famous Spanish bullfighter, El Cordobés, who was in Lima for a momentous bullfight, to appear on a live TV game show. The iconic matador told his manager "No way!" He was not going to appear.

But, our daycare committee's sponsor was the sister-in-law of the Peruvian President, Belaúnde, and she had arranged the details so we could use her name to apply pressure. Sylvia, along with her day care committee president, and I went to the lobby of the hotel where the bullfighter was staying. We turned on the lobby's television and watched the game show host tell the audience that El Cordobés was a little late, but to hold on, he would be appearing soon to benefit the new Day Care Center in San Martín.

Thankfully, the television studio was nearby. We knew if we could speak to El Cordobés in person, we could convince him that the President's sister-in-law was watching the show as well as his adoring public. How could he let them down?

So we found out what room the bullfighter was in and knocked on his door. His manager opened the door, wearing a white T-shirt. I looked behind him and actually saw the bright blue *traje de luces* (suit of lights) that El Cordobés would be wearing on bullfight day. There it was, hanging on the bathroom door, shimmering magnificently with swirls of sequins and reflective gold threads. I couldn't believe what I was seeing and what was happening; that I was only a few feet away from the famous matador's jacket; and that I might see in person the matador himself. The manager tried to shut the door on us saying they wouldn't be going anywhere. We gave him our urgent message again, about how it was a live TV show, about how the audience was waiting for him, and we reiterated the public relations pressure he was faced with.

"Okay. Okay!" the manager acquiesced. "*Vamos, entonces.*" ("Let's go then.")

The two disgruntled men soon pushed past us in the lobby, cussing in Spain's best Castilian Spanish. We stayed by the television and watched as word obviously got to the game show host that El Cordobés himself was about to appear from behind the screen.

Out he came with his best television smile. He bowed with elegance. None the wiser, the audience responded with generous applause. Only five of us were privy to the preceding scene at the hotel. It was dramatic irony turned on its head, where the audience knew less than the actor.

I came away from that experience with a couple of thoughts: first, every story probably has two sides; and second, El Cordobés sure was good-looking—when he was smiling. A third thought was that our measly San Martín de Porres Day Care Center Grand Opening Fundraiser was understandably a nuisance for a transatlantic world famous bullfighter. But a fourth thought was a shoulder-shrugged, *Oh well! We got what we wanted!*

The Day Care Center opened with all the children wearing white tunics and waving red-and-white Peruvian flags for the newspaper's camera. Sylvia faded into the background as several of the committee women exposed their Communist affiliation and grabbed the limelight. I never got a clear evaluation from Sylvia before she returned to the States. Did she consider her work with pride or was she feeling duped by the women who took over her pet project? I was also left amazed that I had actually interacted with real Communists.

In the meantime, I was at a loss for what project to get involved with in my huge barrio. Christmas was coming and I could imagine the excitement building in Bryn Mawr as the street lamps were decorated with lit candy canes and the store windows sparkled with snow scenes. *Dad has probably brought in the live spruce tree and Mom has decorated it with familiar ornaments. Mrs. Stradley's carol sing was probably scheduled, as was turkey dinner at Granny's. For the first time in my life, I won't be there.*

Lima was much more casual about Christmas decor and I couldn't get a feel for any yuletide tradition. Thinking that was okay, and that it didn't bother me, I went to a movie theater on Christmas Eve day and watched Cary Grant's new movie *Father Goose* with a Peace Corps friend who lived on the other side of town. I left her and got home before dark, assuming I would find my local co-workers and celebrate Christmas with them. Without phones, it was not easy to track them down.

By this time, I was hungry. I took the bus down the Avenue in our neighborhood to the home of a Peace Corps friend. I walked three ankle-twisting blocks on the riverbed rocks and knocked on her door. There was no one home. Feeling disappointed, I took the bus in the other direction to another PCV house. Again. No one was home. Where was everybody? Was there a party I didn't know about? Why was I so nonchalant about Christmas Eve coming up. Why hadn't I made plans? There certainly wasn't a turkey dinner waiting for me at my Peruvian home. Nor family. Nor friends.

It was beginning to get dark. I was on foot in an unfamiliar neighborhood. I started walking aimlessly. Tears welled in my eyes. I felt so very alone. Desperate even. *My first Christmas in Peru and look at me. I'm a sad, forsaken outcast.*

Just before the bogeyman of fear was about to capture my mind, I remembered that there was a large Catholic church on the Avenue, where English-speaking missionary priests lived. I walked there fast and went around to the side of the church, through an arched opening into the enclave where I figured the living quarters might be. I knocked loud on the door.

Bingo! The door opened and a very surprised clergyman welcomed me in. The first thing I saw was a brightly lit Christmas tree. Four smiling priests with black shirts and white clerical collars were sitting in the glow of the colorful lights, drinking brandy. Christmas music was playing softly. They were speaking English with Irish and Australian accents. I couldn't tell if they were embarrassed I had caught them drinking, or shocked by the presence of a pretty young woman in their midst. But I put them at ease when I described what a haven they were to me at that moment. They had rescued me from a welling distress.

They added a chair to their circle and I sat with them for half an hour as my spirit was calmed and I regained my self-confidence. I was now ready to return home—not home home, but to my new foreign home.

No, there was no turkey dinner waiting for me. But there was a can of Spam and some Ramen noodles. And three cookies wrapped in a paper napkin one of the priests had handed me on my way out.

Abuela and De Gaulle

The sun shone bright the next day. I went out on my patio and heard the familiar "Sha! Sha!" coming from the open chicken coop below. As usual, old, squat Abuela (Grandmother) was inside the coop. She was seated on a six-inch stool, wielding a bamboo rod to separate feuding fowl. Her apron formed a bowl holding the food scraps which she doled out discriminately to the two-legged critters. Wisps of grey hair hung from beneath her straw hat.

After a breakfast of Post Toasties with instant milk, I peered over the rooftop again to see Abuela now in the narrow alley grinding hard kernels of corn between two large round rocks. The bottom stone was concave from years of grinding. Later, she would be making tortillas for the family with the corn flour. I took a photo of her, reminding myself that I was, after all, an educated outsider in the process of increasing my education. What to me was picturesque, to her was life's necessity.

We had become friends, Abuela and I. I knew she loved me, even though I could barely decipher her Spanish, which was slurred with a mix of Quechua. She often came up to my patio to listen while I read story books to neighborhood children. I imagined what stories she herself could have told me and the children about her life in the Andes mountains. To me she was ancient. She held secrets of antiquity. I knew I was going to treasure the photo I now had of her. How many times had I seen "her" in the stacks of Dad's old National Geographic magazines? Now "she" wasn't a stranger.

A new dichotomy struck my twenty-two-year-old psyche. At the same time that the real world was shrinking for me, my personal world was expanding.

I really needed direction for how best to use my time and energy doing Peace Corps work. I made an appointment to see James Lowery, the Assistant Director of the Lima Peace Corps office. I told him how my community was so large and I felt lost for a project.

When he learned of my past interest in teaching the blind, he soon had me working as a helper at schools and institutions for the handicapped. Through contacts in the social services field, I was invited to attend the inaugural ceremony of a new home for beggars. It apparently was a big deal. They ushered me to the sixth row in a large auditorium with lush red curtains and Peruvian flags. Seated on a platform were three of the country's most prominent men—President Fernando Belaúnde Terry, who was the speaker, Lima Mayor Luis Bedoya Reyes, and the Archbishop of Lima. I held up my camera and took a photo. Afterwards, I mingled innocently quite near them and took candid photos. Unrelated to this, I was given an audience with the Minister of Education to talk about a program to mainstream blind students into the public schools. *Wow*, I thought. *I have complete social mobility here* (a term I had learned in sociology class). *I can as easily wake up on a cot in a barriada as I can be a special guest on a red velvet chair only feet away from the President of Peru.* I truly loved this about my life.

One day, I was at the Peace Corps office on the second floor. There was music coming from the street below. I looked out the window to see the progression of a parade and a marching band. Several uniformed men rode by on horseback in neat rows. A black limousine convertible with the top down came into view. A tall man stood in the back. He was dressed in a tan military jacket and wearing a Charles De Gaulle style kepi cap.

"That sure looks like Charles De Gaulle," I said to a fellow PCV who was standing at the window beside me.

"It is De Gaulle!" he said excitedly. "That's the President of France! Holy crap! He must be here in Lima for an official visit."

I pressed my nose against the glass and watched as this famous elderly statesman acknowledged onlookers with an openhanded wave. The parade and the President of France slowly disappeared out of sight.

A Trip to the Jungle and a Snake

Peru has three distinct geological regions: the dry coast where Lima is, the Andes Mountains, and the tropical jungle that hosts the Amazon River. I had spent my first summer with several other PCVs and some young Peruvians running an American style children's camp on the beach, the dry coast, at the edge of the Pacific Ocean, living in makeshift straw huts and creating an enriching experience for urban barrio children.

I had taken a trip high into the mountains, hitching a ride in the back of an open transport truck, lying on vibrating burlap sacks of onions for hours, zipped up in a sleeping bag, watching the night constellations oscillate in the cold black sky as the diesel engine powered us up the steep switchback roads.

There, I visited my college buddy, Dodie, in the little town of Ataura, where Quechua is the language spoken. The villagers were building a school. The walls were already up, and this day's cooperative project was to fill in the dirt floor with more dirt and rocks. Two by two, women and children and Dodie lugged heavy burlap sacks of dirt from the pile to the future classroom. The men used shovels to spread the surface flat. Old women sat nearby in the sun spinning alpaca yarn on wooden hand-held spindles and chewing wads of coca leaves to stave off hunger, they explained. Dodie appeared to be well acclimated to her stucco house and primitive conditions, but confessed that, though she was fully immersed in her work, she suffered from isolation. I was glad I made the effort to visit her.

I had a separate opportunity to travel to the jungle when fellow PCV Sandy Plate agreed to go with me. The jungle is on the other side of the mountains, so we knew this would be a long and challenging trip. Sandy was from California. Neither one of us had ever been to the tropics. We set out with great anticipation.

We boarded a train in Lima that took us fourteen hours up and over the Andes across the Ticlio pass, which is the highest railroad point in the Americas at almost sixteen thousand feet. At La Oroya, we transferred to another train. I was being affected by the altitude with light-headedness and labored breathing. A train steward in a white coat passed through the railcar with a big hard balloon of oxygen. I was embarrassed to admit it but I was desperate. I hailed him over. He pointed the nozzle towards my face and released a refreshing whoosh of air. That gave me strength to disembark at Cerro de Pasco, a North American mining center with one of the largest productions of lead, zinc, and copper in South America.

My head throbbed from altitude sickness till I wanted to die. Somehow I made it through the night, shivering under six blankets and using the chamber pot for when I had to vomit. Sandy felt fine. She patiently helped me with my ugly needs.

The next morning, she helped me to the bus stop in my weakened condition. The "bus" was actually a squat and wide pickup truck with wooden planks for seats. I didn't care what we used, as long as it was headed downhill. Thankfully, when the "bus" descended towards the jungle, I got immediate relief at the lower altitude. I was glad our plan was to end up in Iquitos on the Amazon River where we could catch a flight back to Lima and skip repeating the mountain passage.

The town of Pucallpa was on the way to Iquitos. It stretched out along the banks of the Ucayali River, which fed into the great Amazon. The townsfolk were Spanish speaking, in western wear. Sandy and I decided to stay there four days. We wandered around the town, enjoying the shops and local restaurants.

One day, as we walked near the river, we saw a group of people dressed in white robes being dunked one by one into the water.

"They're being baptized," Sandy had to explain to me. *Holy Rollers,* I thought to myself. The only baptisms I had ever seen were babies in white gowns being sprinkled. Yet, as foreign as this looked, I lingered awhile, feeling somehow touched by the earnestness of conviction and joy the individuals in this group were demonstrating.

Our quest while in Pucallpa was to visit a Shipibo tribal village. We had studied about the Shipibo Indians in our Peace Corps training in San Diego. These villages were deep in the jungle on the other side of Lake Yarinacocha. We joined some other international travelers and rented a *peky-peky* outboard boat for a full day's excursion to a settlement.

In two hours, we had reached the end of the expansive lake and penetrated far into one of its rivulets. It was so very intriguing winding our way through the thick undergrowth, dodging fallen trees and cutting the motor to pole our way over sunken, soggy logs. Each bend in the narrow waterway brought the hope and anticipation that the tribal village we had set out to see would finally reveal itself.

Finally, we rounded the awaited bend. We pulled up to a grassy bank, alongside two tree-hollowed kayaks. A narrow path led up the hill into the thick jungle. I tried to imagine how I would feel if a large group of white people invaded the peace of my village to stare at me. I decided I had better not stare and suggested this to the others. We agreed that the best approach would be to show them we were friendly, to mix with them instead of treating them as an entertaining sideshow.

Well, we got to the village and nobody was there. Only one elderly man lay in a hammock. The clustered huts were actually open platforms with thatched roofs, like large raised verandas. Soon, a trio of dark-skinned little girls with black eyes peeked out from a cluster of ferns. Then shy, barefooted women appeared. They all had long black hair with straight bangs. They wore wrapped skirts of hand-embroidered white or black fabric. On top, they wore bright-colored, ruffled blouses which almost reached their waists, allowing an alluring peek at their full midriffs.

I noticed how the walk of the Shipibo women was smooth and seductive, compared to the trot of the mountain Quechua Indians in their rubber tire sandals. They spoke quietly in the Shipibo language as they offered to sell us some of their hand-dyed crafts. Some of them wore anklets, bracelets, rings, necklaces, and tin nose disks. Some had geometric designs painted on their skin. A mother and daughter resumed dying fabric with the black dye they had made from berries. Their hands were stained with a purple tint.

It appeared to me that what they were making was for their own use, even the brightly-colored yarn-wrapped hunting bow. None of them could speak Spanish, so we communicated in our own type of sign language. They seemed unfamiliar with the idea of selling their everyday belongings. One woman sold me her own embroidered skirt. Was it possible our enthusiasm as customers in 1965 may have birthed a corruption of their simple, non-materialistic lifestyle?

Soon, a couple of bare-chested men appeared from out of the undergrowth. They were bare-footed and wore baggy pants. Machetes hung from sashes at their waists.

One of them wanted to give us a friendship gift; so he showed us a banana tree and motioned for us to each pick one, which we did. None of us had ever seen a banana tree. Immediately, we started to peel our bananas. Both the men and women watched attentively as we struggled to expose enough fruit for our polite bites. The green peel finally yielded. I took a bite. We all took bites. No longer were we picturesque guests. The raw starch grabbed hold of our tongues and caused our cheeks to adhere to our teeth. We just HAD to spit it out.

The Shipibo natives treated themselves to a good laugh over the suffering *gringos*. It turned out the fruit was not bananas after all. They were plantains, which were never eaten raw, but were always cooked before eating. The joke was on us. WE were the sideshow!

We ventured further into the jungle along a narrow path and came to a clearing where the school and community buildings stood. I saw barefooted children, boys and girls, playing a lively game of soccer, or *fútbol*. No wonder our Peace Corps trainers wanted to expose us to that game. The whole nation of Peru had an obsession with it.

On the way back to Pucallpa, I was about to have an astounding experience. Our young *peky-peky* driver had decided to hug the shoreline of the lake instead of making a straight beeline across it as before. In the distance I saw what resembled an American summer camp, something like Singing Eagle Lodge from my youth. I asked the driver if he would take us over to it, so I could satisfy my curiosity. He pulled up to a boat dock. A few of us got out.

I led the way to the first building which looked like the dining/meeting hall. I pushed the screen door open and stepped inside. There was no one there to give me the scoop. I looked at the bulletin board and quickly discerned that this was a Christian mission outpost of a group called Wycliffe Bible Translators. My fellow travelers were satisfied and returned to the boat. I started to go too, but saw a group of blond-haired, fair skinned people on a beach not far away. Something strong in my spirit made me tell the others that I wouldn't be long, but that I was going to find someone to talk to.

One of the boat group said, "Okay. But don't be long. We all need to get back to town."

There were twenty or so people at the beach. About ten were in the water, splashing and laughing, both adults and children. I could hear them speaking English. The others were standing around, talking or sitting in beach chairs relaxing. Surprisingly, no one approached to greet me. I thought it strange that they wouldn't leap up to meet a visitor. I stood near them for a moment, waiting for a "Hello."

Then, as I looked out at the group swimming, I saw what appeared to be a large stick or branch floating towards them. It moved faster. There was no current in the still lake. As it got closer, I could see ripples emanating from it. The word snake popped into my mind.

I lost all shyness as I turned to the closest man. "Is that a snake moving towards the group?" I asked urgently.

He turned his head and looked out at the water. By now it was obvious that this was a very large snake.

"SNAKE!" he yelled. "EVERYBODY OUT!" Three men grabbed long poles and waded out to the feared intruder. They started whacking at it.

I turned away, stunned by what had just happened. I probably had been drawn by God to that encampment because I was ready for someone to tell me the truth about Jesus, who He was and why He was so important, and what He had to do with my life.

"Jesus saves," Billy Graham had declared in that stadium back in Philadelphia when I went there with Ogden a few years earlier.

Instead, those who were qualified to tell me what being saved by Jesus would look like were preoccupied with a dangerous snake. Jesus didn't save me that day. But instead, I saved a group of Christians. *That probably was an anaconda,* I thought to myself.

I climbed back into the boat, apologizing to the group for taking so long, and thanked them for their patience. I barely had words to describe the immensity of the twenty minutes that had just wedged its way into my life. Years later, I reflected on that incident and how Satan, in the form of a snake, had provided the perfect distraction to keep the missionaries from sharing the Gospel truth with me.

*A*fter twelve international port visits, the Task Force One reached Norfolk, Virginia, on 3 October 1964. The Navy's Nuclear Powered Task Force SEA ORBIT was history. But the task of coordinating the forthcoming repair events was quite vivid in my mind. Time to shift my mental gears to "Think Ship Overhaul."

ENTERPRISE entered the Newport News Shipyard on 2 November 1964. I was most gratified to see the massive work effort that was initiated immediately and it portended that the shipyard's first aircraft carrier overhaul was well organized. The shipyard had proved that eight reactor cores could be efficiently replaced and the ship could be overhauled and finished in eleven months and twenty-one days—a record that has never been broken.

The ENTERPRISE returned to the fleet on 22 November 1965. The Viet Nam war had started. My relief appeared during ENTERPRISE's pre-deployment off Norfolk. Upon completion, I ceremonially cast off Number 1 line of ENTERPRISE as it departed for duty in the western Pacific. I was relieved as Chief Engineer.

Year Two-Arequipa

Working as a Peace Corps Volunteer in Arequipa, Peru.

Upon return from my jungle vacation, Jim Lowery called me into the office. A job had opened up in Arequipa, Peru's second largest city far to the south. It was a teaching position in a fledgling school for retarded children. Peace Corps Volunteers had a major role in helping the school's visionary founder, Mary Luz Barreda, start the effort. Up until that time, children with retardation were being kept at home. It was a revolutionary idea to bring them to a classroom for education. I jumped at the chance to move to Arequipa and take the job. Even though I had no specialized training, I figured no one else did either, so we would all learn together.

When I arrived in Arequipa, the Director had not yet secured a place for me to live. I spent the first night on a canvas cot in a back room of the Peace Corps office, which was near the ancient central square. It felt lonesome and a bit scary to be there all by myself. I fell asleep quickly, though, because it had been a long trip and my body was adjusting to being suddenly higher than 7,000 feet in altitude. The night brought colder air.

I was shivering in my sleep, when I felt the weight of a couple blankets being placed gently on me. I woke up enough to say "Thank you" to the stranger.

A man's voice answered, "You're welcome. I know how cold it can get in this office."

In the morning, I discovered my night angel had been a PCV named Richard. He was a civil engineer whose Peace Corps assignment was designing and building bridges across streams for rural farmers. His drafting table was also in the back of the Peace Corps office, and he often worked late into the night, he told me. Most of the time he was out on a project in some far-away mountain village. I was attracted to his pleasant face, the twinkle in his eyes, and his quiet, caring manner. His design skills impressed me and I saw that he could make a good living.

But he was thirteen years older than I and, therefore, out of the question. On one occasion, when he was back in town, he took me out to eat and we went dancing. He danced well but I wasn't ready for his cheek to be on mine. We sat on some outdoor stone steps and talked. He told me he really liked me. He had a mobile home somewhere in Pennsylvania. He wasn't shy to tell me that he was looking for a wife. But I had to tell him I wasn't ready for a relationship. I was too busy being Miss America.

Richard's kindness to cover a stranger with a blanket set an example for what I would seek in a husband one day. Too bad I met him too soon, and too bad he was born too early. Too bad he lived in a mobile home. He completed his Peace Corps tour soon thereafter and was gone from my life.

Thoughts of Ogden returned. I wondered if he would have cared enough to cover me with a blanket like Richard did. I wondered where he was by now. Maybe working in an office? Or living near a sailboat? Did he ever think about me? I didn't know. He had always wanted me to be more savvy regarding world affairs, pushing *Time* magazine on me, even quizzing me afterwards. *Wait till he hears that I saw in person both the President of France and the President of Peru!*

My new home was located in a suburb of Arequipa, about thirty minutes by bus in outlying irrigated farmland. From my bus window, I saw the dominating inactive volcano known as El Misti and sweeping views of dry hills to each side. The small community was called El Porvenir, The Future. It was one of those *barriadas* settled in a haphazard configuration, a community developer's nightmare or dream.

Even though I would be commuting daily to the city to teach, my other role was to work with the mayor of El Porvenir. He explained to me that his goal was to qualify his little community for official recognition as a municipality deserving of urban amenities, like water, sewer, and trash removal. The first, most obvious obstacle was the irregularity and narrowness of the streets. No trash truck would be able to fit through some of the blocks.

Before anything else, we had to get a surveyor/cartographer to make us a map of what existed. I found a PCV who was qualified and who said he would look into it. My year was up before any map materialized, so I never found out what progress, if any, this *barriada* made regarding its status as a municipality. I threw myself into social work and health projects with the clinic nearby.

Most of the homes were hovels constructed from crude blocks of *sillar*, an inexpensive and readily available white volcanic rock. Mine, however, stood out as if it were a celebrity's manor by comparison. It was red brick and surrounded by a high brick wall that created a large private back yard. The owner was working as a taxi driver hours away on the coast until he had the money to finish building his home and move into it. He was so pleased to find a tenant. He charged me $4.85 a month.

I had electricity but no running water. The village got their water from a community well. Most neighbors were permitted two buckets twice a day, at 5am and 5pm. I was permitted one bucket, being a single person household. I learned to brush my teeth rinsing with just one cup of water and spitting onto the dirt in the back yard. The first day, three PCV guys arrived with some lumber and a shovel to dig a hole and build me an outhouse. It was crude, tilted, with no roof and no door but I was grateful for their efforts and glad to have it. It was kind of fun not having to flush a toilet.

To bathe, I used a wash cloth and a bowl of water I had heated on my kerosene stove. Shampoos were done downtown at a beauty salon, where a woman also set, dried, and styled my hair. I now sported a new bouffant look. I took my dirty clothes downtown to a laundry that washed, ironed and folded them neatly. It was certainly a whole new way of life.

I got to know my neighbors. Children came by to see *Señorita Cecilia*. I soon started a Girls Club where we played badminton in the back yard and baked cakes in the tin box oven on top of my kerosene stove.

Once, I got very ill with a virus. Señora Lorenza across the street heard I was sick. She lived in one large room with her husband and seven children. I had seen the inside of her crude house. There were no windows. The bed areas were divided by clothes hanging from taut ropes. A single light-bulb seemed to make the back corners darker. She came over and brought me a cup of hot chocolate and a bun, their kind of bread. Her gnarled hands were rough and her fingernails dirty but her apron was clean. She sat on the edge of my bed and comforted me with soft words of sympathy.

"*Señorita Cecilia, te triago una taza de chocolate caliente y un trozo de pan pa' que te sientas mejor.*" "Miss Cecily, I brought you a cup of hot chocolate and a piece of bread to help you feel better." With a shy chuckle she added, "*Soy una madre pa' muchos. ¡Ahora también soy tu madre!* "I'm a mother to many. Now I'm your mother too!"

Her kindness touched my heart, as if my own Mom had been there with me. I missed my Mom but already I felt better. *There really is enough love to go around in this world*, I thought.

I got my turn to give help and encouragement to another neighbor, young Carmen. She and her husband had just gotten their first home—one dirt-floored room with only a bed, table, two chairs, a few pots, pans, dishes, and a radio. They both worked in the fields. One day, they returned home to find someone had broken in and taken the radio and dishes. She had no spare money to buy new dishes, so I bought her some in town at the outdoor market and took them to her. She smiled shyly as I presented them to her. It was not supposed to be my role to buy things for any Peruvians but she was desperate and I felt comparatively wealthy with my $105 monthly stipend living allowance.

The mayor and his wife lived two blocks from me. I had gotten to know him a little bit at various community meetings. He shared the desire to see things progress in El Porvenir. One day he asked me to come to his house for dinner. His wife was going to prepare a special meal for me. They wanted to show their appreciation for all I was doing on behalf of their community. I washed my face and hands and put on a clean dress. When I got to their house, they invited me to their eating table within. I was seated on a bench with my back to the stone wall. The mayor sat at the head of the table.

The mayor's wife was peeling some small potatoes at a sideboard in the same room. I watched as she scraped the peelings onto the dirt floor. Four guinea pigs squealed with delight as they scampered from under the sideboard to snatch up and eat the fresh scraps of food. *Pretty neat system,* I thought. *You don't have to worry about your garbage.* The mayor called the little animals by their Spanish name of *cuy,* pronounced "coo-ee," which imitates their sound. They looked so cute to me. We talked as the potatoes cooked in a pot of boiling water.

Soon, the meal was served. I looked down on my plate, and there, to my horror, was a cooked *cuy,* lying on its back with all four feet in the air. Two potatoes and a sprig of parsley sat by. My twenty-three-year-old eyes swept to the other two plates. They were having potatoes and corn on the cob in chicken broth. My starry-eyed, educated Miss America mind made the connection. *You're the honored guest. They have made a sacrifice by preparing one of their treasured guinea pigs for you. Now, suck it up, Cecily. Pick up your knife and fork and eat it!* So without skipping a beat, I did just that. In fact, the skin was crispy and the meat was dark, moist and tender. The whole thing was tasty. As embarrassed as I still was, nevertheless, I was able to be fully sincere when I thanked them for the special dinner.

At a point during my year in Arequipa when I was feeling alone, I met a pretty young woman from Sacramento named Rosemary who had come to Peru with a study group and had decided to stay. I invited her to live in my house. We had such interesting conversations. She was black and told me there was much unrest and dissatisfaction back at her school in California. On her part, she just accepted that she was black, and didn't want to focus on her skin color as a topic of conversation or contention. Instead, she merely wanted to live her life. She was currently on a quest to find out what she believed about God.

She asked me point blank, "What do you believe?" I answered that my Mom had taken me to the Episcopal church all my childhood, and that I guess I believed there was something holy about God, something that required reverence. I told her about how I had gone forward at a Billy Graham crusade to give my life to Jesus, but how that decision had lasted only a few minutes because my boyfriend rejected the idea. So I rejected the idea too. Believing in God, I told her, required my Mom's kind of devotion, where you are on your knees by your bed every night faithfully saying your prayers. Maybe I would acquire that habit too when my life was more settled like Mom's.

"Anyway," I went on, "all that Billy Graham crusade talk about the Gospel seemed like a southern thing to me. In my world, the word Gospel was used only by a minister reading from the Book of Common Prayer during a church service to refer to the "Gospel according to: Matthew, Mark, Luke or John."

Rosemary didn't know what she believed. She had met a Peruvian guy and was going to try the Catholic church with him for awhile. I told her I had gone to an English-speaking Community Church in Lima a few times, but, come to think of it, had not found such a church in Arequipa. Church and religion were not mentioned among the PCVs whom I knew, so I lost interest too.

"I know one thing, though," I told her. "God is nearby."

"How do you know that?" she asked.

"It's because of the words of 'Taps.'" And I sang it to her:

> "Day is done, gone the sun,
> From the lakes, from the hills, from the sky;
> All is well, safely rest, God is nigh."

Just repeating that song was soothing to my soul. Far away in Bryn Mawr, Pennsylvania, I knew that all was well and I could safely rest because Mom would be on her knees praying for me; and not only me—she had a long list of people she prayed for regularly.

"So what's the big revelation that God is nearby?" Rosemary challenged.

"'Nigh' means nearby," I answered. Thus ended the lesson.

fter my assignment to command USS RAY (SSN 653) was announced, I eagerly awaited reporting to the Newport News Shipyard where I assumed the position of Prospective Commander Officer, USS RAY (SSN 653).

The RAY shipyard construction period went smoothly and quickly. We initially devoted many hours a week to all facets of individual and team training so that later when the Engineers were consumed with Reactor and Propulsion system operation and testing, they were also able to assume their watch and other duties with little effort. There was no doubt within senior Shipyard management that RAY outfitting was conducted rapidly and set the record for the shortest amount of time ever seen from keel laying to ship completion. The RAY was launched in June 1966, and sponsored by Mrs. Thomas H. Kuchel, the wife of California Senator Thomas H. Kuchel. The ship was 292 feet long and displayed 4,600 long tons.

Vice Admiral Arnold F. Schade, Commander Submarine Force, United States Atlantic Fleet, stated henceforth his Admiral's flag was to be flown by the USS RAY when RAY was in port. This was a significant honor placed on RAY. From that time on, it also appeared that when a significant mission was needed, the Admiral apparently would choose RAY for the assignment.

Initial launch of nuclear-powered attack submarine USS *RAY* (SSN-653)

Two Girls from Ipanema

In June of 1966, I left my Arequipa teaching job in the school for retarded children and began the process of Peace Corps termination. I had grown to love the little ones I taught, but found out that I didn't want to be a teacher.

There were extensive medical check-ups, language exams, and group conferences. We all felt a certain exhilaration for having successfully completed our two-year tour. The Peace Corps had allotted me a "readjustment allowance" of $550. With some of that money and what I had saved from the monthly stipend, I paid to fly Dita down to Lima to join me on a trip through South America. She had graduated from junior college and tore herself away from a boyfriend to have this adventure.

Dad had wanted to organize the trip for us by making all the reservations. But I strongly resisted. By now, I had the advice of enough world travelers, plus travel books with maps. And besides, we were not on a rigid schedule and would find our own way. We didn't want to commit to a certain hotel or ticket desk. It took the exchange of three letters. Dad finally relinquished control and gave me free reign to escort his youngest girl through unfamiliar lands.

I laid out the itinerary methodically. It began with a trip to southern Peru to see the famous ruins of Machu Picchu—an Inca Indian sanctuary spread along a saddle between peaks high up in the Andes mountains. We climbed one of the peaks. We slept in sleeping bags on a bed of straw in one of the stone relic buildings. Other young travelers had the same idea. They came from faraway places like Australia, Holland and Germany.

Dita and I went on to Puno where we watched Indian dancers twirl in their colorful costumes at the annual Inti Raymi Sun Festival. In the morning, we took a small tour boat out to the famous floating Uros islands to marvel that Uro Indians and their near-naked children were able to live on manmade beds of reeds that undulated under each step. We were permitted to leave the boat to step on the squishy island, and say hi to the native people. The hungry children clamored for the bread we had brought along.

From Puno we slept on a boat for an overnight crossing of Lake Titicaca, which, at 12,500 feet above sea level, was the highest navigable lake in the world. Dita's body adjusted easily to the rare altitude. I did okay too. It was fun to spend this time with my sister. I had to get to know her again after being away for so long. We both had grown up a lot.

The overnight boat dropped us off at Guaqui, Bolivia, where a waiting train took us into La Paz. Dita was all eyes and ears as she watched me speak Spanish fluently and proceed with confidence. We booked a room in a hotel. The next morning, we found out that there was great political unrest in the city. The outcome of some local elections was causing disruption, even gunshots in the streets, right by our hotel! We were told to stay inside for safety. Thankfully, there was a restaurant inside, because we ended up being sequestered until the next day. I told Dita not to worry. Once before, when I was traveling in the Peruvian high plains with some other PCVs, our train's tracks had been barricaded by a protest group. We found a solution by walking across town and finding a paid driver to take us to the next destination. I felt sure that also in this case "all was well" and that "God was nigh," so we didn't need to be afraid.

Soon we were on a bus to cross Paraguay. I was enjoying the scenery, at least I was trying to. The bus driver had the radio blaring with a LOUD sports announcer's incessant chatter that was getting on my nerves. The male passengers obviously appreciated the broadcast, especially when the announcer howled a loud, prolonged, trumpeting sound of "Go-o-o-al!"

The women tolerated it all. One quietly nursed her baby. I looked out the window thinking that this was my one shot to see Paraguay and all the noise was wrecking my pleasure. It was an affront to what I thought my paid ticket had entitled me to. Anger welled up in me until I found myself on my feet approaching the driver.

"Will you please turn off the radio for the rest of the trip?" I asked him in my best Spanish. "It's so loud."

He took his eyes off the road and twisted his fat neck around to see who was asking this obviously asinine question. All he did was just laugh. And so did the men nearby who had heard me. A couple of them spat derogatory words at me as I slunk back to my seat, angrier than before, my mind chewing on the overpowering rudeness of group machismo.

It wasn't until years later that I put two and two together. What the men were listening to that day in Paraguay was a soccer game leading up to the 1966 FIFA World Cup championship. *Oh Cecily! Be humbly put in your place. The world does not revolve around you!*

On the far side of Paraguay, Dita and I squeezed into an eight-seater bucket of bolts that flew us to the edge of the famous Iguazú Falls at the junction of Brazil and Argentina. The falls spanned almost two miles in width. There were 275 individual waterfalls that spilled majestically over terraced layers of ledges. From our viewpoint, though, it was hard to get a postcard type photo through the trees. At least we heard their roaring and felt the exhilaration of being there.

In Buenos Aires, we each ate a huge steak on a wooden plate. I discovered that Argentinian beef was the best in the world.

We hopped excitedly on a hydrofoil boat that seemed to fly us across a wide river basin to Montevideo, Uruguay. Amazingly, the boat was lifted by air above the water. My former Peace Corps director had moved there and was glad to host us for a couple of nights. He took us to a casino, which was not my choice of fun but the meal was good. People were dressed up. Many were smoking—and drinking, of course. There was an ambiance of sophistication, like an adult version of my high school debutante parties. I wondered if I would pick up smoking again now that I was no longer Miss Perfect America. Dita appeared more comfortable that evening— probably because she had recently been May Queen at her college, and debutante parties were not far behind her.

We made Rio de Janeiro in Brazil our last stop. The further we traveled from the poor outreaches of the Andes and the closer we got to a metropolis, the more we became like tourists. Home was beckoning.

Dita had one goal to accomplish while we were in Rio. She said we had to put on our bathing suits and walk along the beach at nearby Ipanema. A new Brazilian song was all the rage back in the States. It had an alluring Bossa Nova jazz rhythm, she told me. It was called "The Girl From Ipanema." Dita wanted to know what it felt like to be that girl.

On a moonlit night, two pretty young sisters swayed their hips as they became "tall and tan and young and lovely, the girl[s] from Ipanema went walking, and when they passed, each one they passed went ahh..."

Peace Corps Recruiter

Back in the States as a Peace Corps recruiter.

After two full years apart, the reunion with Mom and Dad was sweet. I was so glad to see them. I surprised them by showing up as an uninvited guest at the vacation house they were visiting in Kennebunkport, Maine. Mom gasped when she saw me. After a classic double take, she realized it was really me, back at last. "Where's Dita?" she asked. I explained that she had returned home to Pennsylvania.

They could see I had matured with a new level of self-assurance. I told them the Peace Corps was hiring previous Peace Corps Volunteers for the purpose of recruiting new Volunteers. I had applied for the job and been accepted. I was to report to duty soon.

"You mean you're going to be gone again, Cecy?" Dad asked, looking disappointed that I might not be around to enjoy family life once again.

"My office is in DC but I'll be recruiting at colleges in the northeast. So I'll see you, even stay with you, when I'm working at Philadelphia schools. Don't worry, Dad," I reassured him. "I'll be in and out."

A Dark Lobby

I had determined that upon return from Peru I would get in touch with Ogden, to see if he was still single and ready to pick up where we had left off. He may even want to marry me!

I found out that Ogden was indeed single and working in Washington, DC. What a coincidence! I couldn't wait to get to DC.

Once there, I called him at his work. It seemed unreal to actually hear his voice, which was familiar, but stiff. *An office voice,* I figured. I probably sounded awkward too. When you hadn't talked to someone in almost three years, it was hard to sound natural.

Ogden agreed to meet me. He would pick me up at 6:30 at the YWCA where I was staying and take me out for dinner. I was thrilled. This was so perfect. I couldn't believe how my long-term hope and dream was working out with such precision. Surely he had put his social life on hold for me, just as I had for him. Yet, by now, we were estranged. We just needed to see each other to reignite the flame.

At 6:15, I finished primping. My cheeks were flushed with anticipation. *Is he excited to see me too? Will he be wearing the khaki suit that snowed me the first time I laid eyes on him?* I grabbed my trench coat and took the elevator down to the lobby. It was pouring rain and the sky had darkened. Cars splashed by with their headlights on. This YWCA was an elegant six-story building with entrances on two streets. I didn't know which street he would park on, 17th or K, so I stayed closest to the door that seemed the most logical, and kept looking over at the other door in case he appeared through that one. I put on my raincoat so I would be ready. My high heeled shoes began to feel tight as I shifted from one foot to the other. I didn't dare sit down, in case I should miss him.

But 6:30 came and went and Ogden never showed up. The lobby turned grey and colorless. The rain continued to fall in the blackness outside. The receptionist was self-absorbed, not looking up, thankfully, because I didn't want her to pity me. I went back to my room, hungry and alone. And angry. He had stood me up! I sat on the edge of my bed, stuffing emotions inside me, as I kicked off my shoes. There was nobody in my life to share this disappointment with. Rejected once again by Ogden, my heart ached, just like it did in my junior year of college when we first broke up.

The same thoughts battled in my head. *C'mon, Cecily. Be realistic. Ogden is not interested in you. He's all in your mind. He's an empty dream in your heart. It's never going to happen. You're fooling yourself to think he's part of your future.*

I answered myself, *That's not true. I'm back in the States. A recreated woman. Two years spent to grow up and prove I have fascinating capabilities. I can do what I want. The whole world is open to me. Ogden should see me. He should see the new me. I can prove to him that I deserve to be Mrs. Ogden. He is what I want!*

Thankfully, I had a new job to distract me.

Warm Steak and Grilled Cheese

The job was the ideal opportunity—a way to stay within the Peace Corps culture, yet see it from the headquarters' angle. About fifty of us were hired to recruit. We were paid well and treated like celebrities at the home office. Between training sessions, we enjoyed perks like an all-you-can-eat crab feast outdoors under the limbs of a spreading tree. To show us off, we were invited to stand in bleachers behind President Lyndon Johnson in a live television appearance, so he could boast about us. After the show, we each got to shake hands with the President. Up close, as I held his large hand, I noticed that he had a wrinkled, sweaty brow. *He's just a real man,* I told myself.

Once trained, we set out in teams of three. We flew, then rented cars to reach the colleges on our list. We set up a Peace Corps booth, handed out brochures, spoke in classes, and administered the Peace Corps application exam. The students seemed eager to join the Peace Corps. President JFK's mantra about "doing for your country" was still alive in their collective psyche. It was fun being the disseminator, not just for their sakes, but for ours. We were bursting to tell about our ventures and glad to have an audience. They responded to us with awe, that we had actually gone to faraway lands for two years and had returned, unscathed, and obviously inspired by our experiences.

On assignment to a Long Island university, I took a shuttle flight from DC to New York. My teammates were meeting me there, so I traveled alone. I found myself in a VIP cafeteria at the airport. There were only a few tables, and all but one were occupied, mostly by pilots in uniforms.

I sat at the empty table and ordered a grilled cheese sandwich. Soon, an attractive blonde-haired woman asked if she could sit with me.

"Of course," I told her.

She ordered a steak dinner, then said she needed to find a payphone and would be back. Her dinner arrived, but was getting cold. I called the waitress over and asked her to keep the plate warm.

The well-dressed woman returned. The waitress brought her plate out again. The woman thanked me for being concerned that she should have a warm meal. She explained that she was on her way to see her interior designer in New York and there was a lot to discuss. I looked down at my almost gone sandwich and felt the dichotomy between her sumptuousness and my simplicity. Then I thought about her designer decisions and the complexity of a life that needed to commute for such a purpose. *I wouldn't want that kind of life,* I decided internally.

Between small bites (she ended up leaving most of her meal), the woman opened a conversation. "What brings you to travel today?" she asked.

"I'm working for the Peace Corps," I told her, feeling mighty proud. "I'm on my way to Hofstra, then to Columbia University to recruit new Volunteers."

She pulled a wisp of hair from her cheek, then asked, "What are your impressions of the organization? Did you find it worthwhile? Are you glad you..." Then she interrupted herself before I could reply. "I need to give full disclosure why I'm interested in your answers," she continued. "It's only fair to you. My name is Joan Kennedy." She repositioned her silk scarf. "I'm married to Senator Ted Kennedy. My brother-in-law, Sargent Shriver, was the director of the Peace Corps until a few months ago."

I was glad she filled me in, because I hadn't been following politics. I just knew I was sitting with a famous person. Putting two and two together, I realized she was also the sister-in-law of the late JFK! So I sat up straighter and put on my debutante air of sophistication, still embarrassed by my cheapest-on-the-menu grilled cheese fare. My words flowed out glowingly and sincerely as I told her they could all be proud of what they had created. I expressed my enthusiasm for the two years in Peru, how I felt that

I had helped some people, and that the Peace Corps had provided me the opportunity to broaden my view of the world.

She thanked me as we parted to catch our flights and carry on with our lives. I shook her hand, saying I was honored to meet her.

Part 3
ON MY OWN

The Big Apple

Did I want to sign up for another three-month recruiting tour? The Peace Corps wanted to know.

"No, thank you," I told them. I was eager to stash my suitcase and find a home base somewhere. It had been great therapy to let my enthusiasm overflow to others who wanted to hear about my two-year adventure in Peru. However, by now, I was all talked out. In spite of the government's good pay and perks, I needed to move on and discover something new.

I was home just in time to join my siblings and parents for a rare weekend at "Clay Cottage" retreat in Eagles Mere, Pennsylvania. All four of my siblings were either dating or married to Episcopalians. I looked around the living room as they laughed and talked. They seemed happy enough but, now that I was a world traveler exposed to a variety of cultures and people, I knew I was destined for non-conformity from my Main Line upbringing. I would not seek a Philadelphia-raised Episcopalian man for my mate. With a sense of maturity, I made the bold decision to move to a city and seek employment.

"Shouldn't you get a job before you decide?" Mom asked from her familiar position at Cackleberry's kitchen sink.

"No, Mom. Don't worry. I'll find one once I get there." My twenty-three-year-old newfound arrogance caused a deafness to any suggestions, especially from Mom who skipped college to marry at age nineteen. Truth be told, I probably would have preferred her path if fate had not intervened. Ironically, it was Mom who enrolled me in a private school, and who consoled me the night Dad had had one too many and let out with "You're not college material." Mom was my greatest cheerleader, my consoler, my nurturer. Her steadfast faith in God grounded me as I plowed ahead through whatever doors opened.

I pondered whether it should be New York, Boston, or San Francisco. My college friends had mentioned New York the most. Two or three graduates had moved there.

"They call it the Big Apple," I told Mom and Dad at fivesies coffee time. "Isn't that intriguing?" I looked down at my familiar Wedgwood cup, appreciating the moments at home. Mom passed me the silver pitcher of half and half. I poured some in, stirred it with the usual antique Queen-patterned spoon, then took a sip of Mom's love.

The conversation cycled through gentle reminiscences and wishes that I could stay longer, and "I know, I know," until we landed in unison on an understanding of my resolve. It wasn't because my old room was dusty. It was because I was the eaglet now on her own, who was merely a visitor to the nest for old times' sake.

A couple of days later, I had made up my mind to go ahead and move to Manhattan, only two hours from Cackleberry Farm.

With Mom and Dad's blessing, I found a place on East 82nd Street. Dad helped me procure a one-year lease. Together, we drove off pulling a U-Haul trailer loaded with a single bed, my prized Peruvian leather easy chair and hassock, a card table, folding chair, and a few dishes, pots, and pans from the back of Mom's cupboards.

In my naiveté, I didn't consider that you needed to arrange to have your electricity turned on before you moved into a place. My parents didn't think of it either, or they forgot, or they assumed I had taken care of it. We arrived, unloaded, and ate in a nearby Hungarian restaurant. Dad was sure I could handle myself with the electric company, so my parents hugged me goodbye and went back to Bryn Mawr.

There I was in a big city in an apartment with no power. Using a flashlight, I got through the night just fine. The next morning I figured out how to find a pay phone and insert the right coins to call the electric company. I also began the process to contract for telephone service, and it seemed to take weeks before I actually had a phone.

The one friend I knew in Manhattan was my "soda fountain" friend from college years. I had hoped Lee would be my guide and help orient me. I even positioned my apartment to be about four blocks away from his so that we could be friends. He had come from an affluent family in the village of Bronxville, just north of Manhattan. Having graduated from the University of Pennsylvania, he now worked for Campbell Soup. For years, Lee seemed to know when I would be home from college. He would faithfully call and take me out for a soda. We never interacted much more than that. No long distance calls. No kisses. No commitments.

Recently, Lee had met me when I was recruiting for the Peace Corps at Columbia University, and we drove around the city in a convertible with the top down. He knew all the streets and could identify all the major buildings, which made me think he was going to be a great help to get to know the city. He took me to a celebration dinner for his company. He drove me fifteen miles north to meet his parents.

However, Lee was not to be my lifeline. When I actually moved in, there was a note taped to my lobby mailbox which read, "*Hi Cecily- Guess what. I can't see you. I have mono. I don't want to expose you to it. Sorry, Lee.*"

I didn't believe it. I called him and said, "Can't I just help you? You must need meals or something. I mean, can I please help you?"

He said, "No, I have friends who are helping me along." I never saw him nor heard from Lee again.

Ditched and alone in New York City! Was this a predicament or a challenge? I decided definitely a challenge.

I had moved there without a job, which just showed my confidence that I would get one. I went to an employment agency. Without a typed resumé, I gave them a rundown of my experience in the Peace Corps. Based on that verbal report alone, they immediately showed me two potential jobs of interest. One was in the Girl Scouts Administrative Headquarters on 5th Avenue, where my Lima housemate, Sylvia, had worked.

The other was with AFS, American Field Service, a scholarship program for foreign high school seniors to stay a year with American families. They wanted counselors in their home office who would correspond with each of those students once a month. The counselor would become the student's advocate if there were any problems of adjustment to their host family or their school or community. Each student also had a local adult volunteer representative to relocate the student to another family, if needed.

The AFS job appealed to me. I interviewed, was offered the job, and soon began working there. The office was located on East 43rd Street. Across the street was the Ford Foundation with its life-sized indoor forest, a wonderful place for a bag lunch. A block away was the United Nations building proudly displaying many colorful flags. Being a "city girl" was exciting.

I learned how to take the 2nd Avenue bus to work. Wearing newly purchased dresses, high heels, and looking fashionable in my own eyes, I was surprised to discover that city men would allow me to stand. I wasn't the only woman holding the ceiling bar to steady myself as the bus made starts and stops every block for forty blocks. I would have thought men would be more respectful of women and enjoy the opportunity to be gentlemen by giving up their seats to a woman!

What I wasn't aware of was that, during the two years I was in Peru, women were busy asking for "equality" and giving up the idea of being feminine so that they could become manly feminists. *Is this what the "Feminine Mystique" I read in college was portending? Not my cup of tea!* I enjoyed being a girl. And I enjoyed being respected by men because I was a woman. I also wanted to hold men in high regard. However, when they were being rude on the bus, it was hard to do that.

Things at work revved up. The scholastic year was beginning. It was time for the office staff to disperse all over the USA to greet the incoming students. I was sent to California to help greet the students from Japan, Australia, and New Zealand, all of whom were arriving about the same time. My role was to welcome the students and introduce them to their host families, who were excitedly anticipating their new "child-for-a-year." It was my first time meeting someone from these three nations. I enjoyed seeing their fresh faces and hearing their foreign accents. It was a happy scene when they were handed over to their host families.

I had seventy AFS students in my caseload and, therefore, had to write seventy personalized letters a month. In turn, they were supposed to write to me once a month. The territory I oversaw was diverse: parts of Los Angeles, the whole state of Utah, and desert towns in California—like Barstow, Needles and Twentynine Palms. I researched these areas, looking at maps and travel books in order to visualize where my assigned students would be living. To come from Germany, for instance, and suddenly go to the desert was a big adjustment for some of these teenagers.

Even though typing was now much easier on my fingers than was the stiff manual Smith Corona I used in college and in Peru, keeping up with each student was a challenge. We used IBM Selectric typewriters, the newest technology. A type-head ball miraculously moved itself back and forth across the inserted paper. It felt like the typewriter wanted to fill out the page before I knew what I should write.

I started smoking cigarettes again, having stopped the habit while I was "Miss America" in Peru. This new desk job was conducive to inhaling puffs while seeking inspiration for the next sentence. It was a habit for many of us. The large room filled with polluted air. After a murmur of complaint from some brave bothered co-worker, we were issued chunky brown ashtrays with battery-driven fans to pull the smoke into an internal filter. The funny thing was that the suction of the fan smoked the cigarette for you. You rested the cigarette on the ashtray while you were typing, then you looked down and your cigarette was half gone! Plus, whatever you exhaled was still dispersed in the air all around you! The whole staff had to live with the situation. Banning smokers to another location was not yet thought of, much less considered.

It was my distant cousin and classmate, Pepper, who had introduced me to cigarettes back in tenth grade. She had invited me to Long Island for a weekend on her father's yacht, where she pulled out a mint-green pack of menthol Salems, which smelled sweet. She lit one up and I tried it. She taught me to inhale. Propped up on pillows, we used the whole pack, laughing like the schoolgirls we were, and feeling oh-so grown up.

This same friend introduced me to yogurt (I had never heard of it), sliced fresh tomatoes with black pepper on cottage cheese, and, for dessert, oven-baked freestone peach halves with a dollop of sour cream and melted brown sugar. She was also the first close friend to get married and model wifehood and motherhood for me. (And, it was her husband who would later introduce me to marijuana.)

I continued the smoking habit in high school and college. In my senior year at college, there was a short-lived fad of lighting up brightly colored pipes filled with cherry tobacco. I had taken a hiatus from smoking two years earlier on the day I went to Peace Corps training. Now I picked it up again at this job, because so many of the co-workers indulged, and we were under some pressure to crank out our work. Smoking still made me feel grown up and sophisticated, which fit well in the Big Apple.

On weekends in New York City, I was on my own, not having established any social friendships at work and having no affinity for the Lake Erie College grads in the area. I would seek out grocery stores and meat markets and experiment in my tiny kitchen cooking roasts and casseroles.

One weekend, I decided to go to the opera at the Metropolitan Opera House at Lincoln Center. Puccini's *La Bohème* was showing. By the time I got to the ticket window, there were only a few tickets left—standing room only. "I'll take one!," I said. They directed me to the back of the highest balcony, where I was able to stand and prop my elbows on a dividing wall behind the last row of seats. A few other latecomer die-hards were standing with me. I could see the orchestra down in the pit.

The music began and the curtain opened and the singing filled the air. I was mesmerized, never once aware that I had been standing for hours. I was enthralled by the sets and the muted colors and the passionate singing.

I had forgotten how powerful and beautiful the trained operatic voice was. And, this was the best of the best!

It brought back memories of Granny taking me to the opera at the Academy of Music in Philadelphia in the 1950's. I returned to the New York Met to see Giuseppe Verdi's *La Traviata*, this time with a seat! Wonderful! It didn't faze me that, because everything was in Italian, I couldn't make sense of the story. There was dancing, love, heartbreak and death. This I knew by watching. The arias were so melodic and I wanted to hear them again.

Soon I was off to buy a thirty-three rpm vinyl record player. I found a good record store and decided to buy *La Traviata* first. The opera came in a sturdy twelve-inch square box with a colorful label. Inside were three black records and a thick libretto, which had the words of the entire opera typed in two columns, Italian and English side by side.

Back in my apartment, after trying to eat my overcooked roast, I sat on the floor next to my new record player and set the needle onto Side One. With the opened libretto in my lap, I followed along, my eyes zig-zagging down the page to read the Italian as it was being sung, which had a little similarity to Spanish, and the corresponding translation in English. Oh my! The main character, Violetta, was La Traviata, the Fallen One. She was sickly and in love with a man, Alfredo, whom she had to leave because of a promise to his father. She couldn't tell the distraught Alfredo why she had left him. It was to honor Alfredo's family reputation by ending their illicit relationship. It was her secret sacrifice. She died a suffering, unhappy woman. *Poor Violetta!*

I was not one to get moved to tears in movies but this time, as I followed this tragic love story, I was overcome with emotion. I sat there on the floor and had a good cry.

More opera albums followed: Verdi's *Il Trovatore*, Bizet's *Carmen* (this one in French), Puccini's *La Bohème*, and *Tosca* and *Madame Butterfly*, also Verdi's *Aida*. And then one in English, *Porgy and Bess*. I had no television. Instead, I listened to the operas, and learned them in my head, sometimes trying to sing along, but preferring to listen. The operas had become my social life.

Lonely

After months of adjustment to the Big Apple, the day came when I realized that I was lonely. I still hadn't made friends and never went out to eat alone. Plus, I had gotten scared. My narrow apartment building was a five-story walk-up. I was on the first floor. A neighbor told me that a thief had robbed the apartment right above mine. The perpetrator had used the fire escape outside my kitchen window. *Would he come back and break into my apartment?*

Then one night I heard a ruckus in the entry hall. A woman was screaming. I looked out the peephole and saw a man in a long coat drop his briefcase. I watched as he shook the woman and pounded her head repeatedly against the wall. *Not exactly a goodnight kiss!* Instinctively, I opened my door and yelled at the man, "Stop it! Leave her alone!" Then I slammed my door shut and locked it, mad at myself for revealing my presence. Filled with fear and a sense of vulnerability, I crouched down and shivered until the two people disappeared into the night.

Another realization that hit me was that I really couldn't afford my rent. I decided to look for someone at work with a spare bedroom in her apartment who would split the rent with me. Word got out quickly, and I soon moved to a seventh floor apartment on West 106th Street with a pretty redhead named Patricia, whose job at AFS was like mine.

About two months later, I received a dunning notice from my previous landlord. It stated that I had illegally broken my lease and owed him money. He wanted two months' rent, plus I had forfeited my one month deposit. I called him on the phone and asked to see him. He agreed. I found his windowless office up three flights of stairs. He appeared to be self-employed. There was no secretary.

Mr. Cohen greeted me with the statement, "I'm glad I tracked you down, Young Lady. What did you mean by abandoning your apartment and just walking away from your lease?" I looked at him, not knowing what to say. He went on, "Oy Vey! That took guts, Girly! Did you think you would get away with it? You owe me two months' rent. And I won't be returning your one-month deposit."

My mind raced as I tried to think and react like an adult in the circumstance. But I felt like such a child—a country bumpkin, in fact. This man knew the city. He WAS the city. What he said was true and correct. I was embarrassed for my naiveté. I had indeed disregarded my lease. My income shortfall was not his fault. There was no one to turn to. I just started blubbering. He had to go find me a box of tissues.

Through tears, I explained, "I'm a girl who hasn't been trained for these things. I've come to the big city. I didn't understand what my responsibility was, and I'm really sorry. I don't have the money to pay you, and I realize now what I should have done."

He looked at me. With a softer voice he said, "You know what? I'm going to have mercy on you. I hear you. I have a daughter about your age, and I can see that you're caught up, learning how to live on your own. So I'm going to let you go."

And he proceeded to tear up my lease right then and there. I was flabbergasted. That was wonderful, and so unexpected! I was forgiven for the two months' rent.

Well, at least he got to keep my deposit. But I learned that a lease is a contract, and that there are people on the other end of a lease, and the law is in between.

I surely felt safer living at Patricia's. There was a doorman and an elevator. However, although we did take the bus to work together, I found myself no less lonely. It was merely a business arrangement. We kept our food apart in the refrigerator and had meals separately. She ate by the TV in her bedroom. I didn't have a TV. On weekends, she packed a bag and disappeared.

As independent as I wanted to be, there was no doubt that I loved and needed my parents. The only instant communication available was the dial telephone. I usually called collect, which reversed the expense onto Dad's phone bill. Long distance calls being costly, Dad made the whole family nervous by repeatedly saying the clock was ticking. I'd talk to Mom for three minutes. Invariably, I could hear Dad in the background saying, "If this is my nickel, ring off!" He preferred to write charming letters with his fountain pen, which he did every few weeks with impressive regularity, just as he had done whenever I was away.

Mom also wrote letters to me. I always got excited to see those envelopes. The familiar handwriting lifted my spirits. And even in the stretches of time with no communication, the deep bond of unspoken love with both of my parents sustained me now, as it had at college and during the two years in the Peace Corps. I had consolation knowing that assuredly Mom was always praying for me. She had a list of names of people she was praying for tucked in her Bible, and I was on it. She usually pulled out that list when she was alone at the kitchen table. At night, she was on her knees beside her bed checking in with God. Dad would already be under the covers, propped up, absorbed in *Time* magazine.

Now that my rent costs were shared, it occurred to me that I had extra money to buy a train ticket home to Bryn Mawr for the weekend. So I returned to Cackleberry Farm occasionally, and dropped in on Granny nearby on Castlefinn Lane. Mom and Dad were always glad to see me. Instantly, I folded back into their routine, most especially their fivesies coffee time. Their consistency to the lifestyle they had designed together, their love and welcoming manner created a continued sense of security for me and gave me deep roots.

Never mind that they had let me flounder on my own in the Big Apple. I deserved it, even asked for it. After all, by announcing to them right after college that I was leaving for two years to go to Peru, they had already seen that I was ready to venture out, and they had graciously let me go.

Goodbye Ogden

One huge life transition happened for me because of two coincidental encounters on Thanksgiving Day in 1966. I was home visiting Mom and Dad. They had received invitations to two special events and invited me to join them.

The first invitation was to attend an outdoor service early in the morning at a quaint Episcopalian church nestled among horse farms in Pennsylvania's rolling green hills in Chester County. Called The Blessing of The Hounds, this was a centuries-old tradition imported from England. It preceded a horse and rider fox hunt. Its purpose was to bless the riders and all the animals involved, the fox too, I imagined.

We followed the other cars and parked in the field beyond the graveyard. The service was to be held in a clearing further on. There were no chairs. A lady organist sat behind a portable foot-pumped organ that had been placed in the grass. A minister, wearing a white surplice tunic over his black cassock, circulated through the crowd and reached out his hands to greet people. We all gathered to watch as the horses, riders, and foxhounds milled around the ceremonial spot.

The men and women of the hunt wore brilliant red coats with white cravats, white riding pants, black top hats, and tall black boots. They held dignified whips. You could hear the squeak of leather on leather coming from their polished English saddles. Some spoke orders to still the restless hounds that were eager to race toward the distant woods.

The simple ceremony seemed to end as suddenly as it had begun. We watched the varied colored horses, riders, and baying foxhounds bound off in the same direction—as if choreographed—and disappear over the hill. In my eyes, an oil painting had come to life.

Mom and Dad greeted the Hudsons, who lived near this country church and had invited us to continue on to their breakfast party.

I turned around, and who did I see but none other than OGDEN himself! I couldn't believe this random, out-of-the-blue, remarkable coincidence! *MY Ogden!* The one I yearned for all these years. The one I had wanted to marry. The first and only man I had loved. My heart throb! I hadn't seen him since my junior year in college. He had no idea that I was still holding a torch for him. My heart began to pound.

But wait—I looked at him and he did not appeal to me. His face had changed and he was no longer handsome to me. He saw me, approached, and said a dry hello. There was no smile and no sparkle in his eyes. He was reticent. This was the first time we had made contact since the time we didn't meet at the YWCA in Washington three months earlier.

I blurted out the burning question, "What happened to you that day?"

He answered, "It was raining. I waited for you out in the car."

I let out with an incredulous, "Oh!"

"What happened to YOU?" he continued.

My mind flashed to those moments, heart palpitating, holding an umbrella and not knowing through which of the two lobby doors he would appear to take me floating out into that dreary night. "I was waiting for you in the lobby because it was raining. Why didn't you come in?"

He said easily, "Well, there was no parking space. I just waited in my car at the curb and you didn't come. So I left."

"Oh," I said again. *What a lame excuse! Should I have stood outside in the pouring rain to look for him?* The conversation was over. I didn't want to hear another word from him. There was no need to continue, to try to come to an understanding of that awful evening. Ogden obviously had removed me from his life—for real. So it wasn't supposed to be. Just like that, in a matter of minutes, the torch I held for so long got snuffed out. My supposed boyfriend had suddenly become my stranger.

With composure, I was able to say sincerely, "Nice to see you." He was there at the fox hunt blessing with his parents and they were going off to spend Thanksgiving Day together.

I needed this encounter, this fateful coincidence. I was satisfied finally, that, not only did Ogden not appeal to me any longer but, when I thought about it, his personality was not compatible with mine. It never was. His interest in sailing big boats out in the ocean did not appeal to me at all, and that was his passion. And, he really did not smile much. In retrospect, he wasn't even kind. I recalled the times when he pretended to push me off a boulder into the lake below, or grabbed the flashlight and ran off with it, leaving me alone and scared in the pitch black woods until I cried. And then he came back to roughly put me over his knee and spank me hard with the words, "You need to trust me!" He made me read his copy of *Time* magazine, then quizzed me on the content, scolding me to the point of embarrassment when I couldn't recount what I had read.

And, it wasn't like he hadn't broken up with me and moved on. He had, years before. In 1963! I was the one who didn't let go. Did he ever really love me? No. Did I really love him? Actually, no. It was merely a treasured infatuation that I had cherished. I was in love with the idea of being in love. What a blessed release it was after six years to get the hope of being Mrs. Ogden out of my mind and heart.

Hello Ramón

Thanksgiving was not over. Another set of Mom's friends had invited us for dinner so I could meet a group of three young Cuban men, who shared a townhouse nearby. They had graduated from Louisiana State University and two of them worked as engineers for Honeywell, and, as Mrs. Jameson explained to Mom, "They're wanting to meet nice American girls." The Jamesons immediately thought of me, because I had spent two years in South America and could speak Spanish. They set up this dinner party when they found out I was going to be in town for Thanksgiving.

"Ugh. Mom! Please! I DON'T want to meet more Latino men! I've spent two years struggling to get along in a foreign language and trying to understand the Latin way. I'm back in the States now and need a long break from speaking Spanish, and especially from meeting Spanish men."

However, the invitation had been accepted on my behalf, and off we went to dinner.

The three Cuban men were all wearing suits and ties, looking debonair. Their English was polished with a charming accent, and they appeared to be educated and cultured. They were all about my age, twenty-four. I found myself enjoying their company. They had an attractive spark as they interacted, which was enhanced by the fact that they were good friends. One in particular paid the most attention to me. He especially liked that I had joined the Peace Corps and had spent the past two years in Peru.

His name was Ramón. I was immediately fascinated by him. He escaped my rule-out stereotypes. He wasn't an overly romantic Latino nor a fit-in-the-mold Episcopalian. He was different, appealing. He represented a new worldview, which caught my attention. He looked directly into my eyes as we singled one another out, succumbing to a possible new friendship. We exchanged telephone numbers and stayed in touch.

Part 4
Star-Crossed Lovers

Becoming Mrs. Ramón

I got to know Ramón on the weekends I left New York to visit Cackleberry. He loved to talk, especially philosophize about things like honor, duty, and pride. He took my mind to areas that I had never gone before. He loved his family, revered his ancestral past, especially his grandfather, and played Cuban disc records for me. He especially enjoyed Cuban food and ate Cuban crackers with every meal.

He owned a new Sailfish sailboat, which we tied to the roof of his new Volkswagen Beetle and drove an hour to a new reservoir called Marsh Creek. We searched, but couldn't find a clearing through the brush and trees to launch the boat, and there were few roads near the lake. It was a disappointing outing but I was impressed that Ramón took the initiative to at least try sailing in the first place. He seemed to pivot graciously when the plan was foiled.

Mostly, we hung out with his housemates at their "Cuban Embassy," as they affectionately called their town home. We cooked Cuban recipes with black beans and rice and barbecued pork chops outside. We also spent hours at Cackleberry, where Ramón got to know my parents. Mom and Dad seemed to enjoy his company.

He had a stutter that debilitated him, especially out in public. When he needed to talk to a store clerk or the gas station attendant, Ramón couldn't get a word out. His lips pursed and his cheeks blew out and his face got red. Finally, after a long hesitation, he would come out with, "Puh-fill it up!" I really felt sorry for him. But in spite of that flaw, he was good looking with intelligent dark brown eyes and a winning smile. Besides, he

151

was my only friend that first year since returning from the Peace Corps. When he was with me he didn't stutter, and I thought he needed me. There was a rescue thing happening on my part that I never spoke about.

I was unaware that soon Ramón would be rescuing me from a dreaded job assignment. On weekdays, I was back at Pat's apartment in New York. The school year was half over for the foreign students I wrote to. Each high school had a local representative who monitored the student's adjustment. Most of the kids were well suited to their American families. If there were a problem noted, then that representative would call me and say, "I think we need to move John to another family," or, "This is the problem..." I tried to sound professional, but really had no clue for the right solutions. So inevitably, I would go along with whatever the representative suggested. Other than these phone calls, I liked my job.

Soon, it was announced that the following month I would travel in an official capacity to review the conditions of the seventy foreign students in my purview. This involved meeting with the coordinators, not the students. Me? Meet with these mature women who had probably already raised their children and might even be wise grandmothers? In California? In Utah? What could I offer? I felt inadequate and inept, being young and never having raised children. Nor had I ever worked in an advisory capacity with adult women. Besides, what did I know about the dynamics of a public high school community? I had experienced only all girls schools from tenth grade through college. I dreaded the very thought of this trip.

Meanwhile, the relationship with Ramón heated up, and we missed each other during the week. Also, it was expensive and tiring to travel back and forth on weekends to be together. I was the one who brought up the subject. "Why don't we get married?" I asked one Sunday afternoon. I hadn't pre-planned that question. It just popped out of my mouth. Subconsciously, it was a good excuse to leave my job.

Ramón was caught off guard by my proposal. However, he took it seriously, in a humorous kind of way. He paced around the kitchen and tossed green grapes into his mouth from the colander he embraced. I could imagine the wheels of his mind spinning rapidly. His exaggerated steps converted from a parade march to a waltzing swagger. I began to laugh. It seemed the very thought of marriage was suddenly having to be brought forward into his world, and he wasn't sure how to respond.

This hesitation surprised me, though, because I had assumed that the original intent of the introduction to the three Cuban men who were "wanting to meet American girls" was to lead to marriage possibilities. We had never talked about what we wanted to do with our lives. My imagination saw marriage as the ivy-covered cottage with the picket fence around it—pets and children in the yard. I assumed that he had the same vision.

I watched as Ramón's "mind airplane" landed. He put down the near-empty grape container. To my surprise and delight, he was able to agree with me and say, "Yes. Okay. You've come up with a good idea. Let's ask your parents and we will get married."

"But," he added, "does that mean I would have to wear a monkey suit?"

"Of course," I replied. "You will look so handsome in a tuxedo."

Obviously, Mom and Dad were fond of Ramón, and seemed excited that this cosmopolitan man wanted to marry their daughter. They enjoyed his Cuban charm. It helped, too, that he worked just across the river, and that he was an electrical engineer who would provide a good living for me and our future family. I was delighted with the prospect of living near Cackleberry after being away seven years.

It was easy for me to give notice at work. I had my escape from that overwhelming trip out west. Pat, though, was not happy about losing her apartment rental help, and I felt like I dumped her. For one who never exchanged conversation concerning our personal lives, Pat added a dig, something like she couldn't "see me wanting to fly off and marry that man."

Our first hurdle was to decide where we should have the wedding. Ramón immediately zeroed in on the Catholic church.

"I haven't been to mass in years but my heritage is Catholic. I think Mami and Papi would expect me to honor their tradition."

The idea of a Catholic wedding seemed surreal to me. But on the other hand, it would be a bold expression of how I wanted to break out of my own ancestral expectations. And perhaps I would set an example for others who felt caught in the same trap.

We met with a priest at a local Catholic church. The three of us were getting along just fine until the priest said, "You will need to sign a pledge that you will raise your children Catholic." What? Ramón and I looked at each other in disbelief. Ramón stood first and motioned for me to stand too. He shook the priest's hand saying, "Thank you for your time, Father. I'm sorry. We can't sign any promise like that." As we drove away, we both were dumbfounded that the church would try to intrude so deeply into our private lives.

Ramón spoke the words that actually were music to my ears, in spite of my rebellion. "We'll get married in your mother's church. I bet that will make her happy."

Mom took Ramón and me to her church to meet the minister. As we left our session, the minister whispered in Mom's ear, "I don't get a sense that these two are in love." Mom didn't tell me about this observation until after the wedding.

Ramón and I announced our engagement. Mom wrote up a piece for the *Main Line Times* and the *Philadelphia Inquirer*. Coincidently, Dita also got engaged. Mom and Dad looked at their calendar and decided that both weddings would be held that winter. And both receptions would be held at Cackleberry, two months apart. With great vigor, they began to freshen up the old house. They seemed to visualize exactly how the rooms would be rearranged for the best flow of guests—where the food would be served and where the band would be located for the dancing. They were in their element. Dad even made a heated room out of our back porch by adding walls of clear plastic and renting a powerful space heater. There, he set up a cocktail bar. Mom knew where and how to order engraved invitations. Together, we compiled a list of friends and relatives to invite—mine, my parents', and Ramón's. Most of those on the guest list would be meeting Ramón for the first time.

Baton Rouge

While Mom and Dad continued the details of removing rugs and furniture, sanding dance floors, ordering flowers, food, a music ensemble, and borrowing a friend's antique touring car for transport to and from the church, Ramón and I drove to Baton Rouge, Louisiana, to meet his family. I was a little relieved to get away from all the wedding preparation, which included the details for Dita's wedding, which was to be even more formal than mine. I preferred the concept of a wedding over the details of putting one together. Plus, I was excited to travel to a new place and meet Ramón's parents, two brothers, and a sister.

As we drove, Ramón filled me in on their background. They lived in a comfortable, modest suburban home. Ramón's pretty mother had been in the States for six years and had her reasons to not learn English. First, she had no need. Both in Miami, where they first started out, and now in Baton Rouge, she had only Spanish-speaking neighbors and shopkeepers. Her social circle was insulated. As a child in Spain, where she was born, she had been taken against her will to live in Cuba. Always yearning for Spain, she now had to live in yet another country, the United States. Her form of protest was to not learn the language. Playing the piano was her solace. My ability to speak Spanish came in handy, and I felt she was receptive of me.

She had never planned to leave Cuba. It was a sudden necessity. Ramón explained what had happened less than a decade before this. His father, Papi, had worked hard in his career as a heat and air conditioning engineer, to the point where he could afford to send the four kids to Jesuit private schools. He had hired an architect to design his dream house which was set on a slope in the suburbs of Havana. Shortly after they had moved in, in 1959, Cubans took hope when a politician named Fidel Castro emerged to lead an overthrow of the detested military dictatorship of Fulgencio Bautista. Ramón's family rejoiced at first. But, as Castro began to reveal his own revolutionary goals in his public speeches, they became uneasy.

They made the bold and defensive move to send their eldest child, 17-year-old Ramón, and his 15-year-old brother to the States by themselves. They were to find their way to a Jesuit community of priests north of New York City. The two children knocked on the door and asked in broken English for asylum, fully trusting in the Jesuit connection. Unexpectedly, the priests wouldn't even let them spend the night, but chose rather to drive them to the Puerto Rican section of New York City, where the boys found a room to rent. Ramón explained the fright of it all and how he felt such an awesome responsibility for his younger brother as he trusted and obeyed his father's wisdom to get them out of Cuba. They were able to find jobs pushing a coffee cart from office to office in a high rise building.

It didn't take long for the committees of the Castro regime to organize and spread their tentacles into the private lives of the citizens. When the knock came on the door that Papi's new house was being claimed to be converted into a government-run school, the family fled immediately to the USA for safety. They arrived in Miami just in time, before the exit gates of Cuba were closed, having brought a little bit of money, a few changes of clothes, and two of their favorite paintings. Thankfully, the American immigration laws were loosened for the sudden influx of Cubans, and the family was permitted to stay on the basis of asylum. Papi was able to work at HVAC again, and the boys received scholarships at LSU. The family moved to Baton Rouge to be near the boys, and that is where I found them now.

The whole saga endeared me to Ramón and his family.

I Feel Pretty

Back home, Mom and I went shopping for a white satin wedding dress. I chose a floor-length one with lace sleeves to the elbow that matched the lace overlay of the skirt. The dress was scoop-necked with a princess seam at the bodice, allowing a gentle, fairly close flow over my svelte body. It had at least forty satin-covered buttons down the back.

Much to Ramón's displeasure, we decided the men would wear tuxedos. He and Dad would wear the more formal tuxedo jacket with tails. Ramón was experiencing culture shock. I could hear him talking in Spanish on the phone about the long-tailed monkey suit he had to rent. But I encouraged him that it would all be okay and that he would survive such formality.

On the day of the wedding, in December of 1967, Mom herself buttoned me up with her arthritic fingers. It seemed to take forever but neither of us complained. We knew this was a poignant moment. The same girl whose little dresses Mom had buttoned was now a grown woman moving on to her own family.

She then got the diamond and sapphire pendant, the one I wore to the Assembly Ball and she wore in her wedding to Dad in 1933. She put it on me. The tiered veil would be next. I stepped back to see my image in the long mirror.

I stood in my old bedroom, enthralled at what I saw. "I feel pretty," I told Mom.

Pretty Mrs. Ramón.

Cherry Hill on a Winter's Night

I had shed my wedding gown for a bright yellow and grey winter dress and high heels. It was time to go. Ramón and I forced ourselves to leave our own super fun wedding reception at Cackleberry. The party would continue into the night. Even his Mami added to the gaiety with song and laughter. We left in a flurry of hugs under a loving shower of pink rose petals. A chauffeured limousine whisked us away and dropped us off at our car, which had been previously parked out of sight, as planned by Dad.

Minutes later, I was hit with a sober unknown. "Where are we going on our honeymoon?" I asked my new husband.

"It's a surprise," he told me as we drove east toward Philadelphia.

"And where are we going to live after our honeymoon?" I had been so excited about the wedding that I had forgotten to talk about these things. Ramón, himself, had not brought up any details. He appeared unconcerned, like it was a fun game to pique my curiosity for our immediate future.

"You'll see. Soon enough," he seemed proud to say.

I was still floating as we drove past the city and crossed the Benjamin Franklin Bridge to New Jersey. But my heart sank when we pulled into the vast lot of a high rise hotel. It stood sentinel in a sea of empty parking spaces. The fountains and landscape gardens were in off-season slumber. Fortunately, it was a Saturday night and the hotel had enough patrons to activate the restaurant and serve a hot meal. No dancing was scheduled, however. The bandstand was dark.

So this was to be our honeymoon. I saw how pleased Ramón was with himself that he had made reservations for us for the night. Why Cherry Hill? I didn't know what I had expected but this was not it.

I still had hope. There had to be more. So I asked, "What is there for us to do tomorrow?" We were close enough for a Sunday stroll on the Atlantic City boardwalk. We could take silly pictures together in one of the photo booths. The pictures would be fun mementos. We could hear the waves and kick the sand. Then we could move on to another hotel with seafood by candlelight and a live dance band.

"Oh, 'Munch' (Ramón's nickname for me), I told you I have a surprise for you. I'll show it to you tomorrow."

Well, the next morning, his surprise was that he had found us an apartment on Pine Street in Philadelphia. His Cuban friends were showing up to help move a bed in.

My jaw dropped. This time, I could not hide my disappointment. "Do you mean we are spending the first day of our honeymoon moving furniture?"

Then Ramón released another bombshell. "We have to. I need to be at work on Monday."

The Next Surprise

Ramón smoked one cigarette a day, I found out—at night, after supper, lying on his back on top of the covers. It was a filterless Lucky Strike, the closest thing to a Cuban delight.

"It's my special time to unwind and to think," he explained. He tried to draw me into his almost sacred ritual. He wanted me to light the cigarette for him, then lie by his side without talking until the moment was over. I tried to be a good silent muse for him but, for me, it was hard to just lie still and not do anything, especially when it was time to do the dishes. Besides, I was annoyed that our bed and clothes were being permeated by the stinky smoke. I had gotten a job in a dress shop a few blocks away and was arriving there smelling like I had just come out of a bar. Thankfully, Ramón's one-a-day habit disappeared in the upcoming commotion of our new married lives.

During one of his last smokes, Ramón came up with a big idea. He approached the subject gingerly, trying to tell me in just the right way so that I would also get excited and dream along with him.

He started, "You know, Munch, now that you have left the dress shop, you are always wanting to spend time with your parents. And it's good that you have had these four months to live near enough for coffee time with them and with Marion and her children. Your family and Main Line roots run deep, and I know you love them. But I want you to consider something. You and I are married now. We are free to pull up and go and do whatever is out there. We can get our own life going and form our own roots together, however we want. Isn't that a beautiful thought? Do you agree?"

"Yes, I guess so," I said haltingly, not sure where this was leading.

"Well, I have always wanted to live in Europe. I'm an electrical engineer and I feel sure we could find a job there."

Wow! Europe! I suddenly was all ears. Mom and Dad would have to wait to have me live nearby, because this was a great opportunity. We rented a typewriter and set the plan into action. He wrote a cover letter for his résumé which I typed individually and sent to over a hundred American engineering companies in several European countries. It seemed to take forever but he got three job offers—from Switzerland, Germany, and Holland.

After all considerations, he chose The Hague in Holland. Before long, we said our goodbyes and boarded a sixteen-hour flight to Luxembourg on Icelandic Airlines. We linked arms and slept head to head. At pre-dawn we woke up for the two-hour layover on the Reykjavik moonscape.

"Oh No. What Have I Done?"

We both arrived dazed at the Luxembourg airport. I followed Ramón as we carried our luggage to the center of the open concourse. We set the pieces in a cluster. Ramón sat down on the biggest suitcase and was silent. It was an unlikely pose for a handsome man in a blue suit.

"What's the matter?" I asked him.

"I don't know what to do!" he admitted.

I suddenly felt insecure. For the first time since our wedding, my fearless leader, who had taken me to live in a faraway place, didn't know what to do. I knew exactly what to do but I didn't want to be his tour guide. *If he can't do this part*, I thought, *how can he handle the rest of our adventure?*

In nervous reaction, I rattled off how we go to the money exchange window to get some local cash, ask for maps and information at the travel center, get a ride (bus?) to the city, find a hotel for the night, then take a train to The Hague. All this seemed second nature to me after years of travel through South America. Ramón appreciated my expertise. Soon we were in a bus, heading down a romantic lane lined with straight tall trees on both sides. We looked at each other and smiled. We were actually traveling together in a foreign land.

My vacillating mood had lifted, even to exhilaration—at least, for that stretch.

A taxi took us to a fine old Luxembourg City hotel. The room was filled with satin upholstery fabrics of dusty rose and muted blues and peony flowers. I got ready for bed in the antique bathroom with the porcelain handles—emerging a little shy in a new and unfamiliar nightgown and the c'mon-and-get-me dabs of Mom's favorite Arpège.

Ramón had already disappeared under the voluminous covers. Only his face peeked out. He was surrounded by incongruous ruffled pillows. I saw his black eyes looking at me from across the room. A sudden dread overwhelmed me with a wave of strangeness. And regret. Even alienation. My mind flashed with stabbing thoughts, *Oh no! What have I done? WHAT? Am I married to HIM? I don't really know him! What am I doing? Am I going to live the rest of my life in Holland—with a man that the minister said I don't even love, and who doesn't love me? I have made such a big mistake! What am I going to do?"*

But then, just as quickly, in a few barefoot steps, I managed to push that all aside and decided, *Pull yourself together, Cecily. Don't let him know what you're thinking. You're here. This is reality. You chose him. Now go along for the ride.*

I slipped into the bed next to Ramón, and he never knew what my emotional mind airplane had just experienced.

Ik Moet Boodschappen Doen
(I Have To Go Grocery Shopping)

As soon as we got to The Hague, Ramón took over. He found us a furnished second floor apartment with a balcony that overlooked the city's busiest intersection. I mean busy. There must have been eight streets that converged at this one spot. In the center of the bedlam, a uniformed bobby directed traffic from a raised platform. He blew on his whistle and waved his white-gloved hands in perfect syncopation. I pulled back the lace curtain and studied the street scene.

I shook my head in disbelief and announced to my husband, "I'm not going out there, Ramón."

But, Ramón was not cowed. He had gone out to locate his new office and returned with a classified ad in the newspaper that showed a Vespa scooter for sale. "Since my job doesn't start for two weeks, I decided it would be fun if we buy this scooter and explore." He opened a paper bag. "I got us some maps," he added. He pulled out maps of Holland, Belgium, and Luxembourg.

"Oh. You mean really travel. Like to other countries. Overnight? On a scooter?"

"Yes, Munch. These countries aren't all that large, and we have this chance now before I'll be working everyday."

"Do you even know how to drive a scooter?" I asked.

165

"Don't worry about that. I'll learn instantly," he tried to reassure me. Well, we bought the scooter and before two blocks, a policeman pulled us over, asking to see our credentials.

"Your paperwork is fine," the officer said, "but you wobbled like a beginner, so I wanted to check on you. Take it easy. You'll learn." He let us go. I crossed my fingers all the way home as I grabbed Ramón's waist. He amazed me with his boldness and his ability to find our street in the unfamiliar maze of possibilities.

Our rain gear suits and helmets sat in the living room for three days as I worked through my fears of the trip. Ramón was too inexperienced, I told myself. We didn't know the roads, the traffic flow, nor the languages. The view outside our apartment was no less confusing after all these days. Ramón, though, showed great patience. He had bought a new 35-milli-meter camera before we left the States and spent the time learning how to use it. I watched him carefully. His calm demeanor rubbed off on me. I was finally able to put my trust in him once again. I let him take me on a magical tour out of the city, past farmland, through quaint villages, and by stone-walled grassy hills, dappled with happy cows and quiet sheep. He cleverly avoided cities. Every night there was a perfect inn at just the right time around the right bend. There was no need for our rain gear. The weather was magnificent.

I returned with a glow. Ramón's job started up and he was able to come home for lunch. Our landlady lived below us, so I asked her to come upstairs for a minute. I took her to our balcony window. "Helga," I began, "I need to find a supermarket to get groceries for lunches. Can you please show me where to go?"

"Oh!" she reacted. "*Je moet boodschappen doen!* You have to go gro-cery shopping!" Like a kindly mother hen, she pointed to the little shops across the street and explained that the foods I needed were sold from those specialty stores. There was no supermarket within walking distance. I was going to have to cross over to the meat store, the green grocer store, and the cheese shop. She then asked me to notice more carefully the traffic pattern below.

"There's a true order to it," she explained. "The lanes are all clearly marked." She asked me to follow her description. "You see? Pedestrians walk on the sidewalks. Bicycles are in the next lane. Then motorbikes. Then two lanes for cars. Then you stand on the island with the bobby. He will now direct you across the two lanes of opposing cars, and motorbikes and bicycles, until you are safely on the pedestrian sidewalk across the street. You just have to trust the process. It works!"

Thanks to Helga, I crossed over the streets to the shops and got my kitchen up and running. Ramón enjoyed fine spreads of cold cut lunches. I provided pork chop suppers too. We met an ambassador's daughter named Saskia who agreed to teach us Dutch in her home. She became our only friend. Her loving, warm manner made lesson night a highlight of our week as we zoomed to her house on our Vespa. We arrived with rosy cheeks and smiles. She treated us to pastries. The lilt of her voice transferred Dutch to us like a catchy song. No longer newcomers, we settled into a simple routine. I learned how to use the electric washing machine and told Mom in a letter that *"I just love to fold Ramón's underwear,"* and something about how it made me feel important and needed.

The wave of domesticity stirred up my desire to start a family. Ramón agreed that we could stop using contraception. I felt like a horse released from its bridle, free to gallop away to the appealing pasture called motherhood. Pastel blankets, diapers and bassinets swirled in my mind as I envisioned our baby making us three. We were about to redesign our marriage with a new focus, a new purpose. All my role playing with baby dolls was now to become my real flesh-and-blood life.

Weeks went by, however, and I was not yet pregnant. "I guess it's not as easy as I thought," I told Ramón. I tried taking my temperature so we could really go for it when I was most fertile. My graphed charts taped to our bedroom door became like wallpaper. It just wasn't working. We had become too clinical. Ramón agreed with me that we should stop the thermometer idea.

Meanwhile, the months rolled on. I tried to get distracted by signing up for work with a temp agency. The two of us decided to do something naughty, completely illegal. Ramón had acquired some contraband marijuana seeds. Marijuana was talked about when we were back in the States. It was no longer just for the street bums, but was becoming popular with students and young working people as an alternative to alcohol for getting high. The two of us had tried it enough times to make us curious. Ramón and I didn't drink, nor did we really want to smoke the weed. However, for a lark, we planted the seeds in two large flower pots, which we put outside on our balcony. The lacy green plants grew two feet tall. Both of us got an inward diabolical amusement that we were getting away with something so terribly verboten—in broad daylight right in the heart of the city.

Ramón seemed to be changing. He explained to me that his job was making him uneasy. He was an electrical engineer hired by a chemical engineering company. They were using him to introduce the efficacy of a new business system called a computer. The office was linked to a huge computer called a main frame, which they rented by the hour. Ramón was their sole operator. He had never used a computer. He tried to fake expertise while the clock ticked the hours away and the company's rental bills soared.

One day, when I came home from work—at an American oil company where the boss never asked my name but called me "Girl"—Ramón was home and relaxed. He had bought two new books and was already well into the first, a book by French philosopher Jean-Paul Sartre called *Being and Nothingness.*

"What's it about?" I asked Ramón as I sat down on the sofa next to him, glad to be with someone who knew my name, even though it was Munch. Ramón started in on how Sartre was delineating the modalities of being and not being for humans' sakes.

"He's an existentialist," Ramón went on. His eyes sparkled in excitement as he tried to describe that there's a distinction between two kinds of transcendence of the phenomenon of being. "The first is the transcendence of being and the second is that of consciousness," he explained from his understanding of the text. I tried to look intelligent, like I tracked with him. He showed me the second book by Simone de Beauvoir, who, I found out, was Sartre's lifetime lover and also a feminist philosopher of equal renown.

"You are way above my thinking capacity with this new hobby," I remarked as I got up to go fix supper in the kitchen. "I know one thing, though," I turned back with a smile to say, "Roses are red, violets are blue, sugar is sweet, and so are you!" I touched him gently on his nose. *Really, that handsome man should be pitied with such crowded thoughts circulating in his head.* But he couldn't seem to get enough.

He was advised to go introduce himself to a certain retired PhD professor who lived near the university. By this time, we had saved enough to purchase a car, a comical looking French Citroën 2CV, known in Holland as the Ugly Duckling. Ramón invited me to go along. We pulled up to the man's study, which was a wing of his house. Ramón asked me to wait in the car, explaining, "I won't be long." It was already dark. Through the window, I could see a man with a pipe reaching across his desk to shake hands with Ramón. Scores of shelved books surrounded them. Easily, an hour went by before Ramón emerged, so intellectually energized that he forgot to apologize for keeping me waiting.

More meetings with the professor followed but I wasn't invited. There was some talk about a man named Karl Marx and his political views called Marxism. Ramón came home from work one day with a thick paperback called *The Rise and Fall of the Third Reich*. It was about the history of Nazi Germany. He devoured it. I could see his interests expanding from philosophy to history and now to political thought. He took me to the seaside of Scheveningen where groups of vacationing Germans relaxed in beach chairs by their RVs. They slathered themselves with suntan lotion, and called out to one another across the sand grasses with spontaneous outbreaks of laughter.

"It's funny," Ramón noted. "To think, just twenty-five years ago, the Germans were bitter enemies. The Dutch were defending these very war torn, bloody beaches against them. Now, they are free to vacation here as they please, unimpeded." Good, I thought. I'm glad there is peace. I tried to decide if I was envious of people who could laugh so freely like that. I decided it required either friends or family to hang out with, and I didn't have either one of those here. I couldn't wait to start our own family.

"No. I Want To Go Home"

It was Christmas Eve day. We had been in Holland for about a year. Ramón had gone to work as usual. I was very excited that we had a telephone date for that evening with the whole family who would be at Granny's that year for Christmas dinner. I could just picture everyone seated around the lace-covered table, complete with silver candlesticks, a turkey platter, and maybe even a Welsh amber pudding for dessert. At an appointed hour, they expected our call, which we would initiate after midnight European time.

As it turned out, when we made this phone call home, instead of sharing in Christmas joy, we had to broadcast our sudden disappointing news. That day, Ramón had been fired from his job at the chemical engineering company. He came home looking dejected. His boss had pulled him aside to explain he was not a profitable employee–that he had used too much time on the computer, and the company had lost money. So just like that, they let him go. "I thought it was just a matter of time before this would happen," Ramón said.

We spent Christmas day talking about our options. This job was what had brought us overseas to The Netherlands. In my mind, we would, of course, return to Philadelphia. Ramón had another idea. "I'd really like to move to France and study history. Then I'd like to teach in a lycée."

"What's a lycée?" I asked, to bide time while I processed this thunderbolt of an idea.

"It's like a secondary school. I'd really like to live in Paris," he continued.

There was something in me that felt European politics and philosophy were the driving force to steer Ramón in this direction. I needed to veer him away. "No. First of all, you don't speak French. Second of all, the cost of living is too high for us there. I can't see us doing that, Ramón. I can't see ME doing that. Besides, I miss my family. I've been away from them for too many years. I really need to check in with them before I could take off and live in another country. My answer is no. I want to go home."

We talked further and Ramón came up with a compromise. "Alright, what I'll do is, I will go study history then teach history in the U.S. with the hope of maybe, after you've been home a while, going and teaching in France." I still wasn't happy with the France idea but at least we were headed home, and we could take it from there.

Is Marriage Supposed To Be Like This?

Back in Pennsylvania, Ramón enrolled as a history major at West Chester State College and we rented an apartment nearby. I found a teaching job in a research school on campus. I led a class for underprivileged two-year-olds, and then taught English to the children of newly arrived Puerto Rican mushroom farmers. We were not there for long.

Because his high school education was in Cuba, Ramón was required to take freshman American history. He felt like a fool at age 27 in a classroom of seventeen-year-olds, all being patronized by the professor. Ramón also took umbrage with the traditional history texts as compared to the more left-leaning interpretations from his own studies. The mixture of the two created an unbearable unrest in his psyche.

He had gotten a job working for the college using his electrical engineering expertise. They gave him the blueprints of the entire underground electrical system and asked him to go into the manholes to reconcile the actual wiring with the plans on the master drawings. He came home one afternoon and confessed to me that while he was under the sidewalk checking on the electrical grid, he had an overwhelming temptation to cross the wires and thus sabotage the entire campus. He and I knew it was time to quit school and move on.

Ramón seemed to know exactly where he wanted to go. "I've always wanted to live in Boston," he told me. *Wow! How did he pull that one out of a hat?* I had no idea but, as usual, I was willing to go on another adventure. Dad was familiar with Boston because he had gone to boarding school in Massachusetts. I had a Lake Erie friend from there and she recommended it. We packed up in no time, said our goodbyes, and moved up to New England. My thoughts turned to white picket fences again, and children. As we drove, I looked out the window and daydreamed about our new community and all the new friends I would be making.

Ramón, however, had other things on his mind. By now, it was 1969, and the newspapers were full of talk about a country named Vietnam. "There's a war going on between North and South Vietnam," Ramón told me. I had no idea where that was and why it should be such a focus of attention. "While you were in Peru and we were in Holland," he continued, "our troops have been over there fighting in the conflict. So many have died. It's a brutal war, with a hopeless outcome."

"That's terrible," I told him, still not knowing what it had to do with our hopes and dreams of a new life in Boston. Ramón found us an apartment in what I called a grey collar retiree neighborhood in Jamaica Plain. I was miffed. He hadn't even asked me where I wanted to live.

"But, Ramón, there are no young couples living here," I complained. "How are we supposed to make friends our own age?" Ramón convinced me that this was best for our budget and that it was a convenient walking distance to the station for the elevated rail into the city.

We lived on the second floor over our landlady, Mrs. Shimonovich, a fear-filled widow who monitored our every intrusive noise. She would come to the back stairs and bang on the banister to get our attention. "There you go, slamming the refrigerator door again!" she'd say. "And the way you walk! It sounds like a herd of elephants up there! Or what? Are you horses?" She sure didn't help my self image, which was becoming fragile with this confusing move to Boston and my unpredictable husband.

I hadn't known why Ramón wanted to be in Boston but I soon found out. He could go to the Harvard campus in Cambridge to look at bulletin boards, pick up the vibe and tap into the anti-Vietnam War movement. He went to meetings. The outcome was a formulation of anti-war rhetoric, sentiment, philosophy, and propaganda. Ramón became more and more radical in his thinking to where he became an editor of the underground newspaper called *The Old Mole*. It was all he talked about.

173

"Should I be against the war too?" I asked Ramón one morning. I figured if I got on board with him we would have more in common. He jumped at the idea and took me to a makeshift office. There, a group was organizing the busloads for November's Washington DC protest march against the war. I was offered a job to take phone calls and keep names on file cards. They paid me sixty dollars a week, which was to be our only income for the the rest of our marriage. Ramón had been fired from a gas attendant job at a service station because of his cavalier attitude. The owner didn't want him to lean against the building with one foot on the wall between customers. The coup de grâce was the time he let a lady drive off with the gas nozzle still in her tank. By this time, engineering work was a thing of the past.

At my new work office, church groups, other associations and individuals called or came in to sign up for buses. One of the managers was an older Quaker woman who described herself as a pacifist. My immediate boss was with SDS (Students for a Democratic Society), though he tried to hide that identity from me, thinking I would consider him a communist, or something, which I did. There was a callous, shifty-eyed, humorless atmosphere in the office. And a lot of whispering. I just tried to do my job and stay insignificant. At least when I met Ramón after work, I knew I was loved, even though it was in our own gloomy kind of way.

One day as I came up the subway stairs on my way to work, I passed a backpacker who was obviously heading off on a trip. He had a bedroll and wore hiking boots.

I said to him, "Where are you going?"

He said, "Off to the mountains. I'm getting away from here."

I said, "Oh! I wish I could go with you!"

In October, there was to be a trial of seven anti-war activist leaders to be held in Chicago. The "movement," that I was now pulled into, reacted with rage that their leaders might be convicted. So they organized a demonstration called TDA, The Day After the trial, to be held in the Boston Commons.

Ramón took me there. The crowd swelled and became rowdy as nighttime enveloped us. Before I knew it, policemen on horseback appeared from nowhere and stampeded towards us, spraying clouds of tear gas. The crowd dispersed, screaming. I saw many people fall on top of each other as they were pressed against a two-foot wall. There were frightful sirens and red flashing lights. Ramón and I turned to run away from the horses and got separated. I just ran as fast as I could, my heart pounding. I passed wild brick-throwing men who were smashing beautiful plate glass windows with a horrifying crash. I ran desperately for several blocks towards the unknown, to quieter dark streets of the business district, until I was completely lost and exhausted. I sat down on a large window sill, quivering and stunned. Then somehow, miraculously, Ramón appeared at my side. He was unscathed. He took my hand and we walked the long distance back to our car.

There was another demonstration in the making. This time it was to protest the conversion of low rent brownstone row houses into upscale apartments for yuppies, which would push the low income people out. Ramón was part of a men's caucus to help plan it. He encouraged me to meet with the women's caucus, which I agreed to do, thinking it might be a chance to make a new friend. It was held in someone's house. Women sat on sofas, chairs, and the floor. They were all strangers to me but seemed to know each other. No one welcomed me. The meeting was already underway. Women were saying, "We hate this," and, "We hate that," and, "F— this," and ,"F— that," and something about revolution against the Big E, meaning the Establishment, until I couldn't stand to hear anymore. I boldly stated that I didn't hate anybody or anything, and a chorus of women shouted at me, "Don't be proud of that!"

Well, the demonstration was an all night sit-in, whereby a group of us broke into one of the brownstones to occupy it. My body was there but my spirit wasn't, especially when they started to put up chains and barricades to keep the police at bay. I looked at Ramón and wondered if he was really enjoying this revolting, terrifying, rebellious situation. I didn't like these people and would much rather have been home in my own bed. Fortunately, the police never showed up and we all disbanded before daybreak.

The Beatles began putting out songs that spoke to me. In one song, aptly called Revolution, they said, "Don't you know that you can count me out." They made me realize that I didn't have to be in this revolution. I could be counted out. I had a choice to hold onto the things that I held dear, like love, beauty and a peaceful way of life. "Give Peace a Chance," they also sang. The "peaceniks" were anything but peaceful. I had no obligation to identify with this group. But what to do? There was another song the Beatles sang which even sounded religious. It said "Mother Mary, comes to me, speaking words of wisdom, 'Let it be.'" That was my answer! *Let it be! Just let it be. Don't go with that flow. Just return to the peace that you once knew.*

I tried to redirect Ramón back into our idea of becoming a family. I couldn't help thinking if we had a child, things would be better. We still were not conceiving, so I went to a fertility clinic which tested me to find out that I was okay. I was, indeed, fertile. The problem turned out to be Ramón's low sperm count, which the doctor said could be what's known as "hysterical," or temporary infertility caused by stress. "Take it easy," the doctor told Ramón. "Try to enjoy life and this problem might go away."

He took me out to dinner as I clung to the doctor's words of hope. Driving on a high ramp on the way home, I looked out over the lights of Boston, and how they sparkled with reflections on the water.

"Aren't the lights beautiful?" I remarked to Ramón.

He came back with, "How can you say they are beautiful? Those lights are shining on a repressive society. They shine on a world that oppresses the poor. Why should anyone want to bring a child into this?" He paused. "Anyway, I don't plan to worry about it. It's like if you don't need the car, don't fix it."

He might as well have slapped me across my face, or dug my heart out. We drove the rest of the way home in silence. The lights were still beautiful in my mind, no matter what he thought. I wasn't going to feel guilty about it either. I truly pitied him for his outlook on life. At the same time, I tried to put myself in his place to where he had just been told he was not able to produce a child.

The word adoption came to my mind but I pushed it into the deal-with-this-later category. My strong biological need to have a baby wouldn't let me consider such a solution. Then, I thought to myself it might even be a good thing to not subject a child to Ramón's loveless politics. I felt sick. I felt numb. I felt stuck.

That night, I got weepy. Ramón held me in his arms in bed as I cried.

Is marriage supposed to be like this? I asked the moon outside the window.

Ramón comforted me. "It'll be okay, Munch," he said softly as he pulled me closer. The very one who was the source of my sorrows was the only one I knew who could offer me solace.

Divvying Up the Slides

Much to my delight, Ramón stopped going up to Cambridge and *The Old Mole* scene at the same time that I had loosed myself from any identity with that group. We both spent more time at home, reading, listening to his Cuban music, and trying new recipes. Ramón bought himself a new toy one day—a short wave radio and headphones. He carefully tuned in to the available stations until he hit one that caught his fancy. In fact, he became obsessed with it, spending hours at a time adorned with headphones.

He came to the table, his bearded face brightened with a big smile. "I've made contact directly with Cuba," he announced. "I'm listening to Fidel Castro himself, speaking in real time! He's making a lot of sense. He's explaining to the people that because of all the embargoes placed against his country, the only solution is to increase the production of sugar cane to export. He's putting out an edict for all Cubans to work the harvest, even the professionals. He sounds so desperate. It makes me proud to hear his pride for Cuba."

The next day, Ramón had a eureka moment. "I've been fighting the wrong revolution all this time. America's problem with Vietnam is not mine to fight. My allegiance should be to my own heritage, Cuba. My grandfather devoted his life to help free Cuba from Spain."

"But, Ramón," I reacted, "Castro is a Marxist dictator who kills people! You and your family had to flee from him. You even told me what hardship he created for your family."

"I'm just listening and learning," Ramón explained. "They are urgent down there. There's a cry of "*venceremos*" coming across the airwaves." I knew *venceremos* meant "we shall overcome," which singer Joan Baez sang in her lilting anti-war song. "And," Ramón continued, "Fidel is talking more about achieving a social movement that overthrows oppressors, with force, if necessary."

Ramón kept listening. He bought books. He taped a huge red and black poster of a bearded man, Che Guevara, onto our living room wall. I learned that Che was a kind of folk hero for the revolutionary movement in Cuba. He was a handsome man, especially wearing a becoming beret. No wonder he appealed as an icon. But he was a brutal killer with radical ideas. I pulled the window shade down so his face wouldn't be visible from the street. Ramón chided me that no one out there would know who this man was. A young couple had moved into an apartment nearby. I wanted to make friends with them but was too mortified by our Marxist hero on display to invite them over. So they remained strangers to us.

Ramón seemed serious about his new belief in fighting for the cause of the poor masses. One morning, we awoke to a Boston winter wonderland. The snow had accumulated on all the parked cars. Fortunately, we didn't need to go out and were okay to stay put. Ramón had a new political theory he wanted to share with me. We were sitting in our two soft chairs facing the front window. As he talked, I saw a silver-haired neighbor come out with a snow shovel. He began the arduous task of digging his car out of the snow. Another man came out to help, while a third man needed to clear his own car. The three middle-aged men made progress but stopped to lean on their shovels and rest a bit. I was watching them. Ramón was too. But Ramón was not distracted from his train of thought. He stood up to get a better view. He kept talking about helping the poor in far-off lands. Meanwhile, three men right outside our window could have used his help at that very moment. The word hypocrisy came to my mind but I really didn't want to apply it to my husband. Even so, there was a certain comfort thinking that all his talk about revolutionary things was merely cerebral posturing and could be confined to our living room so we could carry on living our "real" lives.

I had enough indoctrination of Ramón's "hypocrisy" to spout off to Dad on a short visit to Cackleberry. Tucked in my mind was Ramón's recent description of how a revolution would look. He had taken out a yellow legal pad and had drawn a line across the upper third of the paper. Below the line, he explained, were the workers—the peasants and proletariat. Above the line, were the people of wealth, the oppressors, who traditionally ruled over those powerless masses.

"They are like a sour cream on the top," Ramón described. "If we can just get them out of the way—do away with them—we will have the perfect society—liberty for the people."

"But Ramón," I argued, "your theory has no merit. It's based on a fatal flaw. If you have to kill a class of people to make it happen, then you have begun your new society with that black blot. And, anyway, a new class of people will rise up to oppress the others." I was proud that my sociology minor at Lake Erie was finally being put to use.

It was like Ramón didn't hear me. He held up the yellow pad and pointed to above the line saying, "Cecily, wake up! You have to realize that your parents are above the line. If need be, take a gun to them!" I looked at him in horror. Surely, this was all rhetoric, like the thought about blowing up the college campus.

I took advantage of Dad's cocktail hour to have a rare moment alone with him. I started to talk. Inside my very being, I was crying out, *Rescue me, Dad!* I was craving my own liberation from a bleak reality. If only he knew how unhappy I was and how I cried at night.

But outwardly, I found myself pontificating to Dad as if I were Ramón. I described Ramón's theory from the legal pad, but didn't carry it so far as to categorize where Mom and Dad fit in.

Dad listened to me with great patience. This was not his idea of "happy hour." He would much rather have been asking how my Ugly Duckling car was running, the one we had imported from The Hague. I paused to let him respond to me. The ice clinked in his bourbon glass. Squirming in his chair, he cleared his throat and leaned his face closer to me. Then he said, "You're no longer my Cecy. I don't love you anymore."

His words hit me like bullets. But they didn't penetrate my heart. My mind raced back to ten years earlier. In the same two chairs, after a second (or third) bourbon, Dad had told me I shouldn't apply to college because I wasn't "college material." I didn't accept his alcoholic words then, and I didn't accept them now. I knew, deep down inside, that Dad really did love me. He always would. We both were victims of rhetoric now.

I returned to Boston where crowds linked arms and sang "Kumbaya." *Did they know they were saying "Oh, Lord, come by here"? Was that rhetoric too? Or did they really want God to intervene?* At that time, the Beatles sang "Get Back to Where You Once Belonged." Now, that song really spoke to me. *Where had I once belonged? And how could I get back there?*

Ramón had something new to tell me. Castro's desperate plea for workers to harvest sugarcane had reached the hearts and minds of Americans from the radical left. A group that called themselves the Venceremos Brigade had chartered a ship to take five hundred sympathizers to Cuba to cut cane.

"They're really going to do that?" I asked Ramón.

"Yes. They are," Ramón answered. "The ship leaves in three weeks from Newfoundland. What I want to tell you, Munch, is that I'm going to be on that ship. But I'm not part of the Brigade. They won't know it until I show up. I'm getting a one-way ticket. I'll stay there and help Fidel with his Revolution. I have to do this in honor of my grandfather. I will show up like a hero on a white horse, ready to help in whatever way I can."

My ears heard Ramón's words. My body went out of itself, and I was floating for several seconds in a seated position in the middle of the living room away from my chair. Later, I learned that I had been in a state of shock. "But, Ramón. What about me? What about our marriage? Are you leaving me just like that?" This time, I could see that Ramón was sincere, and that he really was going to take action.

"I thought about this while you were away." He paused. "If you want, you can come with me." There was no Munch. "We could continue as a married couple, but not in the conventional way. We wouldn't see much of each other. When I work for Fidel, I will have to be where he needs me for the Revolution. I'm sure it will be up in the mountains fighting with the guerrilla forces. That's no place for you. As a woman, you could get a job in a village working in a day care center."

I hated the idea. *How would any wife want to settle for such an arrangement?* I felt like he was throwing me away. There was little emotion towards me in his words. It was like his newfound allegiance to Fidel had captured his heart. *What about our vows?* I had promised to stay with him in sickness and in health, till death do us part.

Determined to find out if there was possibly a better arrangement for us in Cuba, I immediately decided to go to the Swiss Embassy in New York, where consular Cuban affairs were handled. I told them my husband and I were thinking about moving to Cuba. I asked them if I or my future children would have the freedom to visit my family in the States. They told me, "Not at this time."

"Even if the embargo and restrictions were lifted," they said, "you would probably not have the money to make such a trip."

What a dire report! That's all I needed to hear. Ramón was going off to a land with a communist regime that promised me a life of poverty, isolation, danger, no companionship with him, and no visits with my family or my beloved United States. I ceased any thoughts of going with him.

I returned to Boston and told Ramón I was ready to release him from his marriage vow to me. He was free to pursue his dream. He then released me from my vow. We sorted through our things like two college roommates parting ways at graduation. Ramón wanted only his vinyl discs of Cuban music and some photo transparencies of our two-and-a-half years together. He said he was going to be traveling light and these items would give him some memories.

We set up our slide projector. He used it to flash all our captured moments onto the now bare living room wall. One by one, happier times of our life in Holland and at Cackleberry seemed to mock us—there were no pictures from Boston. Ramón wanted to keep about every fourth slide. Most of them were shots of me. In that way, I would be boarding the boat in his backpack, he said.

Gladly, I thought to myself, *I won't be at his side*. I wished he had selected all of the pictures. I wanted all of those memories to leave with him.

We were star-crossed lovers like Romeo and Juliet. Though we didn't have to die like they did, our marriage had to die, because our continued relationship was impossible. Though we weren't from feuding families, our homelands were feuding. Ramón had succumbed to an irresistible calling to cross the littoral blockade between our homelands, thereby renouncing his own family and his marriage to me.

Politics and philosophy were the loathsome victors over love and family.

Perhaps prophetically, I had memorized an old English poem that had touched my heart back in college. It was called "To Lucasta on Going to the Wars." I realized it could have been written now by my husband some three hundred and twenty years later. His version would go something like this:

> Tell me not, sweet [*Munch*], I am unkind,
> That from the nunnery
> Of thy chaste breast and quiet mind
> To war and arms I fly.
> True, [*with Fidel Castro*], a new mistress now I chase,
> The first foe in the field;
> And with a stronger faith [*than marriage*] embrace,
> A sword, a [*white*] horse, a shield.
> Yet this inconstancy [*divorce*] is such
> As thou too shall adore [*come to appreciate*];
> I could not love thee, dear [*Munch*], so much,
> Loved I not honor more.

Richard Lovelace 1649 [*and Ramón 1969*]

I languished on a sofa for the next year at Cackleberry, sad and unable to eat, inconsolable by Mom's and Dad's sweet efforts to help me "get back to where I once belonged." There was no therapy group, no counseling. Just me trying to figure it all out, in a safe place where Che Guevara's face was not looming over me and the police would not be knocking at my door. I went to a lawyer for a divorce. The process was simple.

"Where should I serve the divorce papers?" the lawyer asked.

"I don't know. My husband took off and I don't know where he is," I answered truthfully.

When I received the final decree, the grounds were Abandonment. It cost me three hundred dollars. Just like that, the white dress, the veil, the limousine, the marriage certificate, the vows were to no effect.

I had maintained few friends, the best one being Ellen who lived far away. We wrote to each other because we both had married Cuban men. Unlike anyone I knew, she understood my circumstances.

My up-the-hill cousin, Ross, owned a photography shop in Bryn Mawr and offered me a job at the counter. His mom, my Aunt Ann, was the bookkeeper. In her quiet, non-judgmental way, she loved on me as I sat next to her desk between customers. Ross challenged me to learn how to use the Hasselblad camera on a tri-pod in the back studio.

It was through a photo shoot for a man's publicity portrait a year later that I was invited to a party being held by that man's wife. At that party, I met Levi.

*U*SS RAY had several classified deployments in 1968 and our team was on a roll. I had been awarded the Legion of Merit and other awards. I was detached from RAY in March 1969 and was assigned to be the Commander Submarine Division Sixty-Two which consisted of USS RAY, USS LAPON, USS HAMMERHEAD and USS SEA DEVIL. I later was also assigned to be Commander Submarine Division Sixty-Three. I was very thrilled to still be working for my old bosses, Vice Admiral Schade and Captain Jerry Clarke III. We were a great team. But change was in the air.

I had been promoted to Commander two years early, so after only nine months as a Submarine Division Commander, I was relieved on 17 January 1970. I had gotten orders to proceed to Washington DC to serve in the Pentagon. I had never been assigned to that area but I was informed that eventually all must serve there if they are to have a future in the Navy.

Part 5
Levi

"Wherever You Go, I'm Going To Be There with You."

Ididn't realize how much I was enjoying his company until he got up to leave. His green eyes sparkled as he smiled, and I was attracted to his lighthearted energy. His name was Levi. As he joked, he included me as if I were a longtime friend. We sat in a small group on the floor, eating chips, talking, and listening to mellow music, surrounded by people who also were new to me.

This was 1969-70, when there was a lot of challenge to status quo in all of American culture. Bob Dylan was singing, "The times they are a-changing." The "Dawning of the Age of Aquarius" song was big from the show called *Hair*. The men were growing their hair long. There was an interest in marijuana, and who knows what other drugs were becoming pervasive. They not only hit the urban scene, but also rural areas. People just wanted to find a new way to think and to live.

With his long curly hair and full beard, he wasn't exactly someone I would bring home to meet Mom and Dad. That hippy look might have shocked them. Besides, he was Jewish, which I found out by some of his humor. His friends were all happy. There was no evidence of drugs. And no talk of politics.

I found myself wishing the party wouldn't end. "Do you have to leave so soon?" I asked him. "The party is just starting." I wanted to say, "It won't be the same without you," and something like, "This is my first party since I left Peru four years ago."

But, he was determined to get going. I stood up to walk him to the door. He paused at the kitchen counter to pick up snacks for the road. "Would you like to join me?" he asked. "I'm driving to New York to visit some art studios. I manage my mother's art gallery. I've got to return a couple unsold pieces and pick out new ones. It'll be a long day but it'll be fun."

I told him I was sorry but I needed to use the next day, Saturday, to move from my parents' home into a room I rented in Philadelphia. I didn't tell him that the room was in a student-filled brownstone in a university neighborhood, and that I was planning to throw all caution to the wind and go wild with my life. But he came back with an irresistible offer. If I really wanted to go with him, he would use the gallery's van to help me move on Sunday.

It was a deal. We went the next day. Being exposed to the New York art scene was enlightening. Levi's persona was all business as he handled paintings worth thousands of dollars. He treated the artists with kid gloves, wanting to continue a good business relationship. I sensed he felt tension in his role as representative of his mother's prestigious gallery. He needed to select just the right pieces to please her, and at the same time convince the artists to let go of their precious art creations for possible sale. He also had to use great diplomacy when there was no appropriate piece he wanted to take at that time.

I watched him carefully. He was great at his job but he was not my type of guy. He wore a cluster of keys from his belt loop that jangled when he walked and black tie shoes with saw-tooth black rubber soles.

As promised, Levi moved my mattress and clothes to my new place on Sunday.

On Monday, I went "home" to the student brownstone after working at the photo shop, eager to see how I would fit into this new academic community. I walked into the communal kitchen. AND THERE HE WAS! *Dang!* He had already made friends with housemates I hadn't even met yet. He was cramping my style—making it look like I was spoken for, when I wasn't.

The guy students kindly included us at their meal that evening. Curiously, Levi's joie de vivre seemed to loosen up their otherwise bookish personalities. Soon they all left for their rooms to go study. Levi and I stayed at the table and talked. I was discovering that an age twenty-six divorcée was misplaced among young serious students. I felt more at ease with Levi. We were the same age, and he had been divorced too—both of us jilted.

For days, we met there after work. I asked him why he kept showing up. He told me something I really needed to hear, especially after being rejected by Ogden and abandoned by Ramón.

Levi said to me, "I'm not letting you slip away. Wherever you go, I'm going to be there with you." *Wow. He must really like me.* I received his words into my heart as a welcomed pledge.

The next thing I knew, we were best friends setting off on an eleven year 70's saga together that would bring us three precious children.

An Alternative Lifestyle

Levi's three-room apartment belied my impression of him as an all-business city boy. It was uniquely situated in an original manor house he called "Beverlea," a remnant farmhouse on Philadelphia's city line, now surrounded by hotels and office buildings. Potted plants hung from the ceiling. A calico cat looked at me from the deep window sill where she sat next to a few select books. The living room had two modern chairs. On a table next to the main chair was a harmonica and a pipe stand with four pipes. The smallest one was made from a corn cob, like Popeye's. A guitar stood nearby. A wide slab of walnut served as the kitchen counter. In the bedroom another slab of wood, propped on legs like a low table, served as the headboard above a queen-size mattress with a quilt on the carpeted floor. On this table was an alarm clock and an incense burner. Everything was neat and tidy.

I opened the kitchen cupboards. In the first one I saw stacks of wooden bowls. The others held only large unmarked jars of rice, and beans that looked like tan marbles and hard brown pellets.

"Where's your food," I asked Levi, hoping it was stashed somewhere else because I was hungry.

"That's it," he replied. "You just relax and I'll fix you a nice supper." I was about to have my first macrobiotic meal. Levi explained he was no longer a meat and potatoes man. He had become a disciple of a Japanese health diet consisting of mostly brown rice, beans, vegetables, and seaweed. The rationale for the diet was based on a philosophy of *yin* and *yang*, which are opposites. By balancing the opposites, one becomes "one with the order of the universe." I watched him work quietly in the kitchen. There was no clatter of metal spoons against pots. He was focused like a priest at the altar, deftly chopping vegetables on cutting boards, stirring with wooden spoons, and filling wooden bowls. He showed me how to use chopsticks. We ate his simple meal by candlelight. I was in awe. My little room seemed suddenly so far away.

"Would you please consider staying the night here with me?" Levi asked warmly.

I said, "Yes. I'd like that." My little room in the city now faded into oblivion.

Levi lit up his favorite curved calabash pipe with the meerschaum tobacco bowl. He explained this was his fireplace, his longed-for campfire, his time for reverie. Throughout his childhood, he told me, the living room was off bounds for him and his brother and sister. He could only stand in the doorway and try to imagine a crackling fire coming from the beautiful white birch logs that sat piled neatly on the brass andirons in the family fireplace. The only one to touch them was the maid with her feather duster.

The days and weeks passed. I learned more about him.

Macrobiotics was a new interest, he told me, an attempt to rid his body of marijuana and other hallucinogenic drugs that he had used, especially while in Alaska. He had gone there to work construction for a year to recover from the breakup of his marriage to his high school sweetheart who had fallen for another (wealthy) man.

Levi had returned to Pennsylvania only a few months before I met him. He started working at the art gallery and reacquainted himself with his two little girls. They lived with their mother and stepfather in a fancy glass house with a pool on the side of a mountain. Levi had visitation rights, but was not permitted to take them off the property. Each time we went to see them, the younger one would fly out of the house to jump up onto Levi and cling to him.

"Monkey!" Levi called out to her as she ran toward him, his arms wide open. Monkey's name was Charity. Over the years, she spent time on and off living with us until she reached middle school. She preferred being with her Dad but Levi and I were on the move and, whenever we flunked as

Charity's parents, her mother would give her the structure we didn't provide. Her sweet sister visited us too, but stayed living with her mom.

Levi had no real concept of what I had been through with Ramón. In fact, he was refreshingly apolitical. I wondered if he could even tell me who the president was. He didn't know what it was like to fear the police, to call them pigs. The government was not the monster enemy—the "Big E" Establishment out to get him. Although he had been a drill instructor in the marines, and bore a bulldog tattoo on his arm as proof, he had by now laid down guns preferring to seek quiet and peace.

He and I had met at just the right time. We were both treading water, not sure of our next destination. He was the companion I needed to feel pretty again, and safe, and even free to experiment with getting high on marijuana. Levi had already lost interest in marijuana. But we had friends who supplied me with little bags of marijuana and I learned how to roll a "weed," light it, and hold in the smoke until I felt loosened up to where I would expound on subjects I didn't know anything about. Or I'd dance, or be silly. I discovered different aspects of my personality that fascinated my own self. Like a kindergartener, I was getting my wiggles out. It was all part of recovery from the traumatic two-and-a-half years with Ramón.

Levi was ready to move on to a new phase of life. In addition to macrobiotic cookbooks with the philosophy of *yin* and *yang*, he began reading books like "Walden; Life in the Woods," by Henry David Thoreau. He valued magazine articles about camping, country living, and communal living. I began to read them too. We both enjoyed a new magazine called "Mother Earth News." It proposed a simple, resourceful life, surrounded by nature that sounded so appealing. We had likeminded friends, Jay and LaLa, who taught me how to enjoy macrobiotic foods like brown rice knishes with tamari sauce and hijiki seaweed sautéed with matchstick carrots.

Levi was still managing the Fontana Art Gallery and had left the apartment one morning in the company van. I was commuting every day to the Photo Center. My brother, Bob, and his wife Ann, had sold me their station wagon for five-hundred dollars. They were moving to Mexico City with IBM and didn't need it. Ironically, even though Levi still carried that important bunch of keys for the gallery, we didn't ever worry about locking our own apartment.

I got too blasé and left my car key in the ignition overnight. In the morning, I went to leave for work and the car was gone. I was furious that someone would steal my car. And I felt stupid for not being more careful. But there was no time to wallow in emotions. The fact was that I still had to get to work.

I decided to hitchhike. So I walked half a mile across a grassy field to City Line Avenue. There, I held out my thumb and quickly got a ride to Bryn Mawr. I wasn't even late. After work, I did the opposite. It took two rides but I got home. The people who picked me up were friendly and glad to help me out. Aunt Ann and Ross at the Photo Center seemed shocked that I would lower myself to become a hitchhiker. But at least their employee showed up.

I couldn't wait to tell Levi of my success. "Guess what, Levi. My car was stolen overnight, so I hitched rides to work and back."

"Good for you, Babe!" was his reaction.

In fact, hitchhiking worked so repeatedly well for my situation, that Levi came up with a bold plan one calabash evening. I could tell that he was having that euphoric moment when the tobacco was burning just right. His eyes rolled back as he let go of a staccato of smoke puffs. They smelled like cherry and rose happily to the ceiling.

"I have an idea," he began. He was taking action on many hours of discussions. "We don't have to keep living a nine-to-five existence. I'm sure if we go looking, we can come up with an alternative lifestyle." His concept reminded me of Simon and Garfunkel's "Looking for America" song.

Levi tamped his pipe. "We'll spend our days according to the seasons— not the commercial calendar. I'm tired of working for a paycheck." The "Walden" ideology had captured his imagination.

He continued, "We've both saved our money for the past year. If we pool it together, we'll have enough to travel to find a new life." We had no vehicle, so it was logical, he said, to get rides from others by hitchhiking, which I had proven to be good at.

Then he popped the question, "Are you willing to go with me?"

Go West, Young Man

I t was easy to say yes. Clearly, he wanted me to go along as much as I wanted to be by his side. Levi had an alluring energy, a fun personality, and an adventuresome spirit. I still felt safe with him. He was capable of making this adventure happen. Although I didn't have the urgency to move on like he did, I trusted his vision that there was something special "out there" that we were currently missing.

There was no one else I wanted to be with. Funny. Now I was following him, instead of him following me. Seriously, how could I resist a man who whistled cheerfully in the morning?

We both quit our jobs and cut off our long hippy hair to appear more clean cut to prospective rides. Mine had become full and wild like Janis Joplin's. Levi's was down to his shoulders. His beard crowded his shirt collars. Sitting side by side in the barber shop while committing to a whole new look felt like a wedding. The proud barber pushed our mounds of cut hair into a unified pile. We posed for *before* and *after* pictures of us standing outside the barber shop.

We had mulled over the idea of marriage and how our outlook on it had changed. In both of our cases, divorce had so easily nullified both the promises and the certificates that we had taken seriously. Our conclusion was that we would show the world what a marriage commitment really meant. By sticking together as a loving couple, we would set an example for others. We began introducing ourselves as Mr. and Mrs. We were now married by Common Law, according to Pennsylvania statutes. In fact, if we decided to split up, we would have to divorce. I was glad to find this out. It softened the blow of my renegade ways for my family.

The cheapest way for us to get out west was to hitchhike. We would even keep going south to Mexico City to visit brother Bob. On the way, we hoped to discover a place to put down roots. I held a yard sale at Cackleberry where I sold every single nice wedding gift from my marriage to Ramón—fine china, casserole dishes, lamps and other things. With that cash, we bought hiking boots, warm sleeping bags, backpacks, and a red nylon pup tent.

As it turned out, Dita and her second husband and their baby, Jeremiah, were also seeking a new life. They were heading west in their VW bus and agreed to give us a ride to Kansas City to visit Levi's brother, Jim, who taught law out there. They also happily joined us on two stops that we knew we wanted to make on the way. Baby Jeremiah had all sorts of crawling room in the back of the bus. So Levi and I crawled in there with him.

The first stop was for a week at a no-cost macrobiotic camp on a farm near Binghamton, NY. Under the guidance of teacher Michel Abehsera, we learned to slow down and appreciate our food. We all sat cross-legged, each holding a bowl of brown rice and chewing the grains meditatively until they became like liquid. "Chew your drink and drink your food," he taught us. I watched Levi and Dita and all the other campers. We looked like cows chewing cud but we were healthfully virtuous. We found out that brown rice was the perfect food. It needed saliva to begin the digestive process. I saw mothers of toddlers first chew up the rice then spit it in a spoon to feed the baby. I decided I would do that too for my first baby. Add cooked brown beans to the rice and you had a complete protein. No wonder Levi had already made these two foods his staples.

It was such clean fun being at that camp. In the evenings we would light a little campfire near our tents and laugh, talk, and dream. It was a wonderful time to enjoy the wildflowers, butterflies, the fields around us, the trees, and birds. Baby Jeremiah explored through the grass on his hands and knees. We were among other hippies and women in their bright colored skirts and long flowing hair, some strewn with flowers. We went to sleep in our tents with the feeling of "aren't we all cool?"

Midweek, a large white tent appeared. Two bearded guys, dressed in white, quietly lured campers to sign up for their free one-on-one initiation to the practice of Transcendental Meditation (TM). It had recently been introduced to the east coast by Indian guru Maharishi Mahesh Yogi. Being curious, I was the only one in our foursome who signed up. My visit into the tent was brief. With a holy aura, they ushered me to a chair placed on a small rug. I figured, *uh-oh. I better switch to a really respectful attitude and take this seriously.* One of the guys told me he was going to give me a sound, a mantra, that I was to repeat to myself for twenty minutes in a quiet place twice a day. My mantra was selected just for me and I should never say it aloud or tell others what it was.

I left the tent feeling super spiritual and pretty special that I had my own mantra. It was weeks before Levi and I were alone in the woods and I felt the freedom to withdraw to a favorite rock to sit and meditate. After the first session, I came back to Levi with a smile, mainly because it was a victory for me to go sit alone someplace and be quiet and still. But then, I started getting headaches when I meditated. The more I said the mantra and turned inward, the worse my head hurt. Then something else started happening that I needed to share with Levi. I wasn't sure how to spell my mantra but it had the sound of the word "I'm." For twenty minutes I found myself thinking, *I'm a fool. I'm a dumb woman. I'm lost. I'm terrible. I'm bad,"* or whatever. It was always a negative thought. I let that happen for a couple of days, then decided TM was not for me. So I quit. Levi was fine with that. But I was disappointed that it didn't work out.

The second stop, on our way to Kansas, was also in rural New York. Levi had accepted an invitation to visit a fellow high school student named Emmett, who, like him, had come from a wealthy non-practicing Jewish family. Both boys had been sent to the same dude ranch in Wyoming where they learned to love and ride horses. Emmett, who now had long hair tied in a pony tail, was married to Ginger, also from the same high school. They were creating what they hoped would be a communal farm on seventy-five acres that his dad had bought in the picturesque rolling hills of Jasper. Their first child, Meadow, was born. They wanted other couples to live on their land and share their dream of becoming a self-sufficient community of families, all building their own cabins and pitching in with the farming effort.

Levi was eager to find out if this might be a fit for us. We hiked up the hill to their newly planted vegetable gardens. There were endless rows of squashes, onions, tomatoes, beans, and even a grain I had never heard of called millet. Much to Levi's delight, they were raising horses for income. That clinched it for him. The big barn, pastures, quiet countryside, loving friends were all he had dreamed of.

We decided we had found our alternative lifestyle. But so early in our search! We hadn't even gotten to the west. A travel bug was still in our systems. It was only June. So Ginger and Emmett waved at us as we drove out the dirt driveway, with our promise that we would return to Jasper for the fall harvest.

As we stretched out on sleeping bags in the back of the bus with the baby, Tom and Dita drove us the thousand miles to Kansas City. There, we split ways. They were heading west to wherever. We would be doing the same after visiting with Jim and his family. I took a photo of the two diametrically opposite-looking brothers standing side by side—Levi the farmer next to Jim the law professor—Levi in his new uniform of bib overalls and a misshapen Gabby Hayes style hat, next to Jim in a suit, red tie, and long, curly hair. The two siblings were so glad to be together and could hardly get enough of each other. Having their sister Joy there too made the reunion complete.

The day came when Jim drove us to the strategic highway where we could best catch a ride on the open road. As he pulled up to the drop-off spot, Jim looked at us and said "Geesh! Are you guys sure you want to do this?"

For that minute, I felt a twinge of misgiving, even a sudden fear. The highway was noisy and full of cars whizzing by. But Levi was undaunted, leading the way with his loaded backpack and bedroll. I had mine strapped on my back too. We were on an approach lane with a wide shoulder that headed west.

Levi held out his thumb. A car pulled over and picked us up. We were on our way.

An Experience at the Peak and a Peak Experience

Standing on the Continental Divide in Colorado's Rocky Mountains.

Levi and I were really good buddies. Since we met, we never worried or argued. Now, we were having such a wonderful trip together. We functioned like two people joined at the hip. The summer was still ahead of us and we were in no hurry. We just had to get back to Jasper for the harvest. Levi's idea to simplify our lives and travel was just the right prescription for both of us. It was freeing to own very few possessions. It was freeing to not have a vehicle, to not pay rent, to not have an address. There were no bills coming to us. We owed no debt to anybody and enjoyed each day as it came. We took the time to delight in each other's company and dream about our future on the farm in Jasper.

For now, we thoroughly enjoyed our summer hitchhiking adventure, meeting new people, riding in all kinds of vehicles. One night, Levi and a truck driver slept outside on the flatbed of an eighteen-wheeler at a truck stop, while I slept in the cab. We even rode in an off-duty ambulance where the driver shared his cantaloupe melon with us.

On a hot afternoon in Kansas, we were dropped off next to a cornfield's section line on a rural road, with no food but a small bag of crunchy corn nuts. Every ten minutes or so, a car appeared through the shimmering heat mirage. When it passed us by, we gave ourselves solace by ceremoniously placing one salty corn nut kernel into each other's mouths. I sucked on mine until it became mush. It reminded me of the communion wafer I used to have in church more than ten years earlier.

Levi carried a hardback journal in which he meticulously recorded every ride we took, and the ones we rejected when I didn't feel right about the driver. Levi was amazed at my discernment. When I sensed potential trouble, I let him know and he respected my hunch.

We accepted fifty-two rides total in the long summer's trip. There were a couple of rides we probably shouldn't have accepted. One was in a maroon convertible with the top down that sped too fast, even for the Kansas straightaway.

"Could you slow down, please?" I asked the shirtless driver. He yelled a crude word at the windshield, then turned around to see me in the back seat. Thankfully, he did slow down a bit. I looked like a boy with my short hair and red T-shirt boasting "The Belly of the Whale" over my braless chest. He may have thought I was a boy. I didn't feel like one but twice I was mistaken for one: the time the waitress said to Levi when he ordered a beer, "How about your son. Would he like a beer too?"; and the other time when I was heading into the ladies' room at a service station and a man stopped me to point out that the men's room was "over there."

The other wrong ride was with a talkative man who said he had a pistol under his seat. He was on his way to a shooting range in East Colorado to do target practice. In the next breath, he went on and on about how much he hated his wife. Levi and I both felt uneasy. We were very hungry and asked him to pull over at the rare diner in that Kansas stretch. He said he wasn't going to eat and would wait in the car. We deliberately took our time and were relieved to see that he had given up and gone on without us.

I was taught by Dad to love maps since I was a little girl but, for some reason, I let Levi plot our journey, and went along happily as his companion. I found out why we needed hiking boots in the middle of the summer. It was to walk and climb steep trails in Colorado's Rocky Mountain National Park. Levi wanted to reach the Continental Divide so he could say he slept there.

We found the head of the trail in the wild west town of Grand Lake, Colorado, with its wooden sidewalks and movie set storefronts. The local barber, who washed and trimmed our hair, agreed to guard our unnecessary baggage in his shop while we were gone, which turned out to be nine days.

"Yeah. Sure. Whatever. Leave 'em here," he told us. "I'm not going any place." He was a settled man who looked like staying put had been his lot in life for many years. We thanked him as we moved on.

I felt a girlish elation when we set out into the wilderness. It was reminiscent of me as a twelve-year-old about to climb New Hampshire's Mount Moosilauke while a camper at Singing Eagle Lodge. On this trip, though, it was only the two of us—free adults to go at our own pace, for whatever time or distance we could comfortably handle. The trail was well marked. There were cleared campsites every so often. Occasionally, we met up with other hikers but most of the time we were alone. We found that we hiked at a similar stride. Exhilaration motivated our every step. The scenery kept changing. From a towering pine-scented forest, we rounded the bend to behold a brilliant field of colorful wildflowers spread out before us. Then suddenly we came to a long stretch of tumbled boulders where a little pika rodent peeked out at us.

I followed Levi's lead. He was definitely taking good care of me. He knew how to pitch a tent and how to chop wood and build a campfire. He showed me how to make chapati breads in a pan and how to cook a pot of rice over the burning logs. One day there was a heavy rainstorm. Levi took it in his stride. We put on our ponchos and let the rain come down on us. He smoked a cigarette while we calmly sat it out, staying dry.

Several days in, we went above the timber line. It was dotted with melting snowfields. Finally, we reached what seemed like the top of the world. Off in the distance for 360 degrees was a clear view of other mountain peaks, separated from us by vast valleys.

"This," Levi declared, "is the Continental Divide."

He set down his eighty-pound pack and used it as a headrest as he stretched out on the line that determined which way raindrops would flow. "My left hip is in the east and and my right hip is in the west." I sat down beside him, enjoying his spontaneous bearded smile. To celebrate, we shared a package of McVities crackers and a can of sardines that I had been saving since Kansas City as a surprise for Levi's triumphant moment. We split a tart green apple that a man on horseback had given us two days before. It was a perfect lunch on a perfect day for two perfectly happy people.

The sun began its descent as we walked the long saddle of the rocky mountaintop towards the other side where we would begin the trail back down the mountain. Levi was looking for a place to spend the night while we were still on the Divide. A wind came up bringing a chill to the thin air. We came to a large rock that sheltered a soft grassy spot where we met a lone hiker who was despondent. He had been separated from his friend who had all their food. He was hungry, tired, and had cramps. We decided to make camp there and invited him to eat with us. There was no firewood around, so Levi pulled out a Primus trail stove to cook some of our rice. Fortunately, we still had a box of matches. Our water supply was low but we had enough for this meal and a little extra.

Levi carefully measured the water, rice, and salt into the lightweight cooking pot. He added sesame seeds for taste. In the lee of the rock, he was able to light a match but, try as he might, the stove would not light. Over and over he struck matches. I could see he was getting frustrated. The lone hiker just lay nearby and offered no help. I was of no help either. Outbursts of foul language showed me a side of Levi I hadn't yet witnessed. He continued to try every trick and I admired his persistence. I hoped with all my heart that the stove would light. Sometimes, it seemed to work, but then got snuffed out. We decided it was a problem with altitude.

By this time, the evening was only a couple hours off. Levi was willing to bed down without supper. On the other hand, I began to feel chilled and uncomfortable. Furthermore, our little campsite was no longer attractive to me as it was poisoned with hours of frustrated profanities. And what was worse, it promised no hot rice for supper. Our fellow hiker had wandered off out of sight. I could see both Levi and I needed a change of scene, preferably at a lower altitude and away from the relentless wind.

Below us in the distance, I saw what looked like the perfect place—an area of low bushes and pines forming circles around small green clearings. I figured we could be there in twenty minutes, or less, and still have time to try our stove once again.

My suggestion annoyed Levi. "It'll take us two hours to get there," he protested.

"Two hours, Levi?"

"Well, what're we going to do about this pot of water and uncooked rice?

"I'll carry it."

"CARRY IT?" He was incredulous.

"Yes. Of course." It all seemed so easy to me and so senselessly complicated for Levi. Once again, he was ready to ditch supper for the elation of spending the night far above timberline.

What should we do? I didn't want to be a drag to Levi but I did need at least the comfort of a warm supper if I were going to subject myself to the bitterness of the oncoming night. Levi put the decision in my hands and I decided we should move on down. By this time, my feelings were strong.

Levi agreed, but was fuming at the same time. He gathered our gear and packed it up with loud clatter and fumbling speed—so unlike his usual precise, meticulous manner. I was fascinated. For a man with such great vision, he seemed suddenly blinded. I, the stove, his dreams, the whole situation somehow put a stop to his normal easy flow.

We were ready to go. I was to carry the rice pot. But in case I should drop it, I asked Levi for the plastic belt that holds the lid onto the pot. What happened next was already written in the script. Racing against time—his time—Levi dove into his pack for the belt, then clumsily grabbed the pot which toppled. The rice, water, and sesame seeds flew out. Levi threw the pot down onto the ground with a mighty crescendo. We needed the roll of drums and clash of cymbals.

A silence followed as we stared at the rice on the ground. It lay still—as still as the lone traveler who had been watching from a distance all this time. I felt badly that I had offered him our company and a hot meal, and that we were now so quickly withdrawing. He opted to stay put. I was tempted to scoop up as much of the rice as I could salvage, which I had watched Levi do on other occasions when food was dropped. But Levi made no effort in that direction, so I knew the scene had ended and we were now moving on.

We put on our packs in silence, both a little stunned. Levi came up and hugged me and gave me a gentle kiss and I was deeply touched. I loved him more than ever.

Later that night, when the sun had left us to coldness and we were zipped up in our down sleeping bags, having eaten a much-belabored new batch of hot brown rice with sesame seeds, I thought over the events of the day. This experience on the peak had made a big impression on me. I was understanding something important as I lay there under the stars. It was true what they taught us at camp—"the bigger the back, the bigger the front." High adventure and elation brought a greater response to frustration. An easy lunch led to a problematic supper; a difficult climb to an easy descent. Levi's weakness contributed to my strength.

Through all this, I stayed true to my theme on my college senior essay—that I am responsible for my own happiness in spite of life's ups and downs. I mentally patted myself on the back that I had seen to my own equilibrium.

In the wee hours of pre-dawn, I woke up to find that our unwashed rice pot was stuck frozen to the foot of my sleeping bag. Levi was sound asleep. His head was buried under the down comforter. With a start, my thoughts suddenly shifted. *What became of the quiet hiker? Was he surviving okay? Had he eaten some of our uncooked rice?* Here we were sheltered from the wind that was howling up on the Divide. For my own happiness, I had turned my back on him and left him to freeze. With all my heart, I wished him warmth and peace of mind. I gave thanks that Levi and I were safe and cozy. We were fed and happy.

I recognized this was a new kind of peak experience—a spiritual one. I wrote in my journal, "*I have learned to pray.*"

A Psychedelic Baptism

We left Colorado and continued on our hitchhiking journey. Our ultimate destination for this part of the trip was to go to Mexico City and visit Bob and his wife Ann and their two boys. They were temporarily there on Bob's assignment with IBM.

As we were heading south, we decided to make a stop in New Mexico to visit my Cackleberry neighbor and dear childhood friend, Dee, who had become a hippy even long before I proudly stopped shaving my legs. He had formed a commune in the rural village of Lamy and offered an invitation to any of us Watsons who were "passing by" to stop in for a visit, if we could find it. Levi and I were curious to see what he was up to.

"It's easy," Dee assured me on the phone. "Just off the main highway south of Santa Fe is the road to Lamy, which dead-ends at the region's only railroad station. Look for an old mission church on the left with a cupola steeple and cross, and we're in the bunkhouse behind it."

It was strange to hear his manly voice. I hadn't seen much of Dee since back in the days when we rode on the same school bus. I remembered visiting his bedroom when he was close to death with rheumatic fever during elementary school. He and his brother used to pelt our windows with potatoes. His mother, Mumbles, was famous for wearing a flowered muumuu and crooning "Minnie the Moocher" after a few drinks. (I loved her for that.)

The man who gave us a ride to Santa Fe became intrigued with our quest for the commune, so he went out of his way to help us find it. We turned east on the designated desert road which was flanked by dry, juniper-dotted hills. With so few buildings out there, it really wasn't hard to spot the mission with the cross on it. Sure enough, behind the church was a ramshackle structure. Several cars were parked next to it. As we pulled in, who should we see—standing on the front veranda—but Dita, her husband, and little Jeremiah. So this same couple that we had said goodbye to in Kansas City, not knowing where they were going, nor where we were going, also ended up visiting Dee. The weeks before, while we were hiking in the Rocky Mountains, they were serving as migrant workers picking apples in Colorado. For now, they had created their own private homesite by setting up a tent next to their bus. Other hippy travelers did likewise.

Dee was striking with his very long hair, mustache, and beard. He was happy to see us. He still had the familiar twinkle in his eye and the same demeanor that led me to think I would be laughing with him any minute. Around his neck was a necklace with a large silver cross.

We stayed at the Lamy commune three days. The place was a cultural shock for me. There seemed to be no organized routine for this group, except for Dee and his wife doing their spiritual practices. They got up in the morning to do some yoga, or meditative type things outside. Others would join them or not. Levi and I didn't. We were mainly spectators, trying to understand the dynamic of this haphazard community. There were several families, some with little children, single guys, single girls, the brother of a movie star and his girlfriend, other couples—almost everybody was just passing through. It was like we were all drifting, hopeful, looking for our identity and self-worth in this 1971 Age of Aquarius. Nobody seemed to know where they were heading next. Nobody had money and I questioned whether there was any food at the compound, or toilet paper. I felt uneasy about whether I was going to eat at all—there certainly was no grocery store in Lamy. But somehow miraculously, someone would show up with carrots, and a small group of women would gather in the very primitive kitchen and create a meal that we would all share.

On our second day, I had a surreal and profoundly pivotal experience. It was a psychedelic Christian baptism. It truly happened, but was mostly based on the enactment of a private fantasy that went on for a whole afternoon as I wandered with my mind altered. It began when someone showed up at the commune with a leather bota bag containing a hallucinogenic juice mixture they were calling "orange sunshine." A titter of delight among the commune-ists gave me the impression that this meant it was party time.

Dee told me, "Go ahead, Cec. Take a few swigs if you want a fun mind trip."

I looked at Levi to see what he thought. I knew he had already passed his tripping days but what did he think of me trying it out? I had never taken a psychedelic drug.

"Go for it!" he said. "I'll be the ground man for you when you get back. Have a nice trip!"

So I took my turn on the bota. "Orange Sunshine, here I come."

The first effect was physical, like I was a baby suspended in a "jolly jumper" exerciser. I started to laugh as it seemed for a couple of minutes that I was bouncing up and down. Then I was overwhelmed with a new sense of freedom—like not returning to the past restraints of wearing garter belts and stockings, a panty girdle, and tight flats. I asked the people around me, "Do you think it's true that I don't have to wear a garter belt anymore?"

And they said, "Yes, I think it's true."

I said, "Really?"

And they said, "Really." I started to cry. I was being released from years of that social convention and all its paraphernalia. I looked out the window which hadn't been washed in, who knows, a hundred years? It was clouded over with smears and I was thinking how beautiful it looked.

Dee came by and announced to everybody, "I want to take you to see a cave. We are going to walk there so whoever wants to come, follow me."

"I want to come," I said eagerly. Levi said he didn't want to go and would just stay at the house. I followed close behind Dee as he led the way. He was barefoot and wore a white sheet wrapped around him like a short skirt, and that's all. With his flowing hair, he looked like a character from Biblical times. About eight of us followed him.

I looked down at the ground to behold that this high desert land was now carpeted in sea shells. (Years later, I returned to Lamy and could not see a single shell!) There were ankle-high cactus plants too. (Those were real.) Dee's bare feet maintained a steady pace and I heard him say that he was guided by God to not step on the cactus, so he didn't need shoes. He seemed to be aware of his role in leading us out to his special cave. Dee had a type of personality that you could hardly tell if he was high on something or not. He always seemed to be amazed at the world and everything was wonderful.

We passed a primitive outhouse. It suddenly converted to a cartoon with the grains of the wood exaggerated in black outlines. As we walked, I looked out over the dry hills with the small scrub bushes. I saw beautiful paisley teardrop designs form, and soon the whole countryside was shimmering with bright, neon colors. Never had I seen such rare beauty.

There was chatter about how we were entering a new age where there would be a new heaven and a new earth. Someone asked me, "What's your sign?"

"Capricorn," I answered.

Dee took note, like he was pleased that we were the same sign. "You and I have a big responsibility," he told me. "We are the Original Capricorns in this New Age."

From this moment on, I entered into my trip fantasy. It was like I had a role in a God-written play performed by all the people around me. They all had memorized their perfect lines. I wasn't sure of mine, so I kept quiet, lest I should cause this monumentally spiritual enactment to veer from its purpose—which was my ultimate initiation into something honorable and important. Since I was a key person to usher in a New Age, I wanted to be alert, humble and ready. I felt confident that by the time this preparation period was over, and the ceremony was complete, I would be enabled-from-on-high to be worthy of my calling.

We got to Dee's cave but I saw that its entrance was on the face of a sheer twenty-foot cliff. I was hesitant to go any further.

"You're a Capricorn, Cecily," he said to reassure me. "A Capricorn is a sure-footed goat. You'll have no problem getting over there. God has created rocks to jut out like stepping stones, and other rocks to hold onto." I took his words literally, and sure enough, just like he said, I made it easily across the face of the cliff into the cave.

The cave itself was like an arched room big enough to hold six seated people comfortably. The floor was carpeted with pristine white sand. There were three alcoves evenly spaced across the back where one could sit, as though on a throne. People came and went.

Someone asked me, "What is your name?"

"Cecily," I said.

The same person asked, "What does your name mean?"

At that moment, Dee's wife appeared momentarily in the cave like a blithe spirit and said her perfect line, which was, "It means you love everyone." *Well*, I thought, *that is true of me*. The anti-war women's liberation group back in Boston had tried to shame me when I told them I didn't hate anyone. Now I was validated—that loving everyone was noble. It was a virtue assigned to me by my name.

The next actor came into the cave and swung his young body into one of the thrones. He was a dark black teenager that I had not seen back at the commune. It startled me to see him, because where had he come from? It was like a voice told me, "I have sent this young black man for you to realize that all people are equal and all are loved." As quickly as he came in, he left. I decided God had done that for me. Even though my school was always peacefully integrated and I had no familiarity with racism among my peers, there was definitely a social class difference. God wanted to remind me that segregation, prejudice, and hatred were realities in many parts. And He was just checking my heart.

Below the cliff, I could see Dee on the sandy lane wandering away around a bend. I was now alone in the cave with a lanky, light-haired, good-looking man, who had arrived at the commune with a lady friend the day before. He was wearing a full-length gray woolen coat, like a Confederate soldier's.

The sun had disappeared over the hills and I began to get chilly. The nice man shared his coat, wrapping it around both of us. He began to chant his mantra, which was "ohm." His bass voice reverberated in the cave as he continued with protracted OHMMMM sounds, which were beginning to sound like an instrument.

He looked at me and said, "C'mon, say it with me." I figured this was my part of the script, so I started to vocalize the sound with him. It felt really good. Soon we were a duet of OHMs being blasted out into the countryside. Our two voices became like one. I thought maybe he was also one of the Disciples chosen to bring on the New Age, and we were being used as heralds, like a shofar. I wondered what his sign was, and whether he was the Original Something Else. Or was the Original designation only for Capricorns?

The duet and my reverie stopped abruptly as the man switched gears and went off script. He began repeating quietly a new thought that had come over him. "How can it be?" he asked himself aloud. "I picked Christine. I should have picked Cecily. Picked Christine! Should have picked Cecily!"

He looked at me again, and said, "Cecily, will you start your journey with me? I picked Christine but I should have picked you, Cecily."

My OHM now turned to a NO! and I yelled "NOOOO!!!" in my loudest voice out of the cave. I kept yelling "NOOOO!!!" until anyone miles away could hear me. I thought about Levi back at the house not having taken this drug and how he was my ground person. I was on this life journey with him and I was not about to take off with somebody else. We were committed to each other and to Ginger and Emmett back in Jasper, New York, who were expecting us to return for the harvest. "NOOOO!!!" I cried out again.

Dee came swooping into the cave. "Are you okay, Cec?"

I threw the question back at him because I was confused and a little afraid. I figured the gray coat man was not really a Disciple. He was the Tempter. I still didn't know what my lines were but needed to interrupt the perfect play without ruining it. I just had to have some reassurance. "Dee, am I okay?" I was reaching way back to Cackleberry days in Bryn Mawr, to a place where I knew Dee understood me.

In the play, Dee had the role of Jesus. He looked at me and said, "Yes, Cecily. You're okay. You're fine. Do you want to leave the cave now?"

"Yes," I said. So my familiar friend helped guide me across the protruding rocks.

We walked atop the hill to a clearing. There, sitting on a boulder by himself, was a handsome man wearing pressed trousers and a canary yellow sport shirt. His hair was jet black, neatly combed, and he resembled Elvis Presley. In my mind I said, *He is God.* He was beautiful, perfect looking, peaceful, secure in himself. He was omnipresent because of the way he just appeared out of nowhere. This man had never been at the commune. He showed up here and now because the role of God had to be filled. In the play, I had to be shown that God was real, not an impersonal figment of my imagination. The Perfect Playwright was showing me that I needed God in my life.

Since it was starting to get dark, Dee said it was time to round everybody up and lead them back to the commune for the evening meal. Was the play now over? *It just can't be over!* I waited a minute to see if Dee's next line was to introduce the final act in which I would be formally initiated as a leader in the New Age of Aquarius as the Original Capricorn.

However, Dee seemed oblivious and turned to go back. I was compelled to speak up, even if it meant I was changing the script. If he and I were going to be leaders of such a big movement, I needed to be baptized by Jesus in the Name of Jesus to prepare me for the journey. I didn't know where Levi was going to fit into this but here I was acting out this play. I called out to him, "Dee! I thought you were going to baptize me."

He turned back to look at me and asked, "Do you want to be baptized?"

A weird interlude followed where Dee's face morphed into at least ten different races and nationalities. He went from Tibetan, to Chinese, to Mexican Indian, to Samoan tribesman, to Eskimo, to Norwegian, to Roman soldier, and finally back to Dee. I watched long enough until I was sure he was my friend, Dee, who was playing the role of Jesus. "Yes," I answered.

He said, "Come with me." He led me to another part of the cliff where a natural human-sized birdbath jutted out. We both walked on its rim. "I have never been here and found this little bath dry," he explained. "There's always a puddle of water in it." Sure enough, even after the recent days of dry summer heat, there was a puddle of clear water shimmering on top of the white sandy bottom. "This is the baptismal," he said.

Then, to my great delight, he inscribed a wet cross on my forehead and baptized me in the name of the Father, the Son, and the Holy Spirit. The play was now over. I had the culmination of what I needed. I had seen the purpose of this day's trip. It was for a Psychedelic Baptism. It was amazing.

The Play's Final Act

When I got back to Levi, he was in a bad mood, which didn't fit with anything I had just experienced. Probably he was annoyed with me for being gone so long. Or probably he was hungry or bored. Since I was still processing a fantasy that was mine and not ours, I decided he would just have to work it out on his own. There was no sense in trying to explain the unexplainable. Cosmic highs just didn't mix with silly bad moods.

After supper, people settled in for the night. Dita and her family were out in their tent. Mr. Gray Coat was back with Christine in their travel van. Dee and his wife had their own room. Levi and I found our floor space along with several others and drifted off to sleep.

The next morning, the curtain opened for the dramatic epilogue of the play. I had been sleeping on my back and was still sound asleep. Levi was already up. There was a thick wooden door leaning precariously in the doorway between our room and the kitchen. Since this door wasn't on hinges, it easily toppled our way when a little toddler in the kitchen brushed against it. Bam! It smacked down hard on my forehead, on the very spot where I had been baptized the day before. I awoke with a start. I screamed. Pain shot through my head. Levi rushed over and lifted the door off of me. I sat bolt upright and burst into traumatized tears. The baby's mother brought me a wet compress, feeling sorry that her baby had caused the accident. Dee came in to see if I was okay and apologized for the loose door.

I closed my eyes under the wet towel, sobbing privately. As the pain subsided, an inner voice spoke to me. *That play was all an illusion. The falling door was the bold slap you needed. Welcome back to reality. Don't keep going along with that Original Capricorn thing. Just enjoy your time with Levi and carry on.*

We rolled up our sleeping bags, thanked Dee, and hugged Dita goodbye. Someone gave us a ride to the highway where we stuck out our thumbs and quickly got a ride south. The egg on my forehead was still swelling and turning black and blue. We were leaving the City of Holy Faith (Santa Fe) in the Blood of Christ Mountains (Sangre de Cristo). Something spiritual had happened there.

In all the eleven years we were together, I never found an open door where I could tell Levi any of the details of my Psychedelic Baptism. It was one of those things I hid in my heart.

Levi and Mexico

Mexico is a huge country. Levi and I had no problem getting visas and hitchhiking across the border with a native tradesman who took us all the way from Juarez to Durango. For over ten hours, we drove straight south with nothing to eat but one cantaloupe that the driver kindly shared with us. Much of the highway was dual lane through scrub bush open range. We passed several dead cows and donkeys that had met their fate along the way. I hoped the buzzards would find them, because it looked like the highway department didn't have a clean-up crew.

Levi sat up front in the passenger seat engaged in animated communication with our driver. Levi pulled out all twenty of his Spanish words. I saw him point to a lake and comment, "Mucho grande," which was like saying "much large." The driver got the point and nodded in agreement as the two of them moved along to the next bit of small talk.

From Durango on, we began taking public transportation. The first was a bus to pricy Mazatlan on the coast, where we planned to spend just one night before taking another bus to a simpler town farther south called San Blas. It attracted surfers from all over the world and we wanted to watch them maneuver the gigantic Pacific waves that were famous there. We ended up staying three nights in Mazatlan unexpectedly—to put me in sick bay. On the seemingly interminable bus ride, I had gotten a bad case of *turista*. It started with collywobbles in my abdomen.

"Levi," I had whined with my hands across my middle, "I've got diarrhea. There's no toilet on this bus. I don't think I can stop it. What'm I gonna do?"

Levi craned his neck to see for himself that there was no bathroom. "I don't know, Babe. Can't you just hold it?"

"I'm trying," I said, as the stuff oozed out of me uncontrollably. A stinky smell wafted from my seat. I tried to act nonchalant, like it wasn't me. I felt like a diaper baby trying to keep a secret.

At the coast, Levi found us an affordable room where I could clean up and writhe with fever and more cramps and runs for three more days. It wasn't the best introduction to Mexico with my sweetheart. Our motel was near the beach where there were food vendor carts. He brought me some crackers and fruit juice. I wanted to go out and explore with him, use my Spanish to translate for him, and just enjoy being on vacation in Mexico. But sadly he had to be a tourist on his own at this point. I marveled at the way he could drink the brown *horchata* and eat the street tacos and foods with no bad reaction.

We made it to San Blas, but never got to see surfers. It was the wrong season. The good waves must have been somewhere else. As we pulled into that small town and stepped off the bus, an American guy spotted us. "Do you need a place to stay?" he asked. His name was Mike. He was American and had rented a house. Of course, when we heard it was a free place to sleep, we said yes and followed him several blocks to a pastel cinder block house with square holes for future windows. In exchange for sheltering international sojourners like us, Mike benefitted from the drinks and meals we all provided him. He also had company to go out clamming at the far off beach with its shallow waters. He showed us how to squat down in the knee high water of a receding wave and dig into the sand to feel and retrieve a clam or two with every try.

After several buckets were filled, we boiled the clams over a fire pit back at the house. People brought and shared bottles of beer. Levi, who had taken on a macrobiotic persona for the past year, allowed the romance of tropical breezes to usher him into a drinking frenzy. He talked loud and chain smoked cigarettes, laughed and slapped backs of new "friends." It was like he was back in the marines and on leave. I watched the bulldog tattoo on his muscular bicep get a good workout as he gestured freely with his stories.

With Levi's instigation, the group decided to have a watermelon punch party. It seemed he had totally forgotten I was at San Blas with him. I was the quiet spectator who wished she had a lawn chair to relax in while watching all the shenanigans. He and another guy went to town and returned with a large watermelon, sliced it open, scooped out the pink flesh, then filled it with fruit juices and lots of rum.

From there, who knows where Levi went. He disappeared with other drunken friends and didn't return until I had bedded down on my sleeping bag in a stifling hot, mosquito-filled room with other newly arrived travelers packed in like sardines. I succeeded in saving Levi's absentee place, but had to vie for it, as they couldn't see the sense of his empty sleeping bag taking up the needed floorspace. I felt alone, and estranged. What appeal was it that attracted Levi to this eclectic group? Somebody pulled the string on the ceiling light bulb and we were plunged into complete darkness.

I guess now I understood more clearly how Levi felt when I had abandoned him to go off on my psychedelic trip back in New Mexico. It was his turn to explore and experience whatever wild side adventure he needed. I wasn't mad at him. Or maybe I was. I took it out on the relentless mosquitoes that wouldn't leave me alone. Inside I was fuming. I wanted to hide under my sleeping bag but it was serving as my mattress on the cement floor. Oh, for a sheet and earplugs. The hours passed and I couldn't sleep. It was dark. I had to go to the bathroom but I couldn't find the string for the light, and was afraid to step on someone. Levi wasn't there and I was isolated even in a sea of people.

By the time Levi returned and disrupted the entire room of sleepers, I flew into hysteria over the invisible buzzers that were trying to penetrate my ears. I was glad he woke us all up—glad the light got turned on. No longer caring what the others might think of me, I released my pent-up freak-out. "I can't stand these mosquitos! They're all over me. I can't possibly sleep! Help! Get me outta here!"

A quiet and gentle man came over and put his hands on my stiffened shoulders. "Let me talk to you," he said in a foreign accent. He sat down next to me on the floor. His voice was so soothing that already I became more relaxed. "Think of it this way," he said. "It's like you are in a terrarium space that belongs to the mosquito. This is his world. He is flying around as he should. You are the intruder. So just be at peace with the mosquitos and let them fly around you. Don't flinch at every one. You'll find they won't disturb you so much."

"Thank you," I told him. "I'll try to look at it that way." So after I returned from the bathroom, I lay down next to Levi, who was either asleep or passed out, I wasn't sure, and I soon fell asleep myself, oblivious of the mosquitos. The man's words were to stay with me from then on. I had learned to stay calm whenever a bee or other insect buzzed around me.

A Visit with Brother Bob

W e had tried for days and finally made contact with Bob in Mexico City. He was to be away on business for a week, so we had time to explore more of Mexico. We took a rivulet boat ride through a jungle canopy to a spring-fed pool where we hung out for hours, splashing, swimming, and sunbathing. We ate fruit—bananas, pineapple, mangos, papayas—and lots of tacos. A friendly California couple who were touring Mexico in their van gave us a ride out of San Blas to a lakeside camp-site, where we pitched our red tent and swam, fished, read, and relaxed for a few days. We enjoyed quick visits to Guadalajara and even Guanajuato, the city with no square blocks. Soon we were at a bus station where we got on a bus bound for Mexico City.

I was curious how things would go as we visited my successful businessman brother with his white shirt, tie, and briefcase. What would he think of Levi with his pipe and beard, and me in worn-out hiking boots and bandana?

We were greeted warmly by one of the maids. They were in a modern home. I tried not to be jealous of the apparent affluence—the servant-cooked meals, the country club circuit, air conditioning, picture-windowed guest room, landscaped gardens—and the fact that they were settled with two good-looking eight- and ten-year-old boys. Robbie, the older nephew, built a crackling fire in the fireplace, while Ann served us cocktails. We set about finding topics of conversation that would bridge the gap of our currently differing lifestyles and stages of life. Ann had the gift of gab and filled us in on the boys' schooling and swim club competitions and how she and Bob were in a mixed doubles match coming up. Later, in our treehouse-like guest room, Levi described Ann as charming.

Bob came home for a late roast beef supper, looking very handsome. He was happy to see us. We both were impressed with his sincere and engaging manner. After a couple of drinks, he was ready to laugh and share some Watson humor that gave me Cackleberry nostalgia. His sales work at IBM was not all a bed of roses; it involved business day trips, meetings, and appointments. Ann and the boys filled in the hosting role with metro rides to the zoo, horseback riding in a mountain village, ice cream treats, a drive to Cuernavaca, and chess games.

It was hard to explain to Bob and Ann what Levi and I were seeking. The whole idea of an alternative lifestyle, living by the seasons and not by the commercial calendar, was foreign to their thinking. We tried to describe our direction—how we were about to return to Jasper, New York, to join a couple on their communal farm. The plan was to build our own cabin, have our own children, but share in the farm work. We would all eat the harvest of the gardens that we would mutually oversee.

I could see that Levi and I were veering off into a way of life that would be too earthy, too hillbilly for a couple such as Bob and Ann to understand, much less ever want to visit. It made me a little sad to think that this might be a last encounter with them for a long time.

The conversation turned to the current 1971 marijuana scene, which Bob had succeeded in avoiding. The hippy culture of the U.S. had not hit Mexico City and had certainly not yet hit Bob and Ann, though they had heard about it. Though he would loosen up later in his life, for now, he had a straight and strict view of the world. "If I ever found out that one of my boys started trying out drugs," Bob declared one evening, "I would kick their ass out on the street that very moment!"

On the last day with Bob, Ann and the boys, I sensed that in many ways we had taken advantage of their hospitality and overstayed our welcome. We were actually inconsiderate guests. We were in vacation mode, on our own schedule, waking up when we felt like it. We had no allegiance to place or time—no address, no watches, and I had not been looking in a mirror. Though we weren't demanding, we were insensitive to the fact that, for instance, when we got up late, the cook had to re-open the breakfast kitchen that the family had already vacated, and present us with pancakes afresh. Levi had overheard Ann fussing to Bob over that one.

My personal reaction was to feel quietly embarrassed, but not say anything to them in the way of apology. I didn't have the fortitude to do that. On the other hand, Levi's reaction was to quietly blame them for not giving us more leeway to be a laid-back traveling couple. He wrote about it in his journal, but, like me, did not apologize to Bob nor Ann. I considered it our mutual faux-pas but Levi felt no guilt.

Looking forward and not back, Levi and I pressed onward with renewed vigor for the farm life that was ahead of us.

*M*y first Pentagon assignment was working for Vice Admiral Hal Shear, who held the OP 02 Submarine Office. I held the OP 21 Attack Submarine Desk and Pat McDonald was the OP 22 Strategic Desk. His aide was Commander Liton Brooks, a brilliant naval officer, later to attain the rank of Ambassador for Nuclear Affairs for the United States.

Later Admiral Rickover picked me overnight to be assigned to the Bureau of Naval Personnel as Director of Nuclear Power Personnel and Head of Nuclear Power Distribution Control Branch. Captain Jim Watkins, who had the job, was promoted to Rear Admiral and was being reassigned.

I suddenly realized the importance of what had just occurred. I was totally given the responsibility for all personnel and training aspects of the Navy Reactors Organization under Admiral Rickover. I made a personal resolution never to discuss my responsibilities, misuse my influence, or inflate my ego in any capacity, officially or privately, while I served my country for the U.S. Navy. I feel confident that I kept the oath. I served the Navy in that capacity for a year.

Chain Links at Jasper

Brownsville, Texas, to Jasper, New York, is a long road trip—about two thousand miles. We were glad to be back in the States. The excitement was mounting for the communal farm experience before us. I felt bonded and so in love with Levi. He abounded in energy and zest for life that overshadowed my fondness for melancholy. We easily found rides to take us northeast. One of them was in the back of a VW bus along with other passengers. The driver tuned the radio to a brand new instant hit song by a guy named John Denver.

"Country roads, take me home," Denver crooned, "to a place I belong—West Virginia, Mountain Mama, take me home." The song was so perfect for our moment. We actually happened to be driving through rural West Virginia, heading to our new home. I cuddled with Levi happily as the miles flew by.

What I didn't know was that, in my body, a new life was forming, about the size of a juniper berry. No wonder I was taking frequent naps, and feeling nostalgic about leaving my brother in Mexico. Levi was leading me to a peaceful farm where our little child could play and grow—a place so very different from The Hague or Boston or the Cuban jungle, where, in my previous marriage, the distracted father would have been embroiled in the cutting edge of revolution. There must have been some sort of supernatural favor at work to keep me from conceiving a child with Ramón.

The Jasper screen door opened with the typical squeak of old farm-house hinges. Ginger appeared in the doorway. She had the freshness of a young Vivien Leigh in Gone With The Wind. She greeted us with a happy smile. In her hands was a folded flowered dress, which she presented to me first thing.

"You can wear this on the farm," she told me. "Emmett and I got lucky. We went to the dump and found a whole suitcase of these vintage dresses. A widower must have decided to get rid of his wife's clothes." Ginger was wearing hers. It had large pearly buttons all the way down the front. I received mine with great honor. It was, to me, a sign that I was welcomed as a farmwife's apprentice.

And apprentice I was. She had to show me everything. Even how to sweep a rug with a broom. The house had electricity but no vacuum cleaner. In the kitchen was an oversized wood-burning stove. Ginger taught me how to cook for a crowd. She used only fresh ingredients and produced colorful meals that any homespun magazine would have fought to feature. She puréed baby Meadow's squash and carrots. With devotion in her eyes, she patiently fed her baby one spoonful at a time. It was hard to imagine that Ginger had ever been a bobby-socked Jewish schoolgirl on Philadelphia's Main Line. She exuded a bucolic contentment that a girl like me could envy.

Emmett wasted no time initiating Levi on how to breed the horses. Levi was excited to be working with horses again. There were two mares and a stud. Emmett was starting his farm on nothing, so every endeavor that could produce some income was worthwhile. It would be a year before a colt could be born, then more time to raise it to a salable age. But he was proud of this beginning.

Mostly, Emmett focused on the crops. Levi and I had arrived too late to be of much help with the harvest. We did help load the winter squashes and pumpkins from the upper gardens and stacked them in the cold cellar. The millet had not produced the hoped for volume, which was a disappointment. The onions were plentiful.

In the evenings, we sat in the parlor and reviewed the day. We talked about the upcoming seasons. Already, Emmett was planning next spring's gardens and what seeds he needed. He and Levi wrote out expected expenses and potential income. Together, they had scouted out the most likely place for us to build our cabin, which was on acreage to the east of the main house. We all knew it was a project for the future, since we had to get the core of the farm on sure footing before we spread ourselves out. The hope was that other couples would come along and help fill in financial gaps.

For now, Levi and I were sleeping in the second floor garret room of the main house. A wood burning stove in the living room took the edge off the autumnal chill that crept in after the sun had set. My feet were cold when I took off my boots, especially when we were upstairs. I wasn't looking forward to winter.

One November day, the mail came and I received an early birthday card from Granny, who was always faithful to send me a card and a check. This time, it was a whopping twenty-five dollars. We were all four sitting around the kitchen table when I opened the envelope.

"Oh. Wow! Twenty-five dollars!" I exclaimed. "Granny didn't forget me. Now I can afford to send my thank-you letter to Bob in Mexico by airmail." I held the birthday check to my chest. Looking at Levi, I added, "Also, I'll get some furry slippers to keep my feet warm." Levi knew I was having trouble with cold feet.

Emmett could have bowled me over with what he said next. It was like he hadn't heard me express my desires, nor even cared. "Yeah, wow!" he exclaimed. "This is just what we needed to buy chain links for the manure spreader."

All of a sudden, I saw my life in Jasper in a new light. Levi and I were willingly throwing ourselves into a community pot with little to no income. The land belonged to Emmett's father. Emmett was the boss over us. The kitchen was Ginger's, not mine. After our trip to Mexico, Levi and I were down to five hundred dollars from our year's earnings at the Fontana Gallery and The Photo Center. If our measly cache dwindled further because of the farm's needs, we would have no resources left for our own future.

I felt angry at Emmett's insensitivity. I told Levi that it was a bad situation if I had to feel guilty for looking after my own needs. However, Levi was so enthralled with being on a farm, that he didn't want to hear my complaint nor join in with my resistance. The next day, a visiting friend was returning to Pennsylvania, so I hopped a ride to Cackleberry to go let off some steam.

While there, I found out that Levi and I were expecting a baby. My heart's desire! It wasn't supposed to happen this way. We were supposed to be together when we found out. Since there was no phone at the Jasper farm, I wrote Levi a letter with the news. He wrote me back asking me to please return to the farm, because that was where he wanted to be. He told me he had gotten a puppy and was looking forward to helping Emmett get through the winter. They were about to put new shingles on the barn and were chopping firewood. I wrote back that I wanted to be with him, wherever he was, and that I would try hard to fit in and be content in a communal arrangement. There was a ride that would get me there by Thanksgiving.

I had a few weeks alone to bond with the baby inside me. My body was changing. I had cravings for meat, which wasn't part of the fare on the farm. Mom fixed me up with cans of tuna fish. Plus, Granny sent me back with a complete turkey dinner to share with the community. As I rode back, I felt total resolve. I would greet Emmett with a new attitude. My three weeks away had been a respite. The pregnancy lifted my spirits with a newfound joy. I couldn't wait to be with Levi again.

But within hours, even after hugs from Levi and meeting the new puppy, a heaviness came upon me, and I had to fake it that I was back on board with the group. Emmett infuriated me. He had the gall to thank me for bringing him some tuna fish. I tried to explain that it was my own special stash to give me protein for my pregnancy. Nevertheless, he still proceeded to open a can and gobble its contents. At first, he scolded me for bringing a turkey into the house but then, after we had cooked it overnight in the wood burning oven, he raved about how tender and delicious it was.

I tried to fit back into the routine. We continued to eat at the round kitchen table together, the four of us—Ginger's baby was already asleep in her crib. We each had an enormous wooden bowl and chopsticks to eat our rice, beans, and vegetables. In the center of the table was a bowl of fresh garlic and a garlic press. Emmett pressed clove after clove of garlic onto his meal. There were other condiments. We all ate fast and soon the meal was over.

The gloomy cloud over me thickened. I was confused. *Why am I unhappy? I'm expecting my first baby. I'm with my husband. Maybe it's just the emotional ride of pregnancy.*

Then one day after our noonday meal, a light came on in my spirit. This was our problem—we were not showing any gratitude for our bounty. We were like a business—planning, planting, tending, harvesting, preserving, cooking, then eating to nourish our bodies and keep us alive. We were not recognizing God by giving Him thanks for our provision. We were living with presumption—we were SELF-sustaining. We had developed pride. We lacked humility. I didn't think it was because they all were Jewish. Plenty of Jews know how to give thanks with their special prayers. At Cackleberry, we always had a prayer we called grace, to thank God before we ate our main meal. I couldn't impose that tradition here because they all seemed to be happy to be non-practicing Jews. Besides, grace as I knew it was always prayed in Jesus' Name.

I had to take action. I was desperate. There was no time to delay. Levi and I needed to get away to our own place before our money ran out, before winter came on, and before our baby was born. I pulled Levi aside and pleaded that we go somewhere private where we could talk. Thankfully, he heard me, and took me on a long two-hour walk across the scenic Jasper countryside. I knew I would never forget this interlude. It felt so good to be alone with him. As we walked, we could see the farm in the distance looking very small across the vale.

Levi affirmed that, as much as he loved where he was, he was willing to make a change for the sake of our union. He walked quietly ahead of me for awhile, taking large strides up a hill. Then he stopped to let me catch up with him. He had come up with a creative, outrageous, scintillating plan—one that we could afford, and that would enable us to continue our sought-after "alternative lifestyle." He couldn't wait to tell me his idea.

"Since we only have five hundred dollars left, we need to be realistic. We'll buy a canvas tent, the size of a room, and I'll see if Rowland Buck will let us set it up near the waterfall on his two thousand acre dairy farm in Starrucca, Pennsylvania."

"Really, Levi? Are you serious? Is that really realistic? It would be cold living in a tent! How could we possibly do that, especially with winter coming on?"

"Trust me," he said. "I can picture it and I know how to do it."

We walked back to the farm, only to be greeted with the sad news that Levi's beloved puppy had been run over and killed by the tractor. Although I had not bonded with the puppy, Levi surely had. He actually cried. It was the first and only time I would ever see Levi cry. I was sad for him but I was glad to see him humbled and in need of my consoling hug.

That evening, Levi broke the news to Emmett that we were leaving the farm. I could hear the two of them in the parlor from the upstairs room. Emmett was obviously upset. In an angry voice, he lashed out about how I appeared to be a spoiled city girl.

"Christ, Levi. You can't take Cecily to a tent! She needs a lavish air-conditioned apartment."

I was actually helped by hearing him say that. No. Emmett was wrong. I didn't resonate with the thought of a fancy abode. I wanted to be with Levi while we watched my belly grow. If Levi was happy with the thought of a tent, then I was happy too.

It didn't take long for us to pack our few belongings and arrange a ride back to Philadelphia. Rowland Buck remembered Levi fondly from years back and was ready to accommodate us on his dairy farm, no charge. I hugged Ginger as I thanked her over and over for teaching me so much about how to be a farmwife. I apologized for flunking when it came to their Jasper dream. Levi and I wished them both well as we drove past the barn and on out of sight.

We were about to take on a most out-of-the-ordinary adventure—to live in a tent through the frigid winter in the woods of upstate Pennsylvania. I had presented Mom and Dad with plenty of doozies but what would they think of this idea?

The Blue Tent with Levi

With Cackleberry as our headquarters, Levi and I made trips to sporting goods stores to find the perfect tent and supplies for outdoor living. We were careful to remember that we only had five hundred dollars. As luck would have it, Levi had a wealthy friend who was willing to lend us his brand new, forest green VW bus for an indeterminate time. Starrucca was three hours north, almost to the New York border. Another friend of Levi's named Walter offered us the key to his hunting cabin nearby, saying we could use his shower whenever, and even stay overnight if he wasn't up there hunting.

Mom and Dad listened to our plan at their fivesies coffee table. They both surprised me by not reacting with dismay. In fact, Dad, especially, seemed fascinated. He grilled Levi for details. At this time, Levi was formidable-looking in his fringed Daniel Boone jacket and long curly beard and hair. He still entertained us all with funny anecdotes, yet exuded an air of confidence when it came to wood burning stoves, tents, and living in the woods. Dad trusted that this Marine Corps son-in-law of his could safely look after his daughter and his future grandchild within her.

I thought Mom was going to feel sorry for me. I figured she would be fearful for our safety. However, when we were out of Dad's earshot, she confided to me that Dad, himself, was devising a similarly outlandish plan for the two of them. He had always wanted to live on a tugboat. It had been a mere pipe dream—until that very week when he had found a tugboat for sale. It was located on the east coast and Dad was already negotiating with its owner. Mom was beyond fearful and upset. Every nook and cranny of Cackleberry held decades of tradition and memories. Her life revolved around Bryn Mawr. Dad's mom—my Granny—was elderly and in poor health and needed her attention. How could she possibly leave all that to live on a barnacle-encrusted, stinky tugboat? She told me she had gone to see her trusted Bible study lady friend to ask, "What shall I do?" Her friend advised that she should go along with his dream, trust in God, and see what happens.

"So," Mom concluded, "I'm proud of you for going along with Levi. Go live in your tent and see how God works it out for you." Whew! Now I felt sorry for Mom. I had much rather live in a stationary tent than on a clunky, problematic tugboat!

The one who was the most alarmed about our plan was my Uncle Ross up the hill from Cackleberry. He got emotional as he warned us we were going to either freeze to death or become asphyxiated from the smoke of the wood burning stove. Levi was unfazed by his or any other opposition.

Within a matter of days, we and our supplies were out in the Starrucca woods in upstate Pennsylvania, and Levi was hard at work creating our new home. Thankfully, a 1971 November thaw had melted the early snows. We chose a generous spot of level ground, which was perfectly located in a natural clearing, surrounded by tall evergreens, mostly junipers and hemlocks. It was within sight of the rushing creek and earshot of the thirty-foot waterfall downstream. Behind us loomed a stately, generations-old iron railroad trestle, reminding me of the construction style of my brothers' childhood erector sets. A dirt road on the other side of the creek brought the occasional railroad buff or naturalist up the mile-long dead end road to satisfy their curiosity about these well-hidden wonders—both the waterfall and the railroad trestle. Soon, the hippy couple living in the blue tent would add to the local lore and bring other onlookers.

Dressed in his new daily outfit of bib overall jeans, Levi set six railroad ties flat on the ground in a parallel row, then nailed sheets of plywood onto them. This created a platform which would become the foundation and floor for the tent. The tent itself was a bright blue. It measured ten by fourteen feet and was tall enough for us to stand up in the middle of it. My new home. I couldn't believe it.

I watched with fascination as Levi continued to add features to reinforce the tent for the oncoming winter. He framed out the entire interior with two-by-fours. "This will keep the heavy snows from collapsing the tent," Levi explained to me. This interior framework also provided strategic places to put nails and hooks for hanging our clothes and kitchen cooking pans, and a way to attach shelving.

He also unrolled wide plastic sheeting up and over the exterior to act as a vapor barrier against rain and any melting snow that might drip its way through the canvas. In the left back corner, he built us a platform for our mattress. It sat high enough so that we could slide our trunks full of seasonal clothing and blankets underneath. At the foot of our bed stood a very cute bureau where we kept daily clothing like underwear and socks.

The right back corner was reserved for our heating system, which was our black pot belly stove. Much of me had the same reservations as Uncle Ross. *How was Levi going to pull this off? How could a small tent safely house a wood burning stove? How was the smoke going to be vented?* I would soon find out. Levi placed a large tin mat on the floor as a protection from any flying hot coals or cinders. The stove went on top of that mat, with its four curved legs firmly planted there. This stove would take care of our warmth during the long months ahead.

Levi surprised me by cutting a hole in the back of the tent, behind the stove. He secured sheets of tin to each side of the canvas, lining up their pre-cut holes with the tent's holes. He slipped a piece of galvanized stove pipe onto the vent shaft on top of the pot belly. Using two adjustable elbows, Levi ran the stove pipe like a zig-zag up and outside the tent, where it became a five-foot chimney to give the wood smoke clearance from the roof of our tent. He secured the outside chimney with guy-wires to keep any wind from blowing it over. I was proud of Levi's skill and cleverness.

It wasn't long before the stove was fired up and I saw it in action. It worked like a dream. Without its warmth, we would not have made it through the winter in the Pennsylvania woods.

My belly was growing. My jeans got tight. I made myself a navy blue skirt with an elasticized waistband which could expand along with the baby's needs. I used a cozy velour fabric for warmth. Long underwear, woolen socks and felt-lined snow mobile boots completed my outfit. The floor of the tent was always freezing; whereas, towards the ceiling—since heat rises—the upper half was a comfortable seventy to seventy-five degrees.

We paid a local guy to bring us cut logs. He dumped them near the footbridge that crossed the stream to our tent. Levi split and carried the logs from there to a pile outside the tent. We had to keep the fire burning twenty-four hours. Levi learned all the idiosyncrasies of the Big Black Dragon—as I called it at first. I was afraid to get near it. I left all the handling to Levi. I sure kept him hopping with "I'm chilly," or "I'm too warm," or "Please put a log in for me."

He controlled the temperature with the precise placement and size of the logs, and the correct angle of the chimney's damper. A fully opened damper allowed a draft to flow that set the logs ablaze. We could sit back and enjoy ourselves as the warmth filled the air. It wrapped around us like a down comforter. However, if we had left the hot box going like that, we could have suffered heat stroke. The damper had to be throttled for the fire to settle down to the beautiful orange coals that would allow us to coast happily for awhile before adding the next log. Whenever we left the tent for hours, we were always gratified upon return to see glowing embers, meaning that with little effort we could get the fire going again. On the other hand, if all we had was cold ashes, the tent filled with an outpouring of Levi's choice cuss words as he worked through the frustration of trying to get the fire to roar again.

I learned how to manage cooking on a propane camp stove. It reminded me of my crude kitchens in Peru, though there I used kerosene. I kept a pot of water on the wood stove, so I always had hot water available. Levi ladled the water from the stream into a large metal bucket and brought it to me. We even drank that water.

For refrigeration, I used an empty cupboard on the cold floor. In there, I could keep perishable food from spoiling. For even colder storage, we used the stream itself. Levi had found a watertight metal box that he submerged into the freezing creek. He had put a stash of beer in it, then secured the box to a tree with a chain. I also used the box for storing milk and butter. There was something very exotic about fetching butter from the eddies of a stream.

It was freeing to live without electricity, phone, bills, and debts. We didn't own a mirror nor wear a watch. The days passed easily without differentiation. We turned to entertaining pastimes like reading, writing in journals, doing puzzles, and identifying birds. We learned to read music and play duets on wooden recorders.

A square card table and two folding chairs between our bed and the Black Dragon served as our living room, dining room, library, and office. Our bed was also our sofa. Levi astonished me first thing in the mornings when he would remove the card table to make himself enough room to stand on his head in a yoga pose. That was a sight—to see this bare-chested, muscular man inverted in the middle of a tent. Then he sat down with his legs folded in what he called a lotus pose—on the freezing floor—and did his (noisy) deep breathing and all of the things that go along with trying to do yoga in a small spot.

I looked at him and thought how different, how delightful, how utterly out of the ordinary this "alternative lifestyle" thing was. I was thankful that he had brought me to this tent experience. It was an idyllic spot for an expectant mother.

Spending a winter in a tent in upstate Pennsylvania.

The tent site topography boasted huge grey rocks. For want of a bathroom, Levi and I each chose our own boulder for a hiding place to do our business. We used a portable toilet seat on a metal frame.

One morning, Levi called out desperately as he walked from his boulder, holding the bib of his lowered coveralls, the shoulder straps trailing behind him in the soggy leaves.

"Babe! Quick! I need your help! Get me some paper towels. Christ! I'm covered with sh_t!"

What a sight! The toilet seat frame had given way, and he had flattened his "business" into a pancake with his bare bottom. After we got the mess cleaned up, we were able to have a good laugh.

The snows began falling. Our woods became a winter wonderland. We used a broom to clear off a foot of snow from our roof. The tent remained sturdy and warm. My belly was growing and I was glowing. Levi puffed smoke happily from his pipe in concert with the outside chimney. Levi and I had figured out that living in the tent was fun. What began as a challenging way to solve our housing crisis—on just five hundred dollars—became a peak time in our deepening friendship. We grew in our love for one another, basking in the togetherness of an isolated and simple home. We were enjoying nature and enjoying each other. Levi wrote beautiful love poems to me like:

> Time has no meaning
> Since I am free
> Thoughts softly drifting
> Cecily
> A wave of nostalgia
> Longing to be
> A look to the future
> Soon to be three
> Social commitments
> Planned thoughtfully

Warm thoughts encountered
Cecily
A mutual trust
A desire to see
Together unfolding
Cecily
Clouds slowly changing
Mountains and sea
Forming my image
Cecily

One day, we heard a swishing in the snow behind our tent. Then a man's voice called out, "Halloo!" It was a young man from town named Artie, who was curious about us and ventured cross country on his snow shoes. In his backpack, he carried a complete venison dinner for us. Artie became our first and best friend in Starrucca. The next week, he brought us a white Alaskan husky puppy which we welcomed to our tent. We called the puppy Muk Luk. We tied a red ribbon around his soft furry neck. He became our carefree mascot.

Christmas was coming soon. Mom and Dad invited us to come down to Cackleberry for their party they were having, so we went. We took Muk Luk and stayed overnight. Per tradition, people put their winter coats on an upstairs bed, which happened to be in my old bedroom. I entered the room carrying Levi's and my coats. Marion and our sister-in-law, Mary, were in there talking. I lingered to talk too.

Pretty soon, the conversation turned to Jesus, who, they reminded me, was the reason for the season. Marion was all excited because she had recently "accepted Jesus as her Lord and Savior," thanks to an encounter with an old high school classmate. As happened in my case, the Billy Graham Crusade's call to salvation years earlier had not stuck with Marion either. I graciously told her, "That's nice," and would have left the room to go downstairs but both she and Mary wanted me to consider accepting Jesus too.

"It's important," Marion added. Mary agreed. But I was too eager to see everyone at the party and a little embarrassed by the subject, so I shrugged my shoulders and left the room.

Back in the tent weeks later, in January, I wrote a long philosophical letter to Marion. Basically, I was trying to explain "You're no longer the boss of me." I told her how she had influenced me over the years, set trends for me, swayed my attitude, caused me to think negative thoughts about others. Now, just when I was living a simple life and trying to clear my body of drugs and prescriptions—like marijuana, and the birth control pills that kept me from the natural process of ovulation—she was coming at me high on something new. Jesus was her new high! I told her she was so high she couldn't relate to someone earthy like me. I told her she was only going through a stage in her life in order to eventually feel at one with the earth. She would get through it. I wrote her, "*I am not 'into' Jesus now and you are so 'into' Jesus that it is hard to find you, beautiful Marion.*" Then I wrote, "*But, I am patient. And curious. Where are you heading? Where will your great search take you? Are you asking questions that really have answers? What questions do you have?*"

"*As for me,*" I continued writing, "*I am so quiet these days. It's like I'm just sitting in a patched inner tube on a calm lake, looking forward to gently rocking in the wake of a passing motor boat, and enjoying the stillness in between. A dragonfly lands on my knee. He has a rainbow in his wings. How lovely.*"

A Financial Jolt

The weeks went by and the season was changing. The waterfall began to thaw. My belly got larger and larger. I would soon put away the winter velour skirt. Levi still put out bird seed in the cradle-shaped bird feeder he had made. I enjoyed being able to open the tent flaps to watch the birds—observing how the tufted titmice and chickadees took turns selecting their favorite seeds. The brilliant red cardinals preferred the sunflower seeds, especially the ones that fell on the ground. Levi and I figured we could stay in the tent even with the baby—at least until the baby started crawling. We had created a little utopia and wanted to stay there as long as we could.

One morning, as we were eating hot rice cream cereal for breakfast, Levi reached into the front pocket of his bib overalls. He pulled out a little collection of coins and dollar bills. He spread it out on the table and counted the money. It added up to twenty-seven dollars and fifty-six cents. He looked down at the money, then he looked up at me. My bubble was about to burst.

"This is all we have left," he said. "The fact is, I need to go find a job. Like, now. Today."

Now that was a blow. Reality can oftentimes be a blow. We had chosen a doctor and hospital that cooperated with the Lamaze natural childbirth method, which was going to cost us at least five hundred dollars. Of course, Levi needed to provide that money. But his going off to work meant that I would be left alone in the tent. Things just wouldn't be the same. I braced myself for what he had to say next. I knew this was the end of our Walden Pond experiment.

"I'm leaving this morning. I'm taking an overnight bag, because I don't know how long it's going to take me to find work. I'll be back, Babe, when I get a job. It might even take me two weeks. I need to do this for us."

He hugged me goodbye. I watched as he took off towards the little bridge that crossed the stream over to where the borrowed VW bus was parked. I soon heard that familiar purr of a Volkswagen engine. Then I heard it fade into the distance.

Suddenly it was very quiet there. I wondered how many days it would take for him to find a job. Being in such a small rural community where jobs were scarce, it was a big question how successful he would be. *What if he's gone for days?* Muk Luk came close for me to pet him, as if to remind me that I wasn't alone. I had his company. Then Baby moved a heel or elbow across the inside of my womb. I sat down on our sofa bed and counted my blessings. I decided I was not going to be afraid or lonely—or bored. At least I knew how to tend the wood stove by now. The day's chores needed my attention. I got busy and the hours flew by.

Just as evening set in and I was about to light the mantel lamp for my first night alone, I heard the VW return. Levi came into the tent with a smile on his face. "I found a roofing job," he announced proudly. That was great news.

However, it still meant that he had to leave me every morning, which he did. Some evenings he'd return sore and dirty and bushed. Others, he would say, "Easy job. A straight roof—no gables or odd corners. A gravy run." Gladly, we saved his paychecks for our baby fund.

My solitary days were interrupted by an unexpected visit from Dodie, my college roommate and fellow Peace Corps friend. Somehow, she tracked me down. She brought her husband and baby. They seemed very happy. I couldn't tell if she was impressed by our tent life, or if she felt sorry for me. Bruce also visited. A veteran outdoorsman, he brought his own tent and stayed awhile with us—building camp fires, roasting marshmallows, and telling stories.

It didn't take long, though, for the roofing work to become tedious. Wasting no time, Levi announced that he got a job driving a bulk milk tank truck. That was a wonderful job for him. He picked up his truck, drove to the dairy farms, attached the hose to their collection tanks, filled his truck with the fresh milk, and transported it to the creamery.

I went with him one day to see what the run was like. I took photos at the first stop. The stench of fresh cow manure filled the air. I heard a chorus of mooing. The farmer, who was hosing down the floor of the antiseptic collection room, greeted us with a smile. He said he was always happy when the truck showed up. It was an educational experience for me to see how this part of the dairy business functioned. Levi worked like a pro as he connected and disconnected the truck hose. I looked forward to the next farm visits. But as we pulled away, the milk sloshed back and forth causing the truck to buck. We had barely gone two miles, when I realized that the jolting of the truck on the winding country roads was too much for a very pregnant woman. Levi had to turn around and take me back to the tent.

"I don't know how you can take driving this truck every day," I told him as I got out and waddled to the safety of my home in the woods by the stream.

It occurred to me that I was still in the mentality of living by the seasons. Levi was now a slave to the commercial calendar. *Or, on second thought, were both of us?*

Baby Sunshine

After six months in the Starrucca tent, the weather broke into an April thaw. The farmers released their cattle from the barns to the upstream pastures. This meant the water that rushed by our tent was no longer potable. We had to either boil the water or buy some. Nor was the stream cold enough to refrigerate milk. The cupboard on the floor where we kept vegetables and leftover foods became lukewarm and unusable. Spring rains came too, and our muddy shoes caused a problem in the tent. We were still hoping that we could hold on and stay in the tent even after the baby was born. We had loved it there. But it was obvious, and a surprising conclusion to me, that tent life was easier in cold weather.

Our baby was due about the third week of June. The excitement mounted. We began regular drives to Binghamton, New York, to attend the nearest Lamaze classes for natural birth. In that method, the expectant fathers were called upon to encourage their laboring wives to relax and breathe, a key element to surmount what could be construed as unbearable pain. Natural childbirth was my choice. It was all the rage for couples to cooperate with one another and witness the miraculous arrival of their newborn. Levi stayed focused as he learned how to be my labor coach. I couldn't wait. We were both ready to meet our baby and hold him or her.

We talked about names on those trips to the classes. Levi came up with the name for a son. "Huckleberry," he announced proudly.

"Huckleberry?" I repeated with surprise.

"Sure! We can call him Huck. That would be fitting for a son of mine." I sat there quietly, trying to absorb that idea. Huck actually did sound cool.

Like Huck Finn. I wasn't crazy about Huckleberry, though. It sounded goofy. Then I came up with a girl's name, Willow. We both liked it. Levi added, "What about giving her Sunshine as her middle name." The name made me happy, so I said yes. Willow Sunshine. Beautiful!

Realizing that without refrigeration we would not be able to stay in the tent, Levi scouted the area and found an empty farmhouse for us to rent in the nearby town of Thompson. Suddenly, before we could move there, we were urgent. We heard the news that a hurricane was heading our way. It was about June 24. I saw a tree that leaned towards our tent and pointed it out to Levi. We really needed to leave before the hurricane came—not only because the tent might blow down, but also because that tree might fall on us. Of course there was the stream. Would it flood?

Fortunately, we had the key to our hunter friend Walter's cabin. We grabbed some overnight things and got there before the storm arrived. People called the storm Hurricane Agnes. It was a whopper. The wind whipped through the trees. Sheets of rain pounded the windows. It was so unusual for a hurricane to come inland like that. Thankfully, we were safe in the cabin. We burrowed under our sleeping bags to seek comfort from the fury outside.

During the night I started to get labor pains. By morning, the storm had subsided enough that we didn't have a problem driving to the little hospital in Susquehanna, Pennsylvania. It had a small maternity ward. There were nine bassinets in the nursery. I was the only delivery that day. My progress was slow. The hours passed. Levi, the doctor, and the nurse showed great patience. But when my pain was strongest and it was almost time to push, the men had lost track of my progress and were busy talking about soccer. Levi and I both forgot to utilize the Lamaze breathing technique we had studied.

I cried out to the men, "Stop talking about soccer! Can't you see I'm having a baby?"

It took seventeen tough hours and a lifetime but now, on June 26, 1972, I finally was experiencing my heart's desire. At age twenty-nine, I was about to meet the baby I had so longed for.

"You've got a girl," the nurse said. She held her upside down to make her cry. I saw a beautiful, perfect baby. She had lots of straight black hair and her mouth was wide open as she cried to take in her first breaths. I couldn't hold her soon enough. Then the nurse presented her to me. Her little body was wet and warm against my chest. The miracle of her presence was almost too much to bear.

They moved me and little Sunshine to a room. We had an awkward, but successful first nursing session, then they took her to the nursery while I napped. I rolled onto my stomach for the first time in months and fell into a deep sleep. I woke up sobbing, having dreamt that I was a shell-shocked soldier just returning from the frontlines in Vietnam. The dream was so real that I cried for some time, until the sweet nurse came in to comfort me. Joy and trauma had become a whirlwind of emotion, too much to contain. When they brought little Sunshine back to my arms, all bad memories faded away and the elation returned.

I stayed a few days in the hospital and then was driven to the old farm-house that I had never seen. Levi took down the tent (which had survived the hurricane) and cleared the cobwebs from the upstairs bedroom for "my wife and new baby girl," he said. I settled onto our familiar tent mattress, which he had set on the floor. Sunshine was in a wicker bassinet next to me.

A blissful Cecily with her baby Sunshine.

My world became just me and the baby. Levi kept everything else going. Somehow, he continued to pick up milk at the dairies. A group of loud, unwanted well-wishers brought cake and gifts to the room to welcome baby Willow Sunshine. What I really needed was serenity. Breastfeeding had become complicated by the stabbing pain of a breast infection. Mom, bless her heart, showed up just in time to help. She drove three hours and stayed several days. She unpacked the boxes of kitchen supplies that Levi had moved from the tent and cleaned the kitchen that had vestiges of mice. She brought me a glass of home-squeezed orange juice and a plate of scrambled eggs, sausage, toast and jelly. She soothed me with encouraging words on how to relax as a new nursing mother. She told me the infection would clear up if I just continued to nurse in spite of the pain. And it did.

We enjoyed relaxed coffee times together. She filled me in on Dad's tugboat saga. Because Mom had shown a willingness to go boating with him, he decided to buy a fifty-two foot wooden cabin cruiser instead of the tugboat. He had found it in Crisfield, Maryland. Based on a vivid dream he had had about a voyage to many islands, he named the boat the *ISLANDER*. For now, they were going to keep Cackleberry as home base and travel on *ISLANDER* for leisure. The sale of three Cackleberry acres had paid for the boat. I was happy to hear that Dad had finally fulfilled his dream of owning a motorized yacht.

Shortly after Mom left, Charity came for another period of time to live with us. I was now on my feet and able to fix her meals and keep up with an eight-year-old. To her delight, a mild-mannered swayback horse was pastured behind our house. Charity figured out how to climb on a picnic bench to mount the horse and ride it bareback. Its scrawny backbones tore holes in Charity's jeans and hurt her "privates," so I fixed her up with several menstrual pads stuffed into her pants but they all got shredded. Charity gave up on the horse. She helped Levi clear a plot for a small vegetable garden.

I enjoyed watching them work as I sat in a lounge chair, where I cuddled Sunshine while she nursed and slept. A mother hen pecked and scratched near the barn. Her chicks mimicked her close by. A barn cat appeared with her brood of playful kittens. They skittered among the pink gladiolus by the shed. Muk Luk hunkered in the grass, panting with a smile on his face. Even the horse came up to look over my shoulder.

I called over to Levi and caught his attention. "Look at us. We're in heaven!"

But, it wasn't to be for long. The creamery nearby closed. Now Levi had to drive the milk truck to a creamery way past the New York state line. He left home before daylight and by the time he returned it was already dark. There was no opportunity to tend the garden. He couldn't enjoy family life either.

"This sucks!" he complained. "It's not going to work to stay here. I'm sorry, Babe, but we've got to move back to Philly to get work with better hours. We might as well go now so we can get Charity enrolled in school for September."

I didn't want to leave. It was so very peaceful on this farm out in the country. But I could see that Levi was being realistic and looking out for us all.

We had no place to go but Cackleberry, where Mom and Dad once again graciously opened their hearts and home. Charity briefly attended the local school and then went back to her mother's for a spell. Levi heard about a possible good job. A contemporary named Leon Altemose was hiring non-union workers to help construct a new Sheraton Hotel in Valley Forge. Levi disappeared into Dad's workshop and came out hours later with a handheld wooden toolbox he had created, fashioned after Dad's. He got hammers and other tools. He distressed the tools and the box, to make them appear well used, as though he were a seasoned carpenter. Confidently, and with a bit of cockiness, he went off to the formidable job site. Not only did he make his way past the construction fence and into the boss's trailer but he also came back with a job offer to start the next day!

Levi's drafting skills and architectural schooling served him well. He had a keen sense of how the construction materials should comply with the drawn plans. One day, he impressed the boss by alerting the foreman that the bolts being imbedded in the concrete slab were off by fractions of an inch, and would therefore not be accommodating to the steel girder that would be lowered by a crane. The plans and measurements bore out Levi's warning, so they moved the bolts accordingly, and Levi received a bonus and promotion. One day, they asked him if he knew how to weld. He answered yes. That night, I heard him on the phone with a friend asking for a crash course in welding. I thought, my husband has *chutzpah*, a Yiddish word for shameless audacity!

In the meantime, I enjoyed what seemed like endless fivesies at home with Mom and Dad. Dad kept talking about retirement and fixing up the *ISLANDER* for cruising the eastern seaboard. With their eleventh grand baby living in their midst, they had a new kind of entertainment.

The hardest part for me was trying not to wake them up at night when Sunshine cried to be nursed. Some people believed you could just let the baby cry and pretty soon they would sleep till morning. However I didn't have the option to try that on account of waking my parents. Sometimes, Sunshine cried even after she was fed. She just didn't want to be placed back in her crib. So I found that if I bounced her, she would settle and sleep.

Consequently, Willow Sunshine woke me up to nurse and bounce for two full years before she finally learned to sleep through the night. I may have subconsciously enjoyed that habit. I couldn't get enough mothering done in a day. She was my all in all. I tended to her every meal, diaper change, smile. My eyes and heart were fixed on that beautiful little miracle baby.

Levi, on the other hand, felt left out. He wanted us to bond and eat as a family, with me as a devoted wife, not just a devoted mother. Instead, he saw me regressing as a dependent daughter back into my childhood home. We hadn't yet made enough money to strike out and rent our own place. In fact, it looked doubtful whether we could do that any time soon.

Impatience got the better of him, and one day he announced he was going to go stay with one of the guys from his construction team, Eric, whose wife Maggie had invited Levi to sleep on their living room floor. Levi's obvious desperation to flee the dependence on parents jolted me out of my Cackleberry dreamland. Without hesitation, I told Levi, "You're not going without us. Sunshine, Muk Luk and I are coming too!" Levi was astounded. Would I really leave the comfort of Cackleberry and follow him to camp out on a stranger's floor?

Levi and I were paying our dues for dropping out of society to search for an "alternative lifestyle." While other young people stayed the course in order to build up a bank account to afford their future dreams, we had opted to go the road less traveled to pursue immediately what we considered a more peaceful way to live. Even so, I wouldn't have traded the hitchhiking, mountain climbing and the tent experiences.

However, we were now in for a series of tests and trials to find our way out of poverty. There was no Walden Pond idealism in sleeping on Eric and Maggie's floor. In fact, it was the opposite. Eric turned out to be a mind-blown druggie who, fortunately, waited until we moved out before he took his own life. Muk Luk met his fate under the wheels of a truck on the highway. There was evil in that place. We just had to move on.

*C*aptain Paul Early, who had taken my place in Scotland the previous year when I was derailed in DC to serve in the Bureau of Naval Personnel, was selected to the rank of Admiral after his first year in Scotland. This time the phone call was that I was selected again to be Commander Submarine Squadron 14, based in Holy Loch, Scotland, to report in July 1972. Finally, I received my Captain at Sea command opportunity. My wife and four children were excited to experience a foreign country while serving the Navy overseas.

My flag ship was the USS CANOPUS (AS-34), which was anchored semi-permanently as the host ship for the assigned ten operating Fleet Ballistic Missile Submarines.

I was the first Commodore assigned to Holy Loch who elected to send their children to local Dunoon schools. The school's Head Master and Dunoon's Lord Mayor were elated. This arrangement worked well for solidification of local support, but more importantly for teaching my children the value of experiencing other cultures.

The Flood, Making Plans, and Looking For God

A friend tipped us off about a little cabin for sale in Chester County sitting on the bank of East Brandywine Creek. "You could even fish from the kitchen door," they had said. It was offered at $6,500 "as is." Levi was undaunted by the fact that it essentially needed everything—electric, plumbing, drywall, heat and air. To him it was an exciting project to tackle. He approached his father, Sol, who reluctantly agreed to co-sign a loan. So thanks to Sol's help, we bought the cabin.

Levi scheduled a two-week vacation from his Altemose job to devote that time to restore the house. We borrowed a large camping tent from Dita and another one from Marion and set them up as temporary shelters. I got a crib for Sunshine. Mom let me have one of the hand-painted bureaus she had brought back from Mexico in my childhood to use for Sunshine's baby clothes. Levi and two friends began a whirlwind of construction activity. It was exciting.

Under the autumn trees, I listened to sounds of busy hammers and saws, accompanied by the gentle babbling of the stream. I fixed hoagie sandwiches. Our one-of-a-kind cabin was going to be cute. It sat at the foot of a long driveway in a grassy bowl. Several older houses created a small community above it along the road. I was hoping we would meet nice neighbors who could become new friends.

On the third day of construction, everything changed. A predicted storm hit us with a deluge of rain. I was outside on the porch of the cabin feeding Sunshine, who by now could sit in a high chair. The guys stopped working. We all saw the creek swelling, creeping fast toward the kitchen door. Within minutes, the then turbulent stream flowed over the banks like a tsunami. Our tents were both swept away. The Mexican bureau floated onto its side and started to follow a tent but Levi caught hold of a leg and pulled the family heirloom to the higher ground. The guys began putting our boxes and bags of supplies onto the roof in case water entered the house.

Suddenly, the angry, churning flood surrounded our house. I saw logs and lawn chairs and propane tanks rushing by. I figured, since we were several steps up on the porch, we were out of harm's way. But I was wrong. The water kept rising.

Just in time, I grabbed Sunshine, a box of diapers, and my Minolta camera and lifted them high. With adrenaline soaring, I stepped down into the water, which was up to my armpits. Sunshine's little legs got wet. I put her over my shoulder and held her tight. *Oh God! Don't let my baby slip away!* The force of the current tried to take us sideways downstream but I pushed my body against it. Only by sheer determination, I kept my feet on the ground and was able to walk in a straight line to the safety of the grassy hill thirty feet away.

Out of breath, I plopped down and held Sunshine close to me. God had answered my prayer. The rain continued to pelt us. The house was now submerged in several feet of water. I didn't know whether to cry or rejoice, cuss or laugh. I was speechless, angry, sad for the loss of the house, glad to be safe. We all were safe.

Levi came and sat with us. We both knew the cabin was no longer habitable. It was time to go back to Cackleberry that night to determine our next option.

We barely had time to recover from the flood, when a housing solution fell into place. Near the cabin was a manicured mobile home park, complete with a scenic view of a picture-perfect farm and rolling hills. The park owner was willing to rent us a furnished three bedroom model on a lease-purchase basis. We jumped at the opportunity.

Soon I was cooking our brown rice and beans in the modern kitchen of a mobile home, walking barefoot on wall-to-wall carpet, and feeling luxurious with living room furniture. The master bedroom was not furnished, so we slept on a foam rubber pad on the floor. *Someday*, I told myself, *we will have a proper bed*. We rationalized that it was beneficial to our bodies to sleep on a firm surface but the true reason was we couldn't afford a bed.

The Altemose job ended for Levi when the construction part of the project was complete. Levi had visions of starting his own construction company. He bought a pretty blue van. For now, he tapped into his drafting skills and landed a series of jobs in architectural firms. One job required a long drive into Bucks County just at the time in 1973 when there was a gas shortage—something about an OPEC oil embargo and a Yom Kippur war.

At work one day, Levi lent the van as a favor to a gal who had come into the office. She had wanted it for just a few hours. She never returned! Later, the police found the van totaled on a back street in Philadelphia. It had been used as a getaway vehicle in a drug heist. The replacement car Levi picked up was a gas guzzler. The lines grew longer at the gas stations. Sometimes, there was no gas left by the time he got near the pump.

Both of us were discouraged by the wave of hard knocks. First the cabin flooded, then his van was stolen, and now we were in the middle of a gas crisis. We were trying to make ends meet but we kept sliding backwards.

Undaunted, Levi pressed on and found a temporary construction job closer to home. He also built us a big deck. Sunshine learned to walk. What glee I felt to see her climb onto the wooden rocking horse I had bought in Vermont so many years earlier for my someday baby. "Playing dollies" with Sunshine filled my days with such happiness that all our trials easily faded from importance.

Levi, however, had to shoulder our burdens. We no longer lived an alternative lifestyle. He was in the workaday world with pressures that could rattle even the most stoic of marine drill sergeants. In a way, I felt sorry for him—the man, the provider. I considered myself fortunate to be a woman, a nursing mother. Levi didn't want me to go out and work, and I was glad to stay home.

Among his few prized possessions, Levi had a wooden plaque that he always displayed whenever he set up house. In Elizabethan lettering, it read, "TRUTH is the Highest Thing that Man may Keep." I watched how deliberate he was to place it in a prominent spot on the wall. He had told me how much he valued the saying. It came from Geoffrey Chaucer's "The Canterbury Tales." It was like a creed for him. It got me thinking about myself. I wasn't consciously reaching for high ideals like Truth. But perhaps I should be. I envied this aspect of Levi, that he could be in awe of something like Truth. When he smoked his pipe in quiet moments and rolled his eyes back, was he meditating on Truth? What was he finding out? My mind couldn't ruminate on such things. Maybe re-reading Shakespeare's plays from my college text book would make me more enlightened. What about Honor too? Or Respect? Or Valor? These days, I was more caught up in baby talk and Mother Goose rhymes.

Our second baby was on its way. Sunshine was almost two. I pushed her in the stroller around the neighborhood, enjoying my distant view of the stone farmhouse with its pond and red barn. She pointed her cute finger at some grazing cows and said, "Mooo!" I leaned down and kissed her curly black hair. "Yes, moo cows," I repeated. We passed a walkway to one of the mobile homes where a young mother of three children came out to greet us. She invited us in for cookies. Before long, she started talking about how the world would be coming to an end, probably soon. I could hardly understand what she was saying. We didn't own a television and I never listened to news on the radio.

"Don't you see how the world is having an energy crisis? That's why President Nixon wouldn't let us turn on Christmas lights last winter. There still isn't any gas at the gas stations even now. Yes, for real!" The woman continued, "This all points to God's prophesy that we will be taken up to heaven to be with God. It's called the rapture. There will be an end to this world, before the new heaven and earth come."

I wanted to get out of her house as quickly as I could. It sounded like imaginary science fiction, yet her words reverberated in my mind—especially the part where she talked about God. It was like she knew God. I wondered if knowing God was the puzzle piece missing in our home. I saw her again two days later. She told me that her Baptist church had a bus to take people to church on Sundays, and that it would stop for me and my family, if we wanted to go. I told her thanks but no thanks. It surely didn't fit our picture. I tried to imagine bouncing along in a green bus labeled something like "Gospel Express" with sticky-fingered children dressed in clean Sunday-go-to-meeting clothes. The one subject Levi and I were at odds about was God, so I stuffed all this episode in a back pocket and tried to put it out of my mind.

Levi and I sat on the mustard-colored furniture in the living room of our 1970s mobile home. He had quit his most recent drafting job and we needed to talk. Both the mortgage and lot rental payments were due. We had no health insurance to cover the delivery of our new baby. Cigarette smoke created a fog around him. Our conversation turned philosophical, even esoteric. It seemed to take us nowhere and was as elusive as the dissipating smoke. But at least it was a cuss-free zone, unlike the "real" world where the decisions required to make a living were often punctuated with Levi's emotive expletives.

As we reviewed, it was hard to make sense of our lives. Macrobiotics had temporarily fallen by the wayside, there being no brown rice and seaweed store nearby. Communal farm life with Ginger and Emmett in Jasper had borne no promise of paying the bills. The Starrucca tent experiment to live apart from the civilized world had proved impractical for protection from weather conditions, and now, for raising a family. We were at an impasse.

Levi knew how much I wanted to stay living in the country. I readjusted my position on the couch to accommodate my pregnant belly. The baby's heel or elbow slid beneath my skin. I placed my hand there and transferred silent love to our new child. "What are we going to do?" I asked him. I trusted Levi to come up with a solution. He was good at forging ahead with something new and different, something requiring a different hat.

"I'm going to find a job in the city. You can take me to the train station in Downingtown and I'll commute by train." I thought that was a brilliant idea. Then at least I could stay out in the exurbs, and I'd even have a car to drive.

Looming over us in all of this was the future maternity cost at a hospital. But I had good news for Levi.

"I called a Dr. Carpenter at Bryn Mawr Hospital," I told him. "He does home deliveries and is willing to be my doctor. The only drawback is that he won't come this far west. So I asked Dita what she thought about us coming to her living room to have the baby on the same futon mat where her little girl was recently born."

"What did she say?"

"You know Dita. She's always hospitable and up for hippy adventure."

The evening of quandary was smoothing out with some practical solutions. We already had a crib. We would take it from Sunshine's room and put it in the baby's room. Sunshine could now "graduate" to sleep on a foam rubber mattress on the floor like we did. Levi would get a new job in the city. We wouldn't need to pay for a hospital stay. Both of us felt more at peace. I took the opportunity to round out our twosome interlude by sharing with Levi the amazing revelation that had come to me after meeting with the neighbor Baptist bus lady.

"You know what I've come to realize, Levi?"

"What?"

I actually said it. "I think you and I are looking for God."

Levi surprised me with his negative reaction. I had expected that the idea we were looking for God would have brought a welcomed, life-changing clarity to our collective consciousness. Instead, it was actually met with disdain.

"Not me," he retorted. "I don't know who you met, or what they were trying to sell you but count me out. I'm not looking for God. If you are, you're on your own."

I dropped the subject—for then.

Happily, Levi landed a good job as a draftsman of intricate piping systems for the engineering company Catalytic Construction. It was located in a big office building in center city. We had to buy him a couple of suits and ties. He was visibly nervous that first morning. He said, "I don't know where to go once I get inside the building."

I told him, "Find out where the men's room is." He laughed and seemed more lighthearted as I drove him to the Downingtown train station for his long commute.

I spent precious days with Sunshine. On Thursdays, we went to the Downingtown Diner for chicken pot pie, my pregnancy craving. Afterwards, I indulged in a Dairy Queen cone. Too soon, though, my treat costs doubled. Sunshine discovered that ice cream was cold and delicious. I could no longer get by with buying only one.

*A*bout six months after my arrival in Holy Loch, Scotland, I received a direct telephone call from Admiral Long. After a bit, he said he was thrilled to inform me that I had just been selected by the current 1972 Flag Promotion Board for Rear Admiral. He indicated that the effective promotion date was around 28 March 1973, but that I could expect to remain at the Holy Loch location for six months or more. I was floored to be so recognized. Apparently, only one other of my classmates had also been honored. He was in the Air Force and was currently in space with the Russians. He was Astronaut Tom Stafford. We both had been selected for Flag about six years before our class was even in the normal promotion zone. Tom was an "Okie" as I was, and we both competed for the same Congressional Appointment. I won but Tom got a Senatorial Appointment later.

What a thrill to become Admiral. But get busy Kelln and ensure those submarines, when departing, are repaired, trained and on schedule.

Rear Admiral Albert Lee Kelln.

I received orders for detachment from Submarine Squadron 14 effective 19 January 1974. My orders read that I was to proceed to Charleston, South Carolina, for duty as Commander Submarine

Group Six. I proceeded to Charleston with the concern that there was currently a massive car gasoline shortage in the States. The apprehension I had was, how was I going to get my car from the New Jersey arrival port to Charleston with no gas in the tank?

It was delightful to journey back to the homeland for my new duty in Charleston, South Carolina. We had the chance to see grandparents on both family sides. We welcomed the shirt sleeve warm February weather.

Baby Anna and a Move to the City

On the last day of May, 1974, I got a sudden surge of great energy. On my hands and knees, I weeded the entire vegetable garden Levi had planted. The next day, June first, was Levi's thirty-second birthday. I went into labor. Thankfully, it was a Saturday and Levi was home from work and able to drive me to Dita's. Home births were both a new wave and a curiosity. Word got out that a home delivery was happening at Dita's. Several people came and went. She had a kitchen full of food. It was a party atmosphere. Both of my sweet sisters sat with me, massaging my feet to distract my body from pain and help me relax. Levi coached me with Lamaze breathing.

Just before midnight, when the household had quieted down, our second baby girl was born on her father's birthday. We named her after Levi's maternal grandmother, Anna, who was born in Russia, and had recently died in the States.

Willow Sunshine was still the apple of my eye. Now I had to move her off my lap to make room for the nursing of Baby Anna. As I got to know this sweet blonde-haired bundle, a new kind of love welled up in me. I called her my little Valentine. I sewed hearts on her cloth diapers. She was a calm baby and the love between us was quiet and easy. It was a new depth of feeling, a different kind of relationship. No wonder people said that mothers have plenty of love to go around. I couldn't stop gazing into their fresh little faces. I was full to overflowing.

Levi continued to commute by train to the city. It was wearisome for both of us to pack up two babies to meet the train's schedule both ways.

Charity was with us too. Levi decided to rent a room in the city for week nights. All he had with him was a cot and an alarm clock.

One day he returned to his room to find out someone had broken in and stolen his clock. He came to a conclusion that affected all of us. The family needed to move to the city.

Memories of the overwhelming hubbub of New York, and the loneliness of those first three months in Philadelphia with Ramón, and the turmoil of The Hague and Boston prompted me to tell Levi I didn't want to go.

"It's peaceful out in the country," I told him. Levi eased my mind by offering to drive me through various city neighborhoods to see if one of them looked welcoming. We made several day trips, and I chose Germantown with its tree-lined streets and big old houses with porches.

We found an old three-story townhouse with high ceilings and ornate wood trim. It had six bedrooms, a front porch, back yard, and a laundry area in the basement. Grandmother LoLo gifted us the dining room table from Levi's childhood, which still held Levi's naughty initials etched underneath, and some chairs. Other than that, we had no first floor furniture and only a crib and foam mats upstairs. Charity stayed on, so we enrolled her in an unconventional private school. We resumed our macrobiotic eating of brown rice and wok-cooked vegetables. I bought a hand-crank grinding mill and produced delicious hearty breads from the whole grains I ground into flour—wheat berries, rye, oats, bulgur, millet.

Kneading the doughs on a large cutting board almost put me in a trance. While the babies were napping and Charity was at school, my hands worked the mound in all directions. The fresh scent of uncooked grains took me back to the country. It was my form of meditation to count each fold and push. Then, the loaf pans went into the oven. Soon the delicious aroma of fresh-baked breads emanated from the kitchen and filled the whole house. We slathered almond butter on warm bread slices, topped with honey and toasted sesame seeds.

Because of his association with a chemical engineering company, Levi was inspired to begin the study of engineering. He enrolled in night classes at Drexel University, bought wire-rimmed reading glasses, and soon ensconced himself in an empty third floor bedroom, where he spent all his free time with his nose in the books. He surprised us all, especially himself, by acing his first calculus exam. A new semester started. Levi signed up. He was fascinated and challenged by the grueling subject material. The result was we rarely saw him.

One day, as Levi entered his third floor study, he was greeted by a wooden plaque on his desk with an etched message. In little girl hand-writing, it read in all caps, "ENGINEERING ISN'T EVERYTHING." He brought the plaque downstairs, deeply moved. He recognized that his young girl Charity was missing him, and that he had been spending all his time on what would have been a long process to get a degree. We all had been missing him. Upon reflection, he came to the conclusion that Charity had made a good point.

He admitted to her that engineering isn't everything. "I'm going to give up this plan," he told us.

So much happened in the ensuing weeks. Levi stopped engineering school. In a quiet moment with me, he conceded that he had overreacted when I suggested that we were both looking for God. He now wanted to pursue a study of yoga as a way of seeking God.

He discovered a yoga teacher, named Shanti Desai, who had a yoga ashram in Ocean City, New Jersey, who also gave classes near Germantown. Levi started going to these classes and soon stopped working at Catalytic. He took up yoga full time. The deep breathing, the postures, the lotus position, the settling of his mind, the soothing voice of Shanti Desai, and all of that package became his new passion. He practiced yoga for hours everyday. I made him a white pajama-style outfit that was loose fitting. I embroidered pastel flowers along the V-neckline. He grew his beard. His eyes became sparkly and distant. He began to receive students and charge them for yoga lessons.

I occasionally joined his class on the busy third floor just to get limber, to help me keep up with the demands of caring for Sunshine, Anna, and Charity, plus the meal preparation and house cleaning. Levi was my surrogate, I figured. If he found God, I would catch up with him later. I needed to remain practical while my husband soared into new spiritual highs.

I started giving three-dollar haircuts in our living room. I used a dining room chair for a barber chair. It was easy to sweep up the cut hair snips from the bare floor. Charity was now twelve and wanted her own spending money, so we gave her permission to work at the corner ice cream shop. She posted a hand-written note on their bulletin board that advertised my barber services. "HAIRCUTS $3.00," it said. I soon had a fairly steady stream of customers, mostly long-haired young men. They were living in the city, trying to find their way, and not caring really what their haircut looked like. It was convenient for me.

So as I worked, they talked and shared a lot about themselves. I found almost every one of them was a non-practicing Jew. I heard some fascinating stories about all of the spiritual leaders and teachers they were following out and about. One would tell me about Yogi this or Swami that and others would tell me about Father this and Mother that. I listened with great interest, not memorizing anything I heard, but fascinated that all of these people were excited about the truth or truths they were discovering. Levi and I sensed we were on a path to enlightenment. In fact, there seemed to be an electricity in the air that was turning young people Godward.

Our home in Germantown had an open door policy. We didn't lock our door so that drifters needing a warm place to sit and chat could freely come and go. We were like a little community meeting place. There was one couple, Sam and Judy, who stayed in our spare bedroom awhile. Sunshine called him Mr. Floppy Socks because of how his socks slid halfway off his feet and flopped when he walked up and down the stairs. Sam was a professional comedian looking for work. He and Judy had arrived with the intention of doing a carrot fast. That's all they ate for weeks.

One morning I looked at Sam and noticed his face had turned orange. I said to him, "Don't you think you've had enough carrots?" He looked at himself in the mirror. For the first time I saw this comedian have a good laugh.

*O*n 13 September 1974, I was assigned additional duties as Commandant, Sixth Naval District and Commander, Naval Base, Charleston. As Commander Submarine Group Six, I had operational control of SSBNs in their pre-deployment and post deployment operations, as well as the SSBNs returning to the United States for tender refit refresher training. This included other units as assigned by higher authority. I also exercised administrative control of ships assigned and SSBN off-ship crews home ported in Charleston. This included their schedules and evaluations of off-crew training. I also was to act as area coordinator for Submarine Force Commands in the Charleston area. Submarine Group Six had a cumulative strength of approximately 6,000 officers and men.

In addition, I was assigned to Command other complex activities of the Charleston Naval Base, as well as the Fifth Naval District Commandant. I was very busy but I was needed in the Pentagon to manage the Trident Missile Submarine Program and supervise its approval through Congress.

Is That All There Is?

I did my best to adjust to the change from a quiet mobile home in the country to a bustling city house with four levels. My body was slim because of the fat-free macrobiotic diet. The physical demands of nursing Anna, keeping up with two-year-old Sunshine and lugging laundry to and from the basement were harder with all the stairs. Charity had the interests and needs of a fifth grader that I was inadequate to accommodate. Levi's intense yoga practice lured him to weekend retreats in New Jersey.

Some days I suffered from boredom. On other days, unexpected things happened, like the frightening sudden crash of rocks coming through our front windows. They were thrown by impulsive kids from the Boys' Club down the street. A mentally unstable man, who called himself Six Six Six, wandered into our house and ground up our hamster's food in the grain grinder. I looked straight at him and declared words I'd heard from the Bible, "Get thee behind me, Satan!" The words had supernatural power, because the man didn't hesitate to turn around and walk out.

Somehow, we were paying our bills but we were slipping behind. I hoped Levi would pass through his spiritual quest and come out the other side, ready to work in construction or some other job to support us. He had always shown an honorable work ethic, so this had to be a temporary pause.

For now, though, I was spiraling into depression. I was tired, disillusioned. My heart's desperate cry came from a new sense of hopelessness. I resonated with Peggy Lee's Grammy award song, "Is That All There Is?"

I had so looked forward to being a mother. For years, I practiced with baby dolls in the high attic at Cackleberry. Now I was a real mother. I had not only one, but two real babies, two precious daughters—plus a bonus step-daughter. I loved them dearly. And yet something was missing. Why was I not fulfilled? Why was I asking, "Is that all there is?" I had no answer.

My forward motion came to a halt. Levi arrived home and found me in the bathroom, my thin body sitting on the edge of the tub, crying.

"Levi, I need help," I confessed. "I need someone to feed me three meals a day. I can't go on without help."

Levi was caught off guard. He wasn't aware of my exhaustion. He offered to take over the kitchen and watch the children. I told him I couldn't expect him to do it. "There's only one person in the world I know who can help me, and that is Mom." She and Dad had taken their boat to Florida for the winter.

Levi agreed. "Why don't you take the girls and spend two weeks on the *ISLANDER* with your parents? We'll borrow the money for the plane fare. Charity and I will look after each other. We'll be fine."

Our idea worked out. It was the end of January. I held eight-month-old Anna in my arms. Sunshine trotted alongside me as we entered the boarding ramp of the flight bound for Fort Lauderdale.

"I so 'citing," she chirped. Neither she nor I knew how exciting this trip to Florida would turn out to be. In fact, it was life changing.

Jesus!

Dad and Mom received me and the girls aboard *ISLANDER* with the perfect attitude and solution for healing my exhaustion. Dad proudly showed how they had set up a little crib for Anna next to my bunk in the bow's lower sleeping quarters. Sunshine would sleep in a nearby bunk.

Mom spoke words that were music to my ears. "You, Dear, will rest on your bed for as many hours or days as it takes to start feeling better. Your only job is to nurse Anna when she needs you, and I'll bring her to you. I'll bring you meals, too. Dad and I will take good care of the girls. Don't worry."

Somehow, they all entertained each other while I slept for hours and hours. I barely remember the nursing sessions with Anna. It was like I slept through them too. Normally, I was fully focused on nursing and wouldn't even talk or read because I was immersed in the euphoria of nourishing my baby, my heart's delight.

After a few days, I strengthened enough to go to the expansive Fort Lauderdale beach with Dad and Mom. It being mid-week in winter, there were few people. We had no beach chairs but sat on towels. Little Anna took a fascination to the sand and began to eat it, so I couldn't put her down. We took turns holding her the whole time, even while splashing with Sunshine in the shallow margins of the surf. We went to this beach several afternoons in a row.

My appetite grew and I ate every tidbit of the daily three meals Mom prepared for me. I called Levi, who was suffering from some sort of flu. He had started a body-cleansing fast, but quit, because all he got was "damn hungry," he said.

He asked how I was doing. I told him I was a lot stronger, less depressed. "But, I feel empty. Even though I'm full of food, it's like I have nothing in me. I'm like a jar full of hotdog relish!"

Both of us sounded like two lost people in need of hope to go on.

Wednesday, February 5, 1975, marked a new beginning for me. It was a remarkable day from the moment I woke up because I had had a dream that was so vivid I wrote it down in detail in a little pocket notebook. I joined my parents at the breakfast table to recount my dream. It went like this:

I was in a motel with Sunshine. She was hungry, so I left to go find her a peanut butter and jelly sandwich. While out, I came upon a group of happy people gathered at a familiar intersection near Cackleberry. They told me they were going to a spiritual retreat and invited me join them. I saw their leader from a distance. He was dressed in a long white tunic and I was immediately attracted to know him.

They said, "Come with us. All you have to do is four things: sing, dance, listen, and give."

I was so eager to go. I told them, I could do all of that. The giving part was the hardest but I would panhandle if I had to. But, I told them, I needed to get a sandwich to my daughter and get her settled somewhere. They said, "Okay." A friendly girl named Margaret stayed behind to help me take care of my responsibilities and lead me to the group in case they had moved on.

In the next scene, I was walking alone down Roberts Road to Cackleberry. I sensed someone walking with me. To my utter surprise and deep delight, it was the white-robed man. He didn't say anything to me. Our stride was so unified I sensed that he and I were as one. We got as far as Uncle Ross's house together, and after that I was alone again. I turned into Uncle Ross's driveway and came upon a party of family and friends, whose faces kept morphing from angelic to demonic, and back again.

Then the dream ended. Privately, I decided this dream was a message to me. I needed a spiritual teacher. I decided that when I got home to Germantown, I would listen carefully to my haircutting customers' religious talk. I would choose to join the first group which had a living guru or swami. No matter what he taught, I would go find him, sit at his feet, and place myself in subjection as an avid, loyal follower. This thought gave me a great sense of relief and resolve.

After breakfast, Dad suggested we go to the beach in the morning instead of afternoon. He took us to a different beach where there were young people and families. I spotted a young couple sitting on the beach who were up-north winter-pale, like me. They had two children the same ages as mine. Their baby, however, was happily seated in a sand-free portable playpen.

Without hesitation, I went over and introduced myself. I asked the bold question if I could add my baby to their playpen. They said, "Of course." As I placed Anna next to their little boy, I explained how Anna had eaten sand and that I appreciated the relief from having to hold her. While Sunshine played with her grandparents, I enjoyed the company and friendliness of David and Toni Rose. They were on vacation in Florida from Kansas City. The three of us leaned against the netting of the crib and talked. I found myself spilling out all the sorrows of my life—abandonment and divorce from Ramón, the flooded cabin, the many moves with Levi, and my current state of exhaustion and disillusionment. Somehow, I felt they had some wisdom to give me.

Just before they had a turn to speak, Dad, a man of habit, motioned for me to head back to the car. It was time for lunch. I truly meant it when I told David and Toni that I was sorry we had to cut our visit short. They were sorry, too, so they invited me to meet them that evening after supper.

Dad lent me the car. He and Mom looked after Sunshine. I already felt physically stronger from days of respite—less depressed, too. I set out with my nursing baby in her infant seat to meet my new friends. Visions of sugar plums danced in my head. Maybe they would have wine or a marijuana joint and I could break out of my perfect, macrobiotic, motherhood persona, if just for tonight. It would be my private rebellious moment, away from my parents and away from Levi.

Toni greeted me. "Hi! Welcome! Come on in. Here. Put your baby seat on this bed while I get my boys ready for sleep." She motioned to one of the motel room's double beds. I sat next to Anna. The family's suitcases were on the floor. One was open. I noticed miniature boxes of corn flakes and Cheerios in the pocket. "I'm sorry David isn't here to greet you," Toni went on. "He's the one who wanted to finish our conversation from this morning. He'll be right back. He's getting us some Cokes."

Cokes! Bummer! What could this couple provide to get me high? These were people with a "Betty Crocker mentality," as Levi and our friends called it. They drank soda and ate processed foods. *No one who lived like that could possibly be an enlightened soul!* I figured they were super straight. There would be no eye opening insights about this New Age of Aquarius. Nor would there be any substance to get me high—to give me a temporary escape from my disappointment with life.

I decided to make the best of the evening anyway. Toni finished with the children and gave me her undivided attention. Anna was asleep. I was going to make small talk but then I looked around the room with a sudden realization. What a coincidence! Here I was in a motel, which was the opening scene of my dream. I told Toni I needed to tell her the details of a remarkable dream from the night before.

"Oddly enough," I began, "I was in a motel room with Sunshine..." And I told her the whole dream and all about the man in the white tunic with the group of followers who surrounded him. I told her how it made me eager to find a contemporary spiritual leader to follow once I got back to Germantown.

In walked David with his Cokes. "Here's David," Toni said. "It's so interesting that you are looking for spiritual direction. We know the Guru you need. David will tell you about Him."

I was all ears. David invited me to sit at the little table and chairs at the other end of the room. To my amazement, he pulled out a well-worn, black leather Bible and opened it. *Imagine,* I thought to myself, *a young man, who's probably my age, actually owns and values a Bible!*

I was so impressed that I missed everything he told me. Then, as if out of a fog, I heard David say, "Jesus is looking for you."

It was my turn to answer. "I've heard about that. My sister wants me to choose Jesus. So does Billy Graham. And, my Mom prays I will. I've tried but I guess it's not working out." I pointed to his Bible. "I know He's in the Bible. I've flipped through the pages to see His name. But I haven't heard a voice. I can't hear bells. And I haven't seen a burning bush. I need some indication, something fantastic to show me God."

David patiently waited for me to finish my frustrations. I continued, "Jesus is so elusive. He's not real to me. He died, so what can He teach me? I need to find another teacher who is alive. Real. Someone I can sit with, learn from, and ask questions to. Besides," I told David, "if Jesus is looking for me, why hasn't He found me in all these years? I must not be important enough."

Then, David came through with the word pictures that I needed. I listened carefully. He spoke in such a way that my life would never be the same.

David said to me, "You are like a lost sheep bleating off into the distance." He held his arm out straight with his finger pointed. He slowly swept an imaginary circumference around him. "Baa! Baa! Baa!" he bleated. His eyes followed his moving finger. He continued, "There is a vast universe of 360 degrees around each one of us. Every degree holds possibilities for some enlightening experience, for something attractive to pull our attention and increase our knowledge."

David looked at me to see if I was tracking with him. I definitely was. I felt like I was that little lost bleating lamb. He went on, "Every one of those directions leads ultimately to eternal nothingness. You'd have to pull back and try another direction. At one of those degrees, you will see Jesus, your Shepherd. He is ready to receive you with an everlasting love. His way is the promise of everlasting life."

I wanted that. But I suddenly lost the picture. I was no longer able to see myself as a lost lamb. It was as if David read my mind. He gave me another word picture that I needed. He said, "You don't have to see a burning bush or hear bells. You don't have to be an innocent little lamb. You could be a drunken bum, lying in the gutter on Skid Row. All you have to do is turn your head. You will see Jesus. It's that simple. You turn your head. You keep your eyes on Him."

Pop! Something happened. I was instantly released. Refreshed. Even joyous. My heart went from a hard NO to a definite YES. How easy that was! I knew I belonged to Jesus. This was something lasting, and I knew it.

It was after eleven o'clock when I left the motel flying high. No wine. I was bursting to tell Mom, who had been praying for me for thirty-two years. Mom and Dad were both asleep in their convertible sofa bed in the upper cabin of the *ISLANDER*. I inched by them to put sleeping Anna down in her little crib below deck.

Back upstairs, I knelt down by Mom, tugged gently on her nightie, and whispered, "Mom, I found Jesus! All I did was turn my head and there He was!"

Mom stirred a bit. She opened her eyes to see that it was really me, then said calmly, "That's wonderful, Dear. Jesus found you. Now go get some sleep."

Now this was a woman who had been praying for me, kneeling by her bed every night, reading her Bible every morning, going to church and Bible study three times a week, struggling with a husband who didn't join her in her faith. For years, she had also taught Sunday School and organized a neighborhood ladies' prayer group. And, yet, the best she could do was wake up just enough to say, "Good, Dear. Now go to bed"?

The next day, I asked Mom how she could be so calm when I told her I had received Jesus Christ in my heart. She merely reasoned, "As a baby, you were baptized in the church. You had water and a prayer that sealed you in the Christian faith. I took you to Sunday School so you could learn. I had you confirmed in the faith when you were thirteen. It was just a matter of time before you would hear Jesus knock and allow Him to find you. It happens to all of us."

"Mom," I answered. "You sure are a woman of faith."

The two-week visit with Mom and Dad in Fort Lauderdale had been truly healing in body, mind and Spirit. I couldn't wait to get home to Levi and tell him I had found the truth about God that we were desperately seeking.

I was going to recount all about how Jesus and I had met, how Jesus had found me and I had found Jesus!

But, it wasn't going to go over so well.

A Nunnery Experience and a Wedding

On the flight back to Germantown, I had time to reflect on how amazing God was in the way He paced out my new life in Jesus. He saw how spiritually needy I was, gave me a dream about Him, then had Dad take me to a different beach so I could meet a friendly Christian couple from Kansas City, one of whom (David) was born Jewish. *How perfect this was*, I thought, as I prepared to share all of this with my Jewish-born husband.

When I told him my exciting news, however, Levi lashed out at me with a verbal chastening so brutal, that, if it were possible, I would have put Jesus aside and chosen another guru. Levi made it clear to me any other teacher would have been acceptable to him. But Jesus was "the ultimate in anti-semitism. A Jew who becomes a Christian is no longer a Jew. What better way to do away with Judaism?" I had no way to refute that, except that David Rose, who had been a Jew, was now a Christian, but still claimed his Jewish roots.

Levi made it clear that "Jesus" was not to be a household name. I was forced to hold my Jesus glow deep inside, just like Mary in the Bible who "pondered these things in her heart" after the angel told her she would give birth to a Son and name Him Jesus.

And so a wall went up between us. Levi had thrived on being the spiritual pathfinder in our marriage, and I no longer would be his willing follower. Though I still dabbled in trying to understand Krishna, Brahman and Ascended Masters, I was no longer seeking.

About this time, Levi's guru, Shanti, decided he wanted to start a yoga ashram retreat house in Germantown. He asked Levi to be the resident yogi and Levi accepted. This meant that we would be moving there. I tried to picture my role as Mrs. Yogi and decided that the best thing for me would be to run the kitchen. I would bake breads, which by now I was expert at doing. I bought a sitar hoping to learn Indian ragas which sounded beautiful to me. Ravi Shankar brought the sitar sound into our current music. The Beatles used it in theirs. Levi played the tabla drums, and I pictured the two of us making Indian music together. But then, I realized I would have to immerse myself in that study, and that Indian music was part of a religious discipline that was not mine, nor would ever be. Thankfully, the ashram idea fell through, and I was released from that possible scenario. I sold the sitar.

I continued to love Jesus quietly in my heart.

One very hot summer day, I put Sunshine and Anna in our double stroller to walk down Germantown Avenue. The sun's heat reflected up from the sidewalk, and it was humid. The three of us were sweating and uncomfortable. I spotted some trees and green grass behind a low stone wall.

"Let's go into this yard," I told the girls. "We can get some shade from the trees and cool off." At the end of the walkway was a big church with stained glass windows and gothic wood doors. I pushed the stroller towards the nearest door and tried it. It was unlocked, so we went in. What a magnificent cathedral! Dark wood pews, red cushions, laced wall dividers to the choir loft and chancel, high stone ceilings, fresco paintings—all much fancier than Granny's Church of the Redeemer in Bryn Mawr. Up front, I saw words embroidered in gold filigree across a brocade altar cloth that said, "Man shall not live by bread alone." *Harumpf!* I thought to myself. *What could that be talking about?* I lived by bread alone. Kneading and baking bread was like my religion, my lifeline to sustenance, for me and my family.

I decided to attend a service there. It was called St. Luke's Episcopal Church. Levi gave me permission to go the next day and agreed to watch the girls.

During the service, the minister went up to a raised pulpit where there was a large Bible stand. Two acolytes wearing white cassocks stood below, swinging incense burners on hanging chains. The smoke ascended. The minister bent forward and kissed the open page of the Bible. He stood up and declared, "The Word of the Lord." The inscription on the altar that had stumped me the day before now made sense. *Aha!* I thought to myself. *Man doesn't live by bread alone, but by the Bible, which is God's Word. That's the connection. No wonder they were making such a big fuss over the reading of the Gospel.* I needed to find my Bible.

I hurried home and, at first chance, went to the storage room on the third floor where we had boxes of books. In one, just as I had hoped, was my black leather King James Bible. It had been gifted to me twenty years earlier in 1955 and was signed by Hadley Williams, Rector, for three years' perfect attendance at St. Mary's Church school in Ardmore, Pennsylvania. The Bible brought back a flood of memories. St. Mary's was Mom's childhood church. I held the Bible to my chest as I thought of how Mom had so faithfully driven me there every Sunday to enable me to have perfect attendance. I thought of my Granddaddy Clay, who was a vestryman there so many years earlier. I remembered how he wore a black armband on his suit sleeve as a sign of mourning after Grandmummy Clay died. When I wore my little red choir robe, I walked down the same aisle where Mom and Dad had been married. I had only used that Bible as a child to count how many times I could find the name of Jesus in it. Now, it was time to learn what all it taught.

I started attending St. Luke's often on Sundays. Next door to the church was a retreat house for the convent nuns of the Sisters of St. Margaret. On their bulletin board was an enticing notice. It advertised a no-cost two-week Live-In Program at their summer retreat by the sea in Duxbury, Massachusetts. Without any commitment to becoming a nun, one could sign up and live the life of a novitiate, which included prayer and Bible study.

I jumped at the chance to learn more about Jesus and soon was on a bus to Massachusetts. The girls went with their aunts, Dita and Marion, on their vacations in Eagles Mere, Pennsylvania. Levi took the opportunity to spend time in yoga training with Shanti in Ocean City, New Jersey. I brought my Bible with me. But first I wanted to finish a thick book called *Autobiography of a Yogi* by Paramahansa Yogananda. The nun who picked me up at the bus station saw the book and suggested I wouldn't be needing it, that perhaps I should turn my focus to the Bible.

I kept a journal during my two weeks as a Live-In. The sixty-three handwritten pages chronicled the fascinating taming of me from a wild mustang who wanted to gallop any which way, to me as a quiet, peaceful, joyful member of a highly disciplined community of nuns.

We ate meals in silence. There was no lingering at the table. I was urged, but not required, to attend the five liturgical "offices" held daily in the chapel. Something made me decide to go regularly and not skip any of them. At the beginning, I dreaded the drudgery. By the end, I wrote:

"Sundays are so special here. If you worked it right, you could be in church almost all day! See how I have changed! Now, being in church or chapel reciting scripture is true pleasure for me. The more I repeat the more I believe; the more I believe the more I see; the more I see the straighter my path; the straighter my path the closer I get to God; the closer I get to God the more peaceful I feel; the more peaceful I feel the greater I want to give; the greater I want to give the more I absorb God's love; the more I absorb God's love, the more love I radiate outwards."

Besides chapel, I also helped wash dishes, clean out a storehouse, and weed gardens. I swam in the delicious tidal cove waters. My cheeks grew rosy. I wrote:

"The first week here was like a health spa—restfulness and exercise to strengthen my thin, tense, tired body. Now another kind of healing is apparent—a healing of my spirit. Jesus said, 'Thou shalt have no other gods before me.' Now I understand this. No more questions. No more curiosity about Krishna or Brahman or Ascended Masters. My God is the God of Abraham

and Isaac, of Moses and John the Baptist, of the Apostles—the God who loves human people so much that he gave us a Son, Jesus Christ, to talk to us, live among us and show us the way to eternal life with Him. I want that Way. No other way. I want to walk in the Light of God and follow His path right on to His Heavenly Kingdom. Today, I am no longer a lost sheep. I have found my flock. Thank You, Lord Jesus."

Back home in Germantown, Levi had to put up with me because I was smitten with Jesus. If Jesus were to walk by our windows with a crowd of people following Him, I would be compelled to get in line and go with Him. But being more realistic, I had to stay mum about Jesus so as not to offend my husband. I used the training at the convent to put more discipline into my daily life. I planned better meals, prepared them on time, and scheduled certain days of the week to do laundry.

Levi supported my regular attendance at St. Luke's on Sundays. He seemed to accept my need to do that. I enjoyed the liturgy and the quiet responsive readings between the priest and the congregation and how it all showed great honor to God. The formal Sunday service was not conducive to little children, so they stayed home.

It wasn't long before I realized that I could get the girls baptized at St. Luke's. The next opportunity was super special because the bishop himself was coming to do the baptisms. I talked it over with Levi, and he said, "Why not? Go ahead. I have nothing for them. If you want to take them for baptism, that's fine with me."

I signed them up, bought little white dresses, invited Levi's parents (LoLo and Pop Pop) and family and my family. Several of them came. The service began with a loud banging on the rarely opened door at the back of the church. We all turned around in our pews to watch. The sexton pulled hard to open the gigantic Gothic-arched door. The bishop appeared, wearing a pointed hat and colorful robe. In his hand was the long staff he had used to pound on the door. He approached the baptismal font that held the basin of water.

A line of parents and babies formed for their big moment. The bishop went down the line, holding the babies and repeating their names as he placed the sign of the cross on each little forehead with the water that had been made holy by prayer. He baptized them in the Name of the Father, the Son, and the Holy Spirit. After repeating names like Amy, John, Kelly, and my baby Anna, the bishop appeared visibly amused as he baptized three-year-old Willow Sunshine. I wondered if he wondered whether Sunshine's mother and father had ever lived in a tent! We all enjoyed the ceremony, then the family went back to our house for a little celebration.

Now that my girls were baptized, I wanted to take them to a family-friendly church. Marion and her second husband, David, attended a Presbyterian church which fit the bill. It also provided coffee and fellowship, so the girls and I began going there together on Sundays. It was a great opportunity to meet people and make friends.

It didn't last long, however, because Levi was getting restless with city life. He continued to seek different living arrangements for us. One possibility was a community of Mother Earth type hippies in West Virginia but our friends who were suggesting it decided not to go, so Levi dropped the idea too.

Instead, we rented a row house next to young families and grandparents in the over-crowded suburban town of Drexel Hill. When we were packing to leave Germantown, I took Charity to the school there so she could see where she would be going in September. She was to begin 5th grade. After she saw it, she lost her desire to go on another adventure with us. It overwhelmed her to start over again in a new school with so many strange children that she didn't know. She suddenly said she wanted to return to her mother's house and not move with us to Drexel Hill. She was not an emotional child but she expressed this in a very emotional way and I knew she truly meant it. I contacted her mother and explained that this really was the time for Charity to come back to her. Her mom sensed that Charity was sincere and would return with a good attitude. So Charity happily went home to be with her mother, sister and step-sister.

The new house had a sandbox out back and a little yard in the front. The girls rode tricycles on the sidewalk with neighborhood children. Our neighbors were either Italian or Irish. We saw how the Italian families converted their basement garages into second kitchens for making sausages and hanging salami, while the Irish made hearty stews in their upstairs kitchens and parked their cars in the basement garages. In spite of their ancestral differences, everyone seemed to get along well. We felt welcome but we were a cultural anomaly.

I didn't make any friends there. We were too far away from the Presbyterian church with the Sunday School. I had stopped nursing Anna, so I felt medically released to treat myself to a marijuana joint from time to time for a little escape. Levi was still past his druggie stage. If I wanted to get high, I was on my own.

I came across a weekly meeting of a Catholic charismatic group, which I attended. They were so joyous and expressive in their praise and worship that I was envious. I returned several times but had to smoke a joint before I entered the room so I could appear to be as happy. The nuns would lay their hands on women and pray over them. When they got to me, one said to the other, "Pray hard for this one." I knew I was unworthy of whatever blessing they were trying to impart. All I could come up with was a good snotty cry.

In those days, 1976, there was a big movement in Israel to get more Jews to move to Israel. They called it making *aliyah*. The purpose was to build up the nation and cause the agriculture to flourish. People were encouraged to go live in a community, which was known as a kibbutz. Young people were flocking there from the States. Levi heard about it and was particularly influenced by a proponent, Bruno Bettelheim.

One evening, Levi sat down with me to describe what an Israeli kibbutz was and how he had an interest in moving us there. The married couples would live in one area of the kibbutz, the single women in another, the single men had their own living quarters, and the children would be taken care of in a community building with caretakers assigned to them. Levi said he and I would work in the gardens.

The idea shocked me. The thought of not taking care of my own children was out of the question—totally inconceivable. *Levi couldn't be serious.* However, he was. The idea of moving to Israel inspired him to where he couldn't get it off his mind. He had stopped practicing yoga. Maybe he was yearning to get back to his Jewish roots. He tried to describe it to me in different ways, paint it as something appealing, something we could afford—at least one-way tickets—and a life we would come to love. But no matter how he presented it, I couldn't see moving to a kibbutz in Israel as a solution for our family.

"I'm sorry, Levi. I just can't agree to go," I told him. Levi eventually gave up that dream. I hoped I hadn't ruined his destiny.

I had other things on my mind. I wanted us to get married in a church. And I wanted a ring. What I wore was a brass ring given to me by a woman in the Andes of Peru. It had a little knob on it that I could rotate underneath when I wanted it to appear like I was wearing a traditional wedding band. For six years, we had been Mr. and Mrs. Levi, a binding arrangement by common law that could only be broken by divorce. Legally, we were fine. The difference was that now we were in a suburban community mingling with other families, and I was reading the Bible regularly and seeing myself as a follower of Jesus. The idea that I was Mrs. Levi based on common law felt incomplete. I thought to myself, *We really need to be married in the eyes of God.* I was looking at it more from God's point of view.

I talked to Levi about a ring and a wedding. Much to my surprise, he didn't get riled up. Instead, he listened and said that he would take it into consideration.

One morning, several months later, while I was in the basement transferring clothes from the washer to the dryer, Levi came up behind me. In his open hand was a beautiful gold wedding band.

"I'm willing to get married in a church with you," he said. "I've thought it over. I just want you to understand that any mention of Jesus in the ceremony is for your pleasure. I know that's important to you. As long as you can accept that using the name of Jesus in a wedding is not a commitment to Jesus on my part, then, let's go ahead and schedule a ceremony."

I was elated and sad all at the same time with this good and bad news. But it was what it was. I couldn't twist Levi's arm to make him accept Jesus. At least he was honest about it. Just like Dad told Mom honestly that he couldn't believe in Mom's Jesus because, he would say, "If you can't touch a thing, it doesn't exist." Dad admitted he was a material man. And, really, it was only two years before this that I, myself, was without Jesus in my own life.

I had learned from watching Ramón's choices in my first marriage that you can't control other people. They will do what they want and believe whatever fancies them. Just as Ramón chose to walk away from our marriage and go to Cuba, now Levi was choosing to marry me in a church, but with one foot in and one foot out.

Everything fell into place for the wedding. The minister at the Presbyterian church agreed to perform the ceremony in their outdoor grove. We invited one couple to come as witnesses and no one else. I bought a western shirt for Levi and sewed flowered dresses for me and the girls.

On the day of the wedding, a bit of irony caused us to snicker with hindsight as we drove to the church. I had been upstairs in our Drexel Hill bedroom trying to clasp a diamond and sapphire family heirloom pendant around my neck. Mom had worn it for her wedding and it was passed around for all the women in the family to wear at their weddings. I had worn it to the Assembly Ball and in my wedding to Ramón. It was a valuable piece of jewelry both in sentiment and dollars.

At that very moment, there was a rap on our door. Levi opened the door to find a uniformed sheriff standing there. He had come to confiscate our property because of a debt Levi had acquired before I met him.

"Come on in," Levi told him. He gestured toward our living room, which was arrayed with discarded furniture we had scooped up from sidewalks. "We're all yours. Take whatever you want, if it could help pay off the debt." Even our car was of little value, and the sheriff could see for himself that there was no sense in looking further. The irony was that the pendant, which I now held tightly in my hand, was probably worth enough to pay off whatever debt Levi owed. I didn't want the sheriff to see it and get hopeful, because it didn't belong to us. We settled the matter by agreeing to a payoff arrangement over time, and were able to sign papers and send the sheriff on his way. He never got wind that we were about to be late to our own wedding.

It was a beautiful day for our outdoor ceremony at a stone altar with a cross in a woodsy glade. The minister officiated and two witnesses stood by. Levi and I had written our own vows. Within ten minutes, we had pledged ourselves to one another and received our rings. Then we went over to Marion and David's back yard for a reception. Mom and Dad came, and family and friends. One of Mom's friends gave us six blue-flowered china dinner plates, which we cherished and used in the next few years for special occasions. It must have been confusing for my girls to see their parents getting married. I carefully explained to them that we had been married another way, and now we wanted a wedding at a church.

Levi seemed distracted and restless. His foiled vision of us moving to Israel caused him to think about what other scenario would suit us better than living in a row house in a crowded suburb and commuting to the city for work. I was pleasantly surprised when he revealed his new idea.

I was scheduled to transfer positions about 28 June 1975, as I had been chosen to be Coordinator of the Strategic Submarine Division and the Trident Program. These future assignments were exactly what I had been training for and I was eager to see if I could adequately serve the new Trident Missile Submarine organization as their Pentagon Sponsor.

These upscaled strategic concepts required massive budgets increases to offset improvements being made by the Soviets. One major need was to find and construct suitable Trident Submarine Bases on both sides of the United States. I felt that the initial search for a location should be kept on a low key basis until we had eliminated the candidates to just a few adequate finalists. I was quietly starting a list of possible alternatives as the public debate started. Ultimately, an unused Army Depot near St. Mary's, Georgia, and a west coast property near Bremerton, Washington, were selected. I had an opportunity to visit both locations with Senators Sam Nunn and Scoop Jackson among others during the evaluation process. I agreed completely with their final selections, which sailed through Congress without a hitch.

The first Trident submarine was under construction at Electric Boat Shipyard in Groton, Connecticut. I had the concept and deployment coordination as well as financial and budget sponsorship, but no progress or construction responsibilities, and was able to attain the full support of Congress.

A Horse Farm, A Chicken Coop, and Baby Ezra

L evi decided to return our little family to the country, to farm life. I listened carefully to his vision. He would look for a job on a horse farm. It seemed like a healthy plan. I knew he had loved horses since a child. I saw how happy he was at Emmett's and Ginger's in Jasper when he was working with their horses. I told him to go for it. He was strong and lean and the perfect hard worker that any horse farm owner would want.

Sure enough, his enthusiasm and familiarity with horses won over the owner at the first interview. Mrs. F. was a professional show horse breeder. Her immaculate farm stretched over green hills in Chester County. Breeders from far and wide sought her horses. She showed Levi inside the well-appointed stables. They walked the grassy lanes between the fenced paddocks. Prized horses with shiny chestnut coats dotted the distant pastures. Their black tails swished as they nibbled at the grass. Further on, was another barn where she explained that her new husband, Mr. F., raised race horses. She talked salary and job details. The cherry on top was the inclusion of a three bedroom house for us to live in. Levi took the deal. He came home with the news that he had landed the job of his dreams. His eyes sparkled when he described it all to me. I could tell he was enthralled.

With no problem we disengaged ourselves from the suburbs and moved to our beautiful yellow split-level house. It had three bedrooms on the upper level and stairs going down to the sunken living room, dining room, and kitchen that opened out to a spacious yard and woods of tall trees. In my adult life I had never lived in a home as fancy as this one. Although the inside smelled of mold, I tried to disregard the odor and, instead, show thankfulness for having this home. The girls were so excited. The sloped driveway and two-car garage made a fun play space for them to ride on their big wheels. We got ourselves two kittens and a puppy. Pop Pop came out from New Jersey to spend a day with us. Dita brought all her children out to play and eat. Neighbors invited us for an outdoor birthday party with balloons. I had stopped smoking marijuana and was learning how to look somewhat like a normal housewife.

It seemed Levi was always working, even on Sundays. When at home, he mowed our two acres and kept busy. The horse farm was five miles away, so Levi took our car.

One Sunday, I set out on foot with the girls to attend a church on our road. It was a tough half-mile walk along the uncut shoulders of the narrow road. I had to carry Anna, who was a three-year-old, and try to keep Sunshine and myself safe from passing cars. But the effort was well worth it.

For the first time, I heard a clear presentation of what was described as the Gospel, the Good News of Jesus Christ. The church helped describe the various steps God took to show His love and provision for me.

Finally, I understood why Jesus was so key to the understanding of my place in this universe and my future beyond this life on earth. He created me in God's likeness to be God's child. I just didn't realize it.

The problem, the pastor explained, was that I, like everyone, was born with a rebellious nature called sin. *Who me? I always considered myself a good person. After all, I was the Class President, the Cheerleader Captain, and even Miss America in Peru!* The truth was that I based my goodness on my own perception of righteousness, which the Bible said was as "filthy rags." I was not at one with God. I didn't deserve to be in heaven with God. I actually deserved to die an eternal death.

I heard the rest of the Gospel message. God had a solution for my sin condition. He sent Jesus from heaven to earth to be sacrificed on a cross. Jesus willingly shed His blood and died in my place. By accepting His sacrifice, I received forgiveness of my sin. I also was given *His* righteousness. That was the Good News.

And that wasn't all. When Jesus rose from the grave, He ascended into heaven to provide an eternal home for me. Now, by accepting Jesus into my heart and believing that He died for my sin, I had the assurance of an eternal home with God. *Whew! What wonderful news.* I was on my way to heaven to live with Jesus forever.

I was no longer trying to fit into Dick Tracy's confusing cartoon series, not knowing how it began nor where it was going. I fit into my own story as it related to Jesus! Jesus was now the starting point, the order, the framework, the direction to give meaning to my life. Now my passion was to learn more so I could share this story with others.

I borrowed the car one Sunday to go to the church's evening Bible study. There were at least twenty men and women there. Unfortunately for me, they were reading the last book in the Bible, called Revelation. I wasn't ready to hear about the prophetic future. I needed to hear more about when Jesus walked on the earth, and when He died, and how the early believers lived their faith. I decided I should learn more Bible basics before I returned to that church's "graduate school."

We didn't make as much money as we did in the city. I started to bake quick breads in little tins. I made three kinds—banana nut, lemon poppy seed, and zucchini. I wrapped them in Saran Wrap and applied stickers to describe what type of loaf they were. After a while, the farm gave Levi the use of a pickup truck so I was able to use our black Rambler to deliver the breads to various delis and gift shops. I charged two dollars a loaf to the stores and they sold them for maybe three dollars. That gave us a token side income.

As the school year began, we enrolled Sunshine in the local kindergarten. The school was a mile or so from our driveway. She was such a brave girl to get on the school bus alone and face a whole new world. I was at home with Anna, who was a sparkly, entertaining child.

In quiet moments, I knew I was not finished having children. I knew there was yet another child to complete our family. When I proposed the idea to Levi, he immediately agreed, much to my delight.

Both of us intuitively felt we would have a boy. At the same time, he confided how inadequate he felt to raise a boy properly, since his own father had never so much as thrown a baseball to him. "But," he concluded, "boy or girl we'll just add another cup of water to the soup."

And so, just as with my girls, within weeks of our decision to stop using birth control, I was pregnant. Morning sickness soon stole the enjoyment of baking breads. Nevertheless, I continued the business. We needed the spending money.

There was a problem at the horse farm. The wife had hired Levi. However, since both the wife and husband raised horses, the two different operations overlapped in the upkeep and chores department. Mr. F. began to treat Levi as his ranch hand. But strong-willed Mrs. F. rightfully considered him one hundred percent her hired hand. Levi was often caught in the middle like a servant with two masters. He would get chewed out by the wife or chewed out by the husband if he was not doing what they asked him to do and he couldn't be in two places at once. Besides being a source of their marital conflict, Levi realized that there was no future in this job. He was stuck there. There were no retirement benefits, no raises, and no way for him to advance. He also realized that he really couldn't physically continue doing this.

So all that, coupled with the idea of our expanding family, caused Levi to sit me down and share his thoughts. I had already heard his reasons for leaving the farm.

"I still sense we are going to have a son," he told me. "To prepare for that, I need to be near a synagogue. If I have a son, he will be raised Jewish. I will not drop him off at the synagogue like my parents did with me. I'll become part of a synagogue and he'll go there with me. You have the girls as Christians since they are baptized. Our son will be raised Jewish."

That seemed fair to me. So I agreed. We made plans to leave the horse farm and find a place to live closer to a synagogue.

As it happened, Bruce had the place for us. He had become a custodial parent of his three school-aged children because of divorce. His ex-wife's estate requested that he get a live-in person to clean and cook. I came along just in time to fit the bill. It seemed perfect that I could get an income for just keeping house, something I did anyway. Bruce lived in Wayne, only fifteen minutes from where we both grew up at Cackleberry Farm.

Bruce's dining room was converted to a bedroom for me and Levi. (We had a proper bed by this time.) Our girls wedged themselves to sleep on their teenaged cousin Jenny's bedroom floor. Sunshine resumed kindergarten at the local elementary school and cousin Ben helped walk her there. Levi found work as a draftsman at a construction company. He also got the name of a conservative Jewish synagogue that met in borrowed quarters while their members planned for their own building site.

On the first Sunday, Levi took me and the girls to the weekly Sunday morning coffee at his Uncle Jack's house half an hour away, where Aunt Estelle served pastries with a smile. Levi's dad, Sol, who was Pop Pop to the children, showed up, as was his custom. He drove there from across the river in New Jersey. He lived a lonesome divorcé's life, and the weekly visits to his brother was for him a highlight. With newspapers opened and rattling, they would all peek out periodically to kibitz from sofa to sofa about the major and minor headlines and the stock market. Uncle Jack, a retired physician, puffed on his pipe. Sol had had somewhat of a spiritual turnabout some years before I met him that caused him to eschew his former over-indulgence of booze and tobacco. This transformation led to a stuffiness that perhaps was instrumental in the marital loss of his socialite wife, LoLo, Levi's mother, the art dealer.

Sunshine and Anna left Pop Pop's couch to sit side by side on the piano bench. They soon had to be hushed as their experimental plinking of the keys swelled beyond being cute. I watched all of this, enjoying the spirited interaction of a Jewish family. It made me happy to see Levi so content being with his kin.

The following Sunday, Bruce was headed to his church and invited me to go with him, which I did. Church of the Saviour met in a nearby high school auditorium while its sanctuary was being expanded to accommodate the influx of churchgoers. I could immediately see the attraction. The Gospel message was included in the sermon. There were Bible study groups with both beginner and advanced classes. Free coffee was a plus. And babies, children and teens all had their own Sunday school rooms. I knew I had found a church home where I was welcomed and loved—and I ended up staying there for the next nineteen years.

Our baby was due in April. We needed to leave Bruce's house and find our own place to live. Levi asked around and came up with a most astounding possibility. He had found a large apartment which took up the whole second floor of what used to be a chicken coop during the heyday of a Main Line estate. Never did I think I would live in a chicken coop! But, it was fixed up, and the Chicken Coop it was.

Little Sunshine was enrolled in her third kindergarten. The school bus stop was a quarter mile up a steep paved lane, which was accessed by walking a crossover bunny path and cutting through a small opening next to a locked wrought-iron gate. There were no people around, as this acreage was the private entrance to the large estate. It was reminiscent of Beatrix Potter's "Peter Rabbit" scenes. *Where's Farmer McGregor*, I thought to myself.

I had walked Sunshine to the bus stop for as long as I could, until I was just too pregnant to make the hike. Now I hugged her as she bravely set out on her own. She wore the blue paisley jacket I had made her with the red ladybug buttons and mitten-shaped pockets. She turned around and looked up at me as I watched from the second floor window.

"Bye, Mom," she called as she waved her hand towards me. She walked a few more feet, turned around, waved her little hand and again said, "Bye, Mom."

"Bye, Sunshine. I love you." Her little body was dwarfed by the tall woods outside. "Keep on going, Sweetheart. You'll be fine," I answered. My mother's heart ached as I watched my black-haired child reach the end of our drive and disappear into the thicket. I had to trust she was okay.

And she was. God did take care of her.

The excitement mounted as I approached my due date. My sisters and friends held a baby shower where I received gender-neutral gifts of yellow, green, and white for the mystery baby. I had arranged for a home delivery. My third baby was going to be born in a chicken coop!

When I went into labor, Levi called my nurse-midwife, who came with two assistants. For seventeen hours, I labored with the typical rigors of natural childbirth. Towards the end, I sat propped up with pillows on a plastic lined sheet. At one point, Levi sat behind me and became my pillow as I leaned against him. He was there when my nurse-midwife coached me to begin pushing. The miracle of birth took place.

God blessed us with a baby boy.

At first we were worried. He didn't cry and his skin looked blue. We massaged him and he came to life. He let out a healthy cry and turned pink. A big surprise was his carrot red hair! Levi decided to name him Ezra, to honor a respected cousin in Levi's family who had been a prominent surgeon and had died at a young age.

April 24, 1978, was the happy day we had our little boy. I knew he was to be Jewish but I didn't know what that entailed.

South Merion Avenue– "Barukh Atah Adonai"

The first reality to raise a Jewish son was the traditional ceremony of circumcision, called a Bris, to be held on the eighth day of the baby's life. Levi's family arranged for a Mohel, the one who performs the actual cutting, to come to our Chicken Coop. LoLo and Pop came, as did Cousin Ferne and Jack, who was to be Ezra's godfather. Mom and Dad had already moved away to their retirement home in Virginia, so they didn't come. Dad would not have liked being there and I was having a difficult time myself. It was all so new for me.

The men held my baby. They assigned him a couple of Old Testament names. He cried and cried. All I wanted to do was comfort him at my breast. Sadly, we never wrote down Ezra's Jewish ceremonial names and they fell by the wayside.

We left the Chicken Coop a few months later in time to get Sunshine enrolled in first grade. Levi had purchased our first home in downtown Bryn Mawr, my home town. It was a sturdy old three-story duplex with a front porch. It was just off busy Route 30 across from the firehouse and directly behind the famous Main Point coffee house, which later became Mapes 5 & 10, a fun destination for the children. We referred to our house as "South Merion," the name of our street.

I was to spend thirteen years in that house. They were years fraught with great struggle, but laced with the utmost joy of motherhood.

Levi and I focused on our new home. Without money, we improvised. There was no closet on the third floor where Levi and I slept so the question was where to hang our clothes. Without a word, Levi punched holes in the drywall in a corner of the room, then inserted a broomstick and—voila!—we had a closet. I was shocked.

"Levi!" I reacted. "What did you do? You damaged our walls!"

"Don't worry, Babe," he reassured me. "This is just temporary. I'll fix up this room to be our special space. I have a great design in mind." I felt better. The room had nooks and crannies. I envisioned a sitting area with reading lamps. Maybe even a bureau or two. Downstairs, we still had no sofa but I had found three armchairs on the street that made us comfortable, especially on winter nights when Levi lit one of his crackling fires in the fireplace. I also scavenged desks and chairs for the girls' rooms.

Levi found work in Philadelphia with two wealthy brothers where he supervised upscale construction jobs. The prospect of greater income made us both hopeful that perhaps we could soon buy beds for the children. And maybe a sofa for me. To celebrate, Levi took us on our first overnight vacation to the boardwalk in Atlantic City. Levi even laid down a law, "No more furniture off the street!" I was glad he was optimistic. There would come a day when the girls and I would want to buy department store clothes. Things were looking up.

A big change for me was that Mom and Dad had sold Cackleberry. They had found Mom's requested "corner of a cornfield." The new property also met Dad's requirement of waterfront. It sat by a creek off the Chesapeake Bay in White Stone, Virginia. Even before building a house, Dad hired the construction of a sturdy dock where he tied up his treasured yacht, the *ISLANDER*. They lived onboard for a year while their house took shape.

I missed them terribly. At first when they announced their intentions, and especially when they actually moved, I felt abandoned by them. Why would they leave Pennsylvania where most of their children and grandchildren were, and where they were the hub for family get-togethers and coffee time? They provided tradition and continuity for all of us young families. I blamed Dad for taking Mom away.

But, as it turned out, their absence forced me to grow up and be independent. Plus, their new cottage by the water provided a delightful place to visit, only six hours away. Levi and I packed up the children and enjoyed vacation time there. Dad's vision had become his and Mom's retirement dream.

Our house on South Merion was only fifteen minutes from Bruce's Church of the Saviour (COS). Marion and David attended there too. As a new Christian eager to learn about Jesus and what the Bible taught, I started going to church there on Sundays. I took Sunshine and Anna to Sunday school. Levi told me I could go ahead and take Ezra too, as long as he was still a nursing baby.

I appreciated that COS taught the Gospel message every Sunday. Jesus was their focus. I couldn't hear enough about Him. There was also a class called "Through the Bible in a Year," which I joined. For the first time I studied the Bible along with other believers. It was so refreshing, exciting and enriching.

I think Levi could see my enthusiasm when I got home from church. He would have just returned from his visit to Uncle Jack's. There was always an awkward readjustment as our eyes met. We had to pick up on the relationship he and I shared apart from what our inner souls had going on. It was uncomfortable for both of us, and I sensed bad vibes, so I tried to be specially sweet and accommodating. I got lunch on the table quickly so we could once again be reunited as a family.

Many times I skipped church to go with Levi to Uncle Jack's. It was always nice to be treated to Aunt Estelle's fresh pastries and relax with family. I could see how Levi enjoyed that.

While Levi was at work, I attended a weekday class at COS called "Joy in the Morning." It was a two-year discipleship class, an in-depth study of biblical Christianity led by Joanne Shore. We studied the meaning of Christian terms found in the Bible, such as sanctification, propitiation, justification and discipleship. We were paired up with a partner for Bible memorization. My partner was Gayle. For a year and a half we memorized Scripture verses and recited them to each other. She held me accountable to get the words exactly right and I did the same for her. The biblical Word was precise, and it was penetrating my heart.

The more I learned, the more excited I got about Jesus, Christianity, and the Bible. It became harder and harder to keep all this under a lid, especially at home when philosophical conversations popped up between our friends and Levi who sought after the truth. I always wanted to share that Jesus was the answer to all of their questions. Sometimes I let go of my silence and that boomeranged back to bite me.

In the meantime, as hoped, Levi found and joined a conservative synagogue. The children and I went to services there with him on Saturdays. He also opened a bank account to save up for Hebrew school that would prepare Ezra for his Bar Mitzvah ceremony at age thirteen. I learned that the Bar Mitzvah was a rite for a Jewish boy to become an eligible member of the *minyan* quorum of ten adults before certain religious obligations could take place.

Levi enrolled Ezra (and me) in a Jewish mother-child play group at his synagogue. The purpose was to acculturate the children to their Jewishness. I took Ezra there dutifully and got to know some of the mothers. But I never felt truly integrated.

I did see the value for Ezra, though. These women taught him songs and games. They helped him accept the wearing of a *yarmulke*, the little skullcap used by Jewish men for religious services and at family feasts. I took photos of the children, who one day would be the teenagers with Ezra in Hebrew school.

Now that we were settled in our own home, we began to establish holiday traditions. Christmas and Hanukkah often coincided on the calendar, so there was double joy as we celebrated two holidays at once. We put up a Christmas tree. We invited our neighbor Carolyn and her children to join us at the start of the eight-day Hanukkah season. We all watched as Levi lit the first two of nine candles on our new *menorah* lamp-stand. He recited a prayer of blessing with each candle lit. Ezra wore his hand-crocheted *yarmulke* that Cousin Ferne had given him. I noticed Levi enjoyed his role as priest. I was proud of him.

At Levi's request, we began to honor the Sabbath by having a special family dinner on Friday nights. I always started in the morning to prepare the traditional braided golden *challah* bread. The aroma of freshly baked bread filled the air. I planned our menu carefully so that the meal was memorable.

Normally we ate in the kitchen but these meals were held in the dining room at the family table that Levi had inherited from his childhood. We used our best blue-flowered plates and two brass candlesticks. Ezra was in his highchair, *yarmulke* in place. Sunshine had changed her clothes and put barrettes in her hair. Anna looked pretty in one of her favorite dresses. We were all in our places and ready. Levi lit the candles just before sunset as we recited the prayers. The girls and I learned to say the prayers in Hebrew along with Levi.

"Barukh atah Adonai Eloheinu, melekh ha'olam"—"Blessed are You, LORD our God, King of the universe." It was a beautiful, holy language and an enriching experience to have Levi lead us in worship. The Sabbath was properly ushered in. We were a happy family.

The Beginning of the End

While I was still a new and hungry Christian enrolled in the weekly Bible class called Joy in the Morning, Levi's involvement with his synagogue reached a dead end. He quit for two stated reasons. First, the building committee, for which he was the draftsman, changed their plans repeatedly and Levi felt used. Second, Levi saw my enthusiasm for knowing God but he couldn't find anyone at the synagogue, not even the rabbi, who would talk about God.

Resentment built up and overflowed into our relationship. Levi would have been satisfied if I had chosen any of the gurus out there. Any one of them would have been fine—anyone but Jesus.

"If all Jews became Christians," he told me, "then Judaism would disappear. Christianity is the ultimate anti-semitic movement," he said.

I kind of thought he had a valid idea there. I could see it from his point of view. However, there were Jewish believers in my church, and they didn't dwell on an idea like that. The joyous Holy Spirit they received from their relationship with Jesus overshadowed any sense of lost tradition. In fact, one couple beautifully described the Jewish feasts as symbols of the coming Messiah. They still thought of themselves as Jews.

A highlight of our week had become a "conference call" on Sunday afternoons with Levi's brother Jim and his wife in another state. The four of us each got on a phone. I took the one in the upstairs hall. Levi adored his brother. Usually there was constant laughter.

But one time Jim and his wife had to describe their troubles. I myself had found much comfort from Scripture. I had memorized many verses. The one that came to mind was from a Psalm, so I quoted it to them. I figured since Levi and his brother were Jews, an Old Testament verse would be appropriate. I wanted to say something helpful. Before we got off the phone, the couple thanked me.

Then I went downstairs and received the verbal wrath of my husband.

"How dare you quote scripture to my brother!" He was so livid he banned me from any future Sunday conference calls. I comforted myself with the thought that Levi just didn't understand—not yet.

At home, I tried to keep a low profile. When I tucked the children in at night, I sang Christian songs with them quietly so Levi would not hear me from downstairs. I was especially careful when I sang with little Ezra. By that time, he stayed home on Sundays with his Dad, as agreed. Although Levi didn't talk about it, I could imagine Levi wondered how he was going to follow through with Ezra's Jewish upbringing now that he no longer belonged to a synagogue.

Levi's construction expertise impressed the two builders downtown. They provided him with a vehicle, a credit card, and free membership to a drinking club. We began living two different lives. Levi stayed in town until late at night, skipping supper without advising me of his plans.

But he always arrived home right on time on Friday nights to lead our Sabbath dinners.

In desperation to win his favor, I quit the two-year Bible course. I figured my obligation to homework bothered him. I took the children to one of his construction sites so he could show us his work. I suggested he and I spend an evening together in the city. He said fine—that I should get a sitter, take the train and meet him at a certain spot.

I was so excited. I went upstairs to my thrift shop clothes still hanging on the broom stick in our bedroom. With creativity, I pieced together an outfit that I imagined might pass for the 1981 Philadelphia nightlife scene.

I made it through the confusion of the central train station. We found each other. Levi took me to a smoke-filled bar where we sat on high stools. He ordered a couple of drinks. He lit up a cigarette. We were both nervous, at least I was. Conversation didn't flow, so I made some comment about who the couple at the other end of the bar might be. Levi chided me. He said I sounded catty.

It wasn't going well. He took me to another drinking place that had food. A live band played loud, so there was no way to talk. The next thing I knew, three wealthy-looking women came in with shouts of "Levi!" like they knew him well and were so glad to see him. One by one, they swooped onto my husband and gave him a kiss on the cheek and the caress of hello. One whispered things in his ear. Her words made Levi smile. I was not introduced, not even by pantomime. I sat through two long songs before the band took a break and Levi quickly was able to explain that these ladies were old high school friends.

I felt like an intruder. Levi couldn't get me home soon enough. That was *his* nightlife, not mine. What had come between us? Booze? Other women's perfume? The responsibility of children? I thought back to our compatible days in the tent and his love poems. How we had slept together for months on a single bed mattress with no inconvenience. How we had made friends to laugh with and happily sought after a healthy lifestyle. *He's merely in a phase,* I told myself.

But I was wrong.

The next Sabbath evening, I had the table set, the challah made, a special meal prepared. The children were all cleaned up. Levi never came home. There was no phone call to explain. I knew this was a crisis moment in our marriage.

After the children were in bed, he showed up. We sat in two armchairs in the living room. "I have a problem," Levi began. His problems usually involved sub-contractor issues or even clients' lawsuits. He often spent hours on our downstairs phone to get schedules straightened out to please the boss for the next day. "Sunshine, get me a beer!" he would call out, and we all knew he was under stress.

"Oh, sorry to hear that," I replied, curious to hear about whatever Sabbath-breaking calamity was upon him. I gave him my full attention. "What's the problem?"

"YOU are the problem!" he snapped.

Startled, I sat farther back into my seat. Levi's green eyes glared at me. It seemed like he had rehearsed what came next. "I've tried to be patient with you. I thought your Jesus gig was a temporary fad. But I can see that whatever you're into has taken you over. We can't have a decent conversation anymore. If I have a concern, I know you'll tell me things from your Club's Manual. I'd rather talk to the bartender than you. At least there, the talk is real and we can tell it like it is." He paused a moment, then went on. "You should go marry your Bible teacher. You'll be with her forever anyway."

His words stung like a swarm of angry bees. He just didn't understand. What could I say or do to restore peace for the two of us? It had been six years since I accepted Jesus on the beach in Fort Lauderdale. Why would my Christianity suddenly bring Levi to a breaking point? My mind churned for an idea to defuse his animosity.

In desperation, I countered with, "I'll put my Bible and all my study books in the middle of the floor, and I'll set fire to them right now! I can do that, Levi. I can change!"

But, Levi came back with a wisdom that astounded me. It was so right on. "It won't work. To burn your Bible won't fix anything. I went to your pastor and told him what you believe. I asked him if your belief is what he preaches. He said 'Yes.' So at least you're not crazy. But I learned that it's all deep within you and not something that disappears when your Bible's gone."

Then the full pronouncement of alienation followed. "I'm leaving tomorrow. After the circus."

I looked at Levi. There was a weird deja vu. Levi was seated in the same color armchair Ramón was in when he announced that our marriage was over, that he was leaving me for Cuba.

Levi continued his exit plan but I only heard him through blurred eyes. "We promised the circus for Saturday, so I'll keep my word to the kids. But when we get back and the kids are in bed, I'm leaving. I'm going to the city."

We went upstairs to our room. I stood at the third floor window and looked out. *Damn that city!* The dark night tempted me. In the horror of the moment, I imagined jumping out. My mind wanted to escape, to flee, to be anywhere but there in that reality. My body parts felt dissociated, and my heart was completely broken.

Levi was already snuggled under the wine flowered comforter. He had drifted off to sleep and to his new world.

The next evening, after the tuckered-out circus kids were in bed, I followed Levi to the front door. He held a duffel bag in one hand and his keys in the other.

As he walked out the door, he turned back and said to me, "You go ahead and raise Ezra Christian. I can't expect you to raise a Jewish son." The door shut, and I watched Levi walk out of our marriage forever.

A Fresh Start

The next day was Sunday. We got ready to leave for church. The children asked where Daddy was. I told them, "Do you remember Mr. Floppy Socks?" Sunshine remembered him from our Germantown days. "Daddy has gone to visit him for awhile." That seemed to satisfy them.

As the days passed, I did my best to keep my composure in front of the kids. One late afternoon, though, I was changing the sheets on Ezra's bed when I began to cry. The more the tears flowed, the sadder I got. I tried to pull myself together to go downstairs. My face was blotched. My eyes were swollen and red. My chest heaved. It was past suppertime and the children needed to eat.

I used the hall phone to call church friend, Connie. She had gone through a divorce and I knew she could say something to comfort me. I was right. Connie reminded me how much God loves me. She quoted scripture to me like God's promise of "I will never leave you nor forsake you" and "I have loved you with an everlasting love." She told me I was the apple of God's eye, and He would never take me through a trial I could not bear. She shared the love of Jesus that did the trick.

I was able to wet my face with a cold washcloth and recover enough to go downstairs. Supper was prepared and served without any questions from anyone.

The children were three, seven and nine. I couldn't believe a man would leave his children just like that. Surely Levi would reconsider and come back to us.

A clear image came to me. I saw our family in a rowboat. Levi and I each held an oar and rowed together. The children sat in the front and back seats. But now I was having to row by myself. It was hard to control both oars. In the image, Levi climbed out of the rowboat onto a slapped together wooden raft with no paddle. It was drifting away from us. A coiled rope in our boat was attached to the raft. The coil got smaller as the raft moved farther away. I saw the rope's bitter end go over the gunnel and flop into the water. It was still within my reach. I could easily grab the end and haul his raft close so that Levi could climb back into our rowboat.

The vision motivated me to make a brave and urgent call to Levi. I described my vision and asked him, "Are you sure you want to keep going away from us?"

In few words, Levi made it clear that he was not coming back.

In fact, over the years, he didn't set one toenail back in my direction. He didn't even want to talk to me. Not about the kids or anything else. He established his own relationship with the children that didn't involve any co-parenting communication with me. He wanted to love them in his own way. So I picked up his oar and rowed as best as I could. It was hard. Things around the house needed fixing. The handrail came off the wall and dangled on the back stairs. The toilet leaked. When the children disobeyed me, there was no Dad around to discipline them and say, "You honor your mother and do what she says!" I hated telling my children, "You need to honor me."

One evening, Sunshine asked me, "When is Dad coming home?" It was evident to me that this was the time to let them know.

I gathered them in a circle on the living room rug. I told them the stark truth. "Dad has decided to stay in the city. He is not coming back to live with us. He's going to get his own apartment."

Ezra crawled onto my lap. Sunshine's eyes welled with tears. Anna reached over and grabbed my arm. "But, look at me and remember this," I told them. "We are a family. The four of us. We will always be a family."

"But, what about my birthday party next week?" Sunshine asked. "Will Dad come to that?"

"I'll invite him," I promised.

A couple of weeks after Levi left, I woke up with a start and sat up. I looked over at his side of our bed. His flowered pillow seemed to mock me as it lay there so still and untouched. I flew into a crying rage and punched the pillow hard. Over and over I pummeled it with blows. Wails filled the air from deep within me. *How can this really be happening to me?* PUNCH. *Where is he?* PUNCH. *He belongs here!* PUNCH. *Pitiful me!*

At the next wail, and before the next punch, Jesus showed up and talked to me. I know He wasn't physically in the room but it was like He was. He told me to stop pitying myself.

He said, "Look at Me. Look at what pain I had to endure on the cross. What I suffered is so very much greater than what you are going through. I died for your sake, to give you hope. Keep your eyes on Me, not on yourself. I have come back to life to be your living Savior. I will see you through this. Get to know Me."

I stopped my tantrum and wept instead for my Savior. Then a supernatural peace came upon me. I sat up straight with the awesome awareness that Jesus had just comforted me. He and I were in an intimate and enviable relationship.

There would be years of struggle but I knew without a doubt that Jesus was close by me. He helped me harness rage into determination. Outside, the hedges needed trimming. They lined both sides of the back yard and loomed eight feet tall and four feet wide. Instead of railing that it was a man's job, I brought the ladder and electric hedge trimmer out of the shed and went at the job myself. Anger motivated me to balance on the ladder, flex muscles, lift the heavy trimmer, pull the trigger and lop off wayward growth until the hedge looked better than ever.

With a satisfied exhaustion, I went to the kitchen and poured a glass of ice cold lemonade. "We can do this, Jesus," I said to Him as I plopped into a chair.

The ugly details of separation and divorce usurped any gaiety in my life. Levi did get his own apartment and invited the children for a weekend visit. They returned bubbling over with excitement that Dad had taken them to Sears to help him pick out a sofa. *A sofa! How dare he!* Little things like this poured more salt into my wounds.

I tried to be strong in front of the kids. I didn't want them to be sad, nor biased against their father. I tried to hide from them how much I hated their father for rejecting me and deserting them. Sometimes in the still of the night, a wave of nausea overcame me. I bore the weight of sole responsibility for raising our children.

Someone told me a very helpful reality. When a relationship breaks up and a loved one decides to go in a different direction, one is not to seek that person out to meet their emotional needs. That was a hard one. We had been so bonded. And, one is not to be surprised or shocked at what they do or say, or don't do or say, because it is all part of their process of moving in a direction away from you. So once you accept that fact, stop seeking them. They are no longer in your boat. They are finding their own path. Stop judging their behavior and let them do their own thing. When there are children, though, it's more difficult, because there are more people affected by the brokenness of the family.

Somehow, Levi and I would have to struggle through our alienation to make responsible parenting decisions for the sake of our children.

As if God knew what I needed, a new program appeared on the Church of the Saviour campus. It was a three-day seminar called "Fresh Start" to help people get through separation and divorce. I signed up immediately. I was not alone in my plight the way I was when Ramón left me and I languished for a year at Cackleberry. About fifty participants, men and women, came to the seminar. Each of us was in our own phase of pain. We were divided into discussion groups each led by someone who had been divorced.

To my utter amazement, my group's facilitator, a woman, greeted us with a pleasant, sincere smile. What an encouraging revelation it was to see that one could smile after divorce.

It had been Levi's preference that I not work during the eleven years we were together. He decided to send me a monthly check that was based on our prior budget. He made sure to keep the payments coming. Other separated and divorced women shared harrowing stories of neglect. At least he cared about a financial responsibility. I was fortunate in that department.

After six months, Levi said he would no longer pay for mortgage and food, so I should work to make up the difference. This prospect set me into a tailspin. I had no idea what type of job I would seek. I was unsure of my skills. By this time, I ran a little business to watch a handful of children at home. But that income was not enough to make up the future deficit. *What should I do?*

What I did was establish personal discipline by pretending I had a job. I got up before my children and dressed for the workplace, not in jeans. I filled a purse with things I needed, like an I.D., lipstick, cash, and tissues, and placed it by the door. Then I fixed breakfast, saw the girls off to the bus, and got Ezra ready to go out the door by a certain time. After many days of rehearsal, the timing worked out. I rented a typewriter and practiced typing in case I would be a secretary.

The most difficult hurdle was to visit child care centers for Ezra. At each interview, I broke down in tears. The sorrow of giving up my days at home with Ezra and entrusting him to others overwhelmed me. I had cherished the precious preschool years with Sunshine and Anna. I was not prepared to let go of Ezra's company and the care of him so early in his life. He was a delightful three-year-old.

My neighbor, Carolyn, advised me to look in the newspaper for a help-wanted ad with the words "will train." Sure enough, a part-time "will train" bookkeeping position appeared and I got the job.

I found an affordable day care center for Ezra to attend. Thankfully, my new work desk was by itself on the third floor of an insurance agency. While I quietly shed tears between training sessions, little Ezra was being taught a new order in his life by always putting his toys away before starting anything new. This day care training was to stay with him even into adulthood! I discovered good things can come out of what I thought was bad.

I learned at the Fresh Start Seminar that recovery from a broken love relationship requires a gamut of stages. I went through them all: denial (*this can't be happening*), bargaining ("I'll try to do better—I'll burn my Bibles on the living room floor"), anger, fear, self-pity, and the pit of depression. Then finally one looks forward to an upward path to acceptance, forgiveness, new relationships and a new lease on life. It was called a slippery slope, they told me, where one progresses and regresses along the way.

As I processed my pain, I grew stronger. Soon, I was the woman facilitator who smiled at at my own group of newly hurting people at the opening of a new Fresh Start Seminar. I worked in the capacity of group facilitator at Fresh Start for a couple of years. I even gave an elective talk on how to return to the workplace.

Levi filed for divorce and gave me full custody of the children.

Two months after the divorce was final, the children received a post card from him that said something like, "I've gotten married on the beach in Maine. Her name is Linda. We saw Andre the famous seal. We'll come see you soon."

Linda, I found out, was the hostess at the drinking club Levi frequented. I was livid. I slipped back into the anger phase of the slippery slope.

I pictured them pulling up in their car. I felt adamant. *Linda will have to stay outside in the passenger seat. I refuse to invite her in. That is that!* But, on second thought, she was now his wife and a step-mother to my children. *I should at least invite her into the front living room.* So in my imagination, I allowed her entrance. *But wait. What if she wants tea? Should I offer her tea? Yes. I should be hospitable. But then again, what if she follows me into the kitchen? No way!* There I drew the line. *Linda is not welcome to enter my inner sanctum. Never!*

The day arrived for the big visit. I watched Linda, a young redhead, get out of the car. Levi brought her to the door. The children were excited to meet her, so I stayed in the background. She was smiling and seemed nice enough. Anna had brought her sticker collection to the living room. It was a tattered composition book, her favorite possession. She opened it on her lap. Colorful stickers appeared in lopsided rows. I had never looked through the book. I didn't have time. In fact, with my new full-time job at John Hancock, it felt like many of those little details of life, those loving moments of undivided attention to the children, had to be traded for the practical necessities of keeping house and home.

Linda, however, seemed like she had all the time in the world. She spied the sticker book and, within moments, wedged herself into the armchair with Anna. They pored over every page. I heard Linda say, "Oh look! You have that teddy bear in five colors, and they're all side by side!"

"I know," Anna agreed. "And wait till you see the next section where I put all my spotted ponies!"

The Lord gave me a sudden revelation. Linda was not my adversary. She was my helper. She could dote on my kids and give them attention in ways I couldn't manage. She could help me love my children. I needed that help.

As Levi and Linda got up to leave, I noticed a knick knack on my mantelpiece. It was a blue porcelain seal, an antique I cherished from Cackleberry. God's love is supernatural, because my next gesture could not have come from my own bitter heart. I offered the seal to the newlyweds to remind them of their visit to see Andre the Seal. I wished them much happiness in their new marriage. They were both taken aback by my sentiment and thanked me for the gift.

Levi and Linda moved to a nice old house two hours away in the quaint town of Barnegat, New Jersey. The children went to see them occasionally for the weekend. Either Levi picked them up or I dropped them off. Linda was always friendly to me when I arrived. Sometimes they would invite me to sip a mint julep on their porch before I had to take the drive back. It seemed as though Linda's presence helped Levi to be more cordial towards me.

There are always surprises in life and things I will never understand but that marriage lasted a very short time. Levi suddenly called it off. Linda slipped out of our lives as quickly as she had slipped in. He married again, this time for several years, to a woman with a wonderful sense of humor. She called herself the "Step-Monster," and lavished gifts, clothes, and love on Sunshine, Anna and Ezra.

If it weren't for Levi's animosity towards me, I felt I could be friends with each of his other wives.

*M*y last two active duty jobs were also based in the Pentagon. First assignment was to be the Deputy Director of Strategic and General Operations (J-34) in the Office of Joint Chiefs of Staff. The Strategic Operations were well in hand by the Omaha Strategic Group. I made several visits to Omaha and to various locations of the Air Force Missile Launchers. The attitude and professionalism was clearly evident. I saw that no improvements from my position in the Joint Chiefs was necessary.

My last assignment on active duty was as Deputy Director Defense Intelligence Agency (DIA). I spent some interesting times in council or debate with Vice Admiral Stansfield Turner, the Director of CIA, discussing some of their positions. But my most rewarding task was to get all DIA activities under one roof. Those issues consumed most of my time and I was the person in 1980 to present our DIA needs for efficiency and consolidation to the Congress. The presentations proved effective after so many disappointing years of trying. Congress appropriated $32 million in fiscal year 1981 and $73 million the following year. Ground breaking was held on 21 April 1981 by Lt. General Eugene Tighe. The DIA complex was completed in April 1984.

With no major sea command in sight, I retired from Active Duty on 30 September 1980 at the age of fifty, after twenty-eight years of Active Duty. My retirement ceremony was held in the Washington Navy Yard. The primary speaker was Lt. General Tighe. I was pleased to see the great number of active duty and retired Navy personnel and their wives in attendance. I accepted my retirement and was "piped off" from the ceremony. One of the first persons to approach me at the following reception was a representative of Woody Ramsey, who was the President of American Systems Corporation. The company was interested to discuss my possible future employment with them. I accepted.

My service awards included:
Defense Distinguished Service Medal

> *Defense Superior Service Medal*
> *Legion of Merit with Gold Star*
> *Meritorious Service Medal*
> *Navy Commendation with Two Bronze Stars*
> *Navy Meritorious Unit Commendation with Two Bronze Stars.*
> *And others.*

Immediately upon retirement in 1980, I focused on gathering any-thing that would eventually help me fulfill the need that Bill Wegner had postulated in our Navy Yard meetings years before. My problem was that I was not schooled in such an effort but I had a scissors to cut out ideas from others' writings, paste them into a document, and a desire to learn. Of course, I was disappointed not to have achieved my goals for active duty positions. But I was sufficiently motivated not to cry over spilt milk. I was focused on what I had come to believe, and agreed with Admiral Rickover that the Submarine Force Public Relations was in desperate need for fruition.

After a few months and many visits, the answer came to me during one of my normal 3:30 a.m. inspirational awakenings. I decided the skeleton for structure of a future submarine organization would be to use the model of the Naval Aviation community—just eliminate what could be their weak factors and document Submarine Force needs. Now, I needed to assimilate a group to give me flexibility both with time and income. God provided me both.

I met with Woody Ramsey, a Naval Academy Class of '52 class-mate, and Jim Austin, who headed the Applied Physics Laboratory (APL) Submarine Division. Both strongly encouraged me to GO FOR BROKE. Now it was time to assimilate the solutions that Bill Wegner identified five years before. My first step was to brief Admirals Al Whittle and Jack Williams about the concept and get them onboard. Both were completely supportive and agreed to step in whenever it was appropriate.

Now the task was to originate the organizational paperwork. From the start, we always kept the concept that a Symposium content be

unclassified and open to all. We would hold our classified NSL brief-
ings for contractors at Applied Physics Laboratory to protect the level
of national operations and equipment. Admiral Whittle and I knew
that there would be some individuals who would like to keep all subma-
rine matters and support submerged. Times had changed. The Naval
Submarine League was born in 1982 and has contributed to the Navy
for over thirty-seven years.

    About that time, Prudy and I agreed to separate and divorce to
fulfill our very different individual life endeavors. I then became com-
pletely immersed into the research, foundation, and growth of the
Naval Submarine League, as well as earning consulting income.

Part 6
Returning to Me

Dennis

Accepting single motherhood—"We are a family."

The years passed. I was growing in my knowledge of the Lord and His promises for my life. I began to see myself from God's loving point of view, rather than the judgmental attitudes of mankind. I was God's beloved and forgiven child. The rejection pain was lessening and I started to accept my circumstances. There was surely a hope and a future for me. I had finally come to identify as a single, not a married woman.

My children were my world. We shared a close bond of love. What we lacked in worldly goods was compensated by a quality in our commitment to one another. I loved them with all of my heart. In the difficult moments when I lacked discernment and stamina to keep it all going, I tried to ask God for wisdom.

I joined the new singles group at Church of the Saviour called "Focus." It met after the worship service on Sundays and grew to about a hundred people. Soon it needed its own pastor. Focus provided my Christian social life. Besides Bible study and special speakers, there were picnics, dinners and weekend retreats. My children also had active COS youth activities to attend. We all learned more about Jesus and made new friends. As much as I was sorry to lose Levi, I recognized the freedom we now enjoyed to express our faith in Jesus and live openly with Him as our Lord and Savior.

In 1987, a mission opportunity caught my eye. Six COS families would go to Venezuela for two weeks. They would live with separate native families and help in their local churches. I applied, not sure if a single parent and her children would be acceptable. To my surprise, Families With A Mission put us on the team. I took a break from Focus to meet on Sundays with this group where we studied Spanish, trained, and bonded. Sunshine used her language proficiency from school to teach Spanish to the young children on the team.

We flew to Caracas on a huge 747. Our host, Sonia, made us feel most at home. She confided to me that Venezuelan currency was slipping dramatically and she was worried for her husband's job and the future of her family. She took us to her Presbyterian church where I was asked to lead a Sunday School class in Spanish.

We went to a park with others on our team. My children impressively shared the Gospel with strangers in an outdoor café. They had a technique where they pointed to each of their five fingers. Each finger represented a different aspect of man's need for salvation and God's provision in Jesus Christ. Anna ran up to me rejoicing that one of the teenaged girls in the café booth had prayed to receive Jesus as her Savior.

Back home in the States, when Anna was in middle school, she became the daily target of several bully girls for whatever reason. Most often it was for her curly hair, which they pulled, especially on the bus. They even began to punch her.

Without telling me why, she decided to carry a brown bag lunch to school, which I allowed. Normally Anna was a self-assured, happy-go-lucky girl, free to be herself. But when I found out that my sunny dispositioned daughter had begun to eat alone on a rock behind the school so she could cry, I knew I had to take action to get her out of that school. The bully girls were most likely spoiled kids from wealthy homes, and the problem seemed greater than I could tackle as a single working mom. I decided not to seek help from the administration.

The solution I came up with was a transfer to nearby Delaware County Christian School. Anna blossomed there, once she adjusted to their structure and expectations of personal discipline.

The next year, I enrolled both Sunshine and Ezra too. The school preferred that all siblings in a family attend. Sunshine was a good sport to enter a new school as a junior. She made friends easily and even performed as Golde in "Fiddler on the Roof."

Ezra was displeased, however, particularly because they required him to sing in the fifth grade choir, which had an upcoming obligatory concert. He tried his best to wriggle out of performing with the others on the basis that he was new. But the headmaster explained to me that Ezra was merely being obstinate. He insisted that Ezra should not be permitted to consider himself special or different, for his own good.

The result was that Ezra sang in the choir. I noticed that the headmaster's wisdom had great merit. Ezra seemed released after that concert. He smiled more and even stood a little taller. He settled in and developed some close buddies. I, too, grew from this experience. As a coddling parent, I would have done him no favors.

The tuition load sent me running to a bank for a loan. Then I had trouble paying the loan debt too. Levi aggravated my shortfall by cutting off support payments in protest against Christian school for his kids. The court defended me saying that, since I had full custody, it was my prerogative to choose where they went to school. I tried to tell Levi how unhappy Anna had been and how comparatively joyful she had become. He wasn't interested in anything I had to say. He just preferred public education. However, the court made him resume the support payments.

Personally I was going through a letdown having to reorient to the singles group again after spending a year on the Venezuela team socializing with intact families. I had been rowing my boat as a single parent for eight years. I felt tired and discouraged. I thought, *What's next? Is my life going to continue like this forever?*

I accepted a table leader position at the Sunday Focus group. I chose the newcomers table because I knew well what it was like to show up for the first time. Faced with sudden and often unwanted change, one's whole identity was challenged. Now a singles social scene was hitting them in the face. They needed the interaction with other people but didn't know how to act.

And for some, the Christian aspect of Focus may have been unfamiliar too. A person in these circumstances needed to feel welcomed, accepted and not rejected. For me, to be the smiling face to greet others was like the Golden Rule—do unto others as you would have them do unto you.

With this role I had a refreshing sense of purpose.

One day, a new guy sat at my table. He caught me off guard. His name was Dennis. He asked to borrow my pen, which was equivalent to taking my gavel. We began to talk. After church, he invited me into the empty sanctuary and charmed me by playing beautiful songs on the piano. His hands swept the keyboard like a maestro with a flair. I found out that he also had three children at a Christian school. *What a coincidence*, I thought.

Dennis continued to show up at my table. When he discovered my financial plight, he used his paperwork skills to apply and succeed in getting me scholarships for all three of my children. I was most grateful to him.

In subsequent days, we volleyed at racquet ball and tennis together. He took me to the Focus holiday dance and led me around the dance floor with fun rhythm. It was a new kind of gaiety.

But I soon discovered that with Dennis there were highs and lows.

Dennis's children were each one talented and good-looking. Together, our six children seemed to get along. We looked like the Brady Bunch, a well-known blended family on TV.

It seemed as though love was in the air at Focus, because at least six couples from Focus got married. They formed a new social circle which Dennis and I wanted to join. We allowed ourselves to get swept up in the romance of it all.

Before long, much to the chagrin of our friends, family, and pastors, Dennis and I decided to get married. And we did.

It was a fateful decision with disastrous consequences. I had unknowingly entered into the daily life of a bi-polar person. In the one-and-a-half years of our short-lived marriage, I had to separate from Dennis several times.

I myself lost my footing with the Lord and my own mental well-being. I plunged into depression.

Sitting alone in my car over lunch hour one day, I began to cry. I allowed myself to truly feel the sadness, then took my own photo with my camera. *This will be a portrait called 'Sad Cecily,'* I thought. And, indeed, that one photo told the whole story of this disastrous marriage.

I returned to my desk and couldn't see my computer screen through my tears. Thanks to my supervisor, I was approved for an eight-month disability leave from John Hancock. Anna sought safe housing with her school counselor to finish her senior year. Sunshine had already left for college. Regrettably, I had been like an absentee mother to her. Ezra weathered the storms with me.

A counselor advised me to have a Plan B in the event I had to flee urgently. I used that advice after midnight on December 23, 1992, landing on friend Francie's doorstep. Just as she had described, her front door key was hidden under the trash can on the right.

"Come anytime, day or night," she had said.

Dennis's frequent manic rage outbursts had exceeded my bounds of Christian tolerance. I had tried to honor my vow of marriage to him. I kept returning to try again. This time, if I had felt safe, I might have stayed merely to watch in fascination that a human being could act and speak as he did. But skipping medication and adding alcohol can be lethal.

So instead, I woke Ezra with the frantic words, "Quick, Ezra. Dennis's coming home and he's angry. Grab your book bag and pack three sets of clothes in it. We have five minutes to get out of here."

This time, I knew I wasn't going back.

Ezra was in eighth grade and had returned to public school. I had filed for bankruptcy. With no savings and no credit, there were few options for a place to live. I needed a free place to stay for awhile in order to save enough money to open a credit account. Thankfully, I still had my job at John Hancock and Levi's support payments. But for now, I was homeless.

The next day was Christmas Eve and I had no place to go. Francie's college-aged daughter came home for vacation and needed the room where I was sleeping. Dita had a full house with all five of her children visiting for their traditional get-together.

"But," she said, "you and Ezra can come live with me on Christmas Day after my kids have left."

So I had the unique experience to spend a made-to-order Christmas Eve at a Marriott. Not only did the lobby have a decorated tree and cheerful holiday music, but also complimentary eggnog and cookies. There was even a sunken living room with a lit fire and sofas where we could sit and enjoy the evening. What's more, the motel was known for serving a full Christmas morning breakfast. And the bonus was an indoor pool.

On Christmas Day, Sunshine, her boyfriend, Richard (who would later become her husband), and Anna all joined Ezra and me for breakfast, a swimming party, and exchange of gifts. It was a special interlude for a scattered, shattered family to reunite. We were celebrating the birthday of Jesus. It was apparent to me that He wanted us to have a good time.

In reality, I didn't deserve God's favor. I had truly messed up. I had married Dennis even in the face of dire warnings. "You'll be like two vacuum cleaners sucking on each other," someone had said. "You both are too needy and won't have enough to give each other."

What's more, I had become a financial drain to Dennis, who was already struggling in his own business. According to my divorce agreement with Levi, I had to sell South Merion if I married. But it turned out that I owed more than the selling price and had to take a loan in order to sell it. What I thought would be a windfall turned out to be a loss.

On Christmas night, Ezra and I knocked on Dita's door. We stepped into the front hall as she came to greet us. There was peace in the air. Her warm hug and soft words were like the balm of Gilead to my wounded, sin-sick soul. "Welcome home," she said. "I'm glad you're safely here."

Returning to Me

Enabled by thousand dollar gifts from both the COS benevolence fund and Dad, I found an apartment for Ezra and me within his school district. Anna opted to finish out her school year living with her guidance teacher's family. It was a period of precious mother/son time with Ezra. He learned to play the drums, raised two black-and-white kittens, worked at odd jobs, bought himself a car, and started to date classmate Lisa, before graduating from high school.

There was no grief in the loss of Dennis—only relief and regret. Dennis moved on in his life. He wrote me a masterful letter of apology. In spite of his hurtful behavior, his best attribute was asking forgiveness. He modeled that humility over and over in the period I knew him—not just to me, but to his children and others as well. I hadn't learned to do that at Cackleberry and was grateful to see and hear how the humble process of admitting fault and asking forgiveness worked.

Dennis had also given me the reason and impetus to break out of the stalemate I had felt in the South Merion house, which had been deteriorating around me.

> Peter, Peter pumpkin eater,
> Had a wife but couldn't keep her;
> He put her in a pumpkin shell
> And there he kept her very well.

Attributed to Levi, that nursery rhyme had swirled in my head for years. Although the process had been fraught with great repercussions and upheaval, Dennis had helped put that perceived conundrum behind me.

My task at hand was to regain my equilibrium in the Lord. I knew I had lost my way and needed to "get back to where I once belonged," as the Beatles sang. *Where had I strayed away from my God-given path? How did I fall into such a co-dependent relationship with Dennis?*

The little girl named Cecily started out with such hopes and dreams, security, and happiness. I prayed, "*God, you created me and gave me a happy childhood. Lord, let me get back to being that girl.*" I missed what I had always called my Cecilyness.

God's answer was to give me the idea of gathering photos of myself as a baby, a child, and a young girl and post them all around the walls of my bedroom. There were pictures of me as a two-year-old in Mexico City, as a happy child at Cackleberry and as a fresh college graduate. It lifted my spirits to see them. Slowly, I found myself returning to me. In the ensuing divorce, I took back my maiden name of Cecily Clay Watson.

I returned to the Focus singles group at Church of the Saviour and, once again, threw myself into a leadership role of being a table group facilitator on Sunday mornings. An added highlight was getting baptized in the main church with the entire congregation present.

I heard about a singles weekend retreat for women being held at Sandy Cove in Maryland. Two speakers were scheduled, one of whom was also a musician, named Nancy Honeytree. I signed up on my own, not seeking a friend to go with me. I wanted to be among strangers and allow myself to absorb the message I sensed was going to be given. It was a good move and it worked out as a momentous step in healing for me.

When the final talk was given and the event was over, everybody left to pack up and return to their various homes. I stayed seated and had a cathartic weep. With my head held down, I allowed the salty tears to flow. It was a deep, wonderful weep. I knew that I was getting rid of anger and sadness. When it stopped and I had wiped my face with tissues, I went up to the singer and speaker, Nancy, who was gathering her things. I thanked her for sharing her own painful testimony. I then asked her to pray and rejoice with me because I was walking out as a healed woman who was never going back to such sorrow.

Nancy and I faced each other and held hands. I reaffirmed my faith aloud in front of her. I confessed to her, "I am a child of God. I believe the truth of the Bible and the truth has set me free. It's because God's Son, Jesus, died on the cross in my place that He has become my Savior. I have been forgiven of my sin. And since Jesus rose from the dead and ascended to heaven, I am promised eternal life with God." Nancy gave me a hug in agreement. We were sisters in Christ. She didn't need to hear any sad details of my life. She knew she was sharing my moment of release. We both were recipients of Jesus' love and victory.

I drove home from Sandy Cove as a free woman, full of anticipation for what lay ahead. I had fallen hard but Jesus forgave me, lifted me up, and restored my soul.

Praise God! I was an overcomer.

Changes

E zra spent another year with me in the apartment after high school. Then he left to study Industrial Design at University of the Arts in Philadelphia, the same school as Anna. He was still a delightful guy to be with. I enjoyed how he shared the changes he noticed about himself. "I'm paying more attention to finer details," he told me, "like I care about washing my hands in hot water, instead of cold. Also, I want to put a saucer under a mug. And, I take the time to button up my coat when it's cold." He asked me to teach him how to tie a necktie. He didn't know it but within a few years he would become an industrial designer, he and Lisa would be married, and they would live near San Francisco.

Ezra was currently the drummer in a Christian rock band. He gave me gratuitous "do-it-again" physical therapy by drumming his hands on my back to Pearl Jam songs. He was still a tease, too. I had started turning all the food labels in my kitchen cupboards facing out, and one morning I found them all staring at me backwards. I loved getting that special attention.

On the weekends when he went to visit friends, I discovered how quickly I felt lonely. I found myself walking to the front window wishing I would see a car pull in, wishing somebody was coming to see me.

Anna was between drama jobs so I invited her to come live with us. She had graduated from University of the Arts with a degree in Theater. She and Ezra filled the apartment with laughter. The three of us spent precious remedial months together.

Sunshine and her husband joined us for special occasions. She had become a teacher and was married to her God-given longtime sweetheart, Richard, whom she had met at COS in ninth grade. They lived in northern Maryland.

But change was in the air. Ezra and Anna moved onward and outward. In the same period, my employer, John Hancock, where I had worked for thirteen years, sold their group health business to another company, which relocated out of state. I received a good severance package, enough to tide me over for almost two years.

Endless options were open to me. I could move anywhere and work at whatever. I knew I would not stay in the apartment. I wrote my resumé, then called my friend Ellen in Colorado (from Ramón days) to see what she was up to. This would be a good interlude to visit her. Much to my delight, she was about to leave for a Spanish language school in Guanajuato, Mexico. What a perfect way to enjoy a reunion with Ellen and find out how much to emphasize Spanish on my resumé. She got me enrolled in the language school and arranged my travel. Off I went to Mexico.

Ellen and I stayed with a widow who rented modest rooms to students. We had an invigorating two weeks with lots of reminiscing and laughter, navigating the narrow, curved streets of that European style town, and being challenged by the study of advanced Spanish grammar. I learned that, unless I could master the subjunctive, I would always butcher the language. Although I understood most of the spoken word, I could not pass myself off as professionally fluent on my resumé.

I flew home to Philadelphia. To my great surprise, all three of my children met me at the arrival gate. They had news to tell me.

While I was in Mexico, my Dad, their beloved grandfather, had died of pancreatic cancer. They had no way to call me. Lying on his bed overlooking *ISLANDER*'s empty dock, Dad drew his last breath on July 11, 1997. On his desk was the map of Montana where he was going to take Mom for their next road trip. The previous year, when he was eighty-seven, they had been passengers on a postal supply ship all the way up the coast of Norway. There, they met a railroad engineer who invited them to ride with him while he drove a train from Billings to Missoula. Instead, Dad had taken the eternal train.

I knew Dad had lost weight. He had been telling me he felt weak for months. Cancer was not mentioned, nor did it occur to me. But I was concerned that he was getting old and had not accepted Jesus into his heart. I didn't want him to miss Heaven. I had visited him in November of 1996. We had talked together. As he shared his thoughts, he revealed to me that what he lacked was a sense of peace.

Dad was never a believer, but occasionally went to church with Mom and us children on Easter and/or Christmas. "If I can't see it or touch it, I can't believe in it," he continued to say, referring to the divinity of Jesus. His years at St. Mark's boarding school in Massachusetts endowed him with a fine classical education but not with a love of the Bible. What he lacked as a spiritual role model for me he made up in personality with whimsical story telling and his inventive enterprises.

I told Dad during that visit that I could lead him in a prayer to accept Jesus as his Savior. He replied, "Oh no. I don't want to do that too soon."

I left White Stone at that time to return to my apartment in Malvern, PA. In a eureka moment, I realized it was not salvation that Dad sought. It was peace. On the way, I pulled over and wrote my inspiration to him. I worded the letter this way:

> *"Dear Dad, Remember our conversation on Saturday about eternal peace? You gave me the impression that one enters the state of eternal peace only at one's death.*
>
> *But Jesus said, 'My peace I give to you.' Dad, you can have peace immediately at the very moment you trust that Jesus meant it. You don't have to wait till the end of your life. Anyway, if the end comes suddenly, it will be too late."*

Then I continued writing:

"The way to be assured of eternal peace with God is through a simple, sincere prayer. Dad—Please pull away to a quiet spot and pray this prayer. Take your faith as small as a mustard seed and become a child of God. He loves you and He is good. Pray something like this:

'Dear Jesus, I have such a load of impropriety in my life—things that I have thought, done, or said—that there is no good reason, no way in and of myself, that you should accept me into your eternal peace. Finally, after all these years, I realize that you already knew this about me. And that's why you took all my sin when you died on the cross. You forgave me and washed me as white as snow. Thank you, Jesus. I receive your free gift of forgiveness. I receive your peace. From this moment on, You are my Lord and Savior.'"

I ended my letter by giving Dad some poignant Bible verses:

"'But as many as received Him, to them He gave the right to become children of God, even to those who believe in His Name.' John 1:12

'Most assuredly, I say to you, he who believes in Me has everlasting life.' John 6:47

I love you so much. Your daughter, Cecily."

In December, Mom wrote this to me in a letter:

"I think you opened a door for Daddy, though he's afraid to do more than just peep in. God will pull him through the crack."

And, also in December, I received this from Dad in his last letter to me:

*"I thank you for all the neat stuff you've sent me...The prayers
were particularly nice. I've tested the prayer routine and I'll
report on that when you come down."*

I never did see Dad again. He had died peacefully that summer at age
eighty-eight in his bed overlooking the scenic Antipoison Creek. His treasured wooden cabin cruiser, the *ISLANDER,* had long since been missing
from the dock. It had sunk years earlier at the boatyard in Little Bay closer
to the Chesapeake where he had taken it to be looked at for leaks.

"Hoist her to dry dock now," Dad had told the boatyard owner. "She's
leaking fast."

"Yessir," the salty man had replied. However, the yard had only one boat
lift. In an ill-fated move, the boat repairman gave preference to a sailing yacht
that was en route somewhere and in a hurry. Mercifully, the *ISLANDER*
had sunk at a faraway marina and not in Dad's bedside window view.

Brother Bob was with him and told me that, just before he died, Dad
had spread his arms out like Jesus on the cross and had asked Bob to take a
picture of him. Was Dad offering his life to Jesus? I didn't know. But it gave
me comfort to believe that when I see him in Heaven, Dad's report that he
had accepted Jesus will be obvious. I had no tears, only joy at that thought,
and happiness that I had known and shared a love with my earthly father.
He had enriched my life with whimsy, curiosity, love of travel, invention,
honesty, and love of people.

At the funeral in Kilmarnock, I watched Mom graciously greet us all and
act as hostess. The house was full afterwards with my four siblings, spouses,
and most of the nineteen grandchildren, including my three kids.

"What do you think you will do?" I asked her. "Will you stay here at
"Watsons' Landing" by yourself?"

"I don't know," she told me. "I married young and have never lived alone.
Daddy always took good care of me."

Young Dorothy Clay was a devout Episcopalian when she married him.
She was so drawn by his charisma that somehow, for sixty-four years, they
created a solid marriage that worked. How ironic that all five of their children experienced divorce. It must have been the turbulent era we lived in.

My heart went out to her. We had something in common. We were both about to live alone. Another marriage was not in my radar. *Three strikes and you're out,* I had told myself. Maybe God had just come up with a solution for both of us. I had used my coping skills and God's scriptural comfort to help others who were going through the pains and sorrows of marital separation and divorce. Now I could help a widow.

"Mom!" I said excitedly. "If I can find a job here, I would be willing to move in with you. Would you like that?" She was overjoyed.

I found the job of my dreams as an assistant at Brandylane Publishers right there in White Stone. It was perfect for the English major in me. It must have been worked out by God, because what were the odds that a job like this would be nearby, and that the owner and I would have connected? He had advertised only once in the weekly paper, which happened to be the paper I bought.

I returned to pack up and say goodbye in Malvern. The adults at my table at Focus tried to dissuade me. "Are you sure you want to leave COS? Your roots are deep here in Pennsylvania, and we friends don't want to lose you. We'll miss your leadership. Are you sure you want to live out in the country by a creek? What if there are no new friends and you are stuck?"

Their pleadings couldn't sway me. I had a supernatural peace about this move. Mom needed me and the fact was that I needed her. She was eighty-four. I was only fifty-four. So while I saw her through her older years, she would provide me with a roof over my head—and a very nice covered porch for fivesies from which we could watch the sea birds fly and the ducks swim.

Ezra, Lisa and a nephew helped load my U-Haul and moved me to White Stone.

On the way down, I thought, *I've had such an out-of-the-ordinary, interesting, sad and happy, challenging life. This will be a good time to write my story.* A Barnes and Noble store caught my eye. I pulled into the parking lot, entered, and came out with four books on how to write one's memoir.

I felt refreshed as I headed south. I was entering a new phase of my life.

White Stone with Mom

The frightful prediction I wouldn't have new friends in Virginia proved to be unfounded almost right away. Before going to work in the mornings, I had established a routine of taking a walk on the long lanes and roads that surrounded the planted fields. The corn had grown tall. As I rounded the corner between rows, I almost bumped into a cluster of three women who were walking fast and talking. Each held a handcrafted wooden walking stick.

We introduced ourselves. "My name's Joycelyn," the leader said, "and this is Fran and the tall one's Doris. Do you walk every morning?" I told her yes. "We do too. Three miles, unless it's raining. We pass your house about eight o'clock. Come join us."

"Sure," I answered.

"We'll look for you." I smiled as they left. If they only knew what a blessing it was to meet them.

The next morning, I fell right into step with the "Little Bay Walkers and Talkers." They became my first set of friends. We ended up walking together for years. There was no gossip, no bad-mouthing, only good clean chatter. Others joined us. Some fell away. We wrote poems to each other and celebrated birthdays and Christmas, or sorrowful times like funerals. Husbands were included at the get-togethers, so I brought Mom too.

Mom spent little time grieving over Dad's passing. She adjusted well to my presence in her home and seemed pleased to have fivesies out on the porch with me when I returned from work. We sat on white wicker chairs viewing the subtle ebb and flow of the tidal creek. We got along like good friends. Both of us were easy-going and life was sweet. She told me about her day, be it the healing prayer service at her Episcopal church, or serving communion at the nursing home, or playing bridge with her friends. I described the happenings at my book publishing office. Then she took to the stove to prepare supper. The table was set with the familiar silverware I remembered from Cackleberry, all carefully laid out on bright place-mats, fork on the left, knife and spoon on the right. Mom had settled into a simple style of cooking. Although it wasn't the labor-intensive, freshly hand-picked crab cakes she'd prepared for Dad or the "floating island" for dessert, it was more than ample and always delicious.

I was being pampered. I knew it. But at the same time, Mom had someone to care for, which she needed. It was a win-win situation. My role was to be her assistant. I'd do the dishes and clean up the kitchen, vacuum the floors, wash the sheets, and get the groceries. We spent the evenings quietly reading, working on jigsaw puzzles, playing Scrabble, or watching the "telly." She had two huge old cats, Purrington and Ceremony, who took turns weighing down our laps.

Mom kept the flower gardens. During growing season, her exquisite flower arrangements enhanced the beauty of our glass-walled cottage. Everywhere I looked, there was something lovely or scenic to see.

The creek disappeared around a bend about a quarter mile from our porch. It beckoned me—a watery highway that I was helpless to travel on. I got curious about Dad's old runabout skiff tied at the dock. If I learned how to start and drive it, I could explore the creek up into the tributaries and even go all the way to Little Bay. I took a boat safety course. But, although they awarded me a certificate, they hadn't given me the hands-on experience of operating the boat.

The 4th of July was coming up. I really wanted to decorate the skiff in patriotic colors and enter the contest in the upcoming Antipoison Creek Neighborhood Independence Day Boat Parade. Thankfully, a neighbor came over and showed me how to start the engine and putter around the wide area of water by our dock.

Anna had come to visit just in time to help me slap together some decorations. The object was for the decorated boat to drive back and forth in front of the picnic area about a mile up the creek. Two so-called judges would be seated in the middle of the lawn on white Adirondack chairs under the cooling shade of tall trees—one was Mom with macular degeneration and cataracts. The other judge was her ninety-year-old friend, Celia Atwood, who quite possibly could also not see well. They looked so official holding clip boards to record their results.

Anna and I put on red-white-and-blue outfits and climbed into the skiff. This was going to be a lark. Off we went into the great unknown, around the bend, and another bend, and a third.

Suddenly, I saw an armada of colorful boats ahead, some of them proper multi-dollar yachts. I gasped inside myself. *How am I going to maneuver safely into the huddle of this parade? Where was Dad when I needed him?* He was the one who always took us out for rides. I tried to hide it from Anna but I knew I wasn't yet ready to skipper a boat. I put on a smile and acted like this was a blast even though I felt inept and out of control.

I held the tiller and forgot to steer while I increased the throttle of the engine. Our boat bucked like we were on a wild sea. By the grace of God, we made our passes successfully before the "reviewing stand" and landed without crashing into the dock or any other boat. Not that I expected differently, the "judges" paid us no attention when it came to awards. For me, though, that was okay.

As I sat with Mom and an elated Anna among the crowd, eating hot dogs and singing patriotic songs, I felt victorious. No one else knew it but I was the true winner. I had overcome a fear and acquired a budding new skill.

Across from my office in downtown White Stone was a large, tan, three-story house with a wide wraparound front porch and a sign that read, "White Stone Church of the Nazarene." What fun it would be, I thought, to have church in an old house. I missed COS and needed to find a church family. It turned out to be a right fit for me.

Pastor Jimmy and his wife Julie greeted me warmly, as did the others in this small fledgling congregation. They held adult Sunday School in the kitchen and the church worship service in the expanded living room. The kids' classrooms were upstairs in the second floor bedrooms. I attended church regularly. Word spread that there was a new church in town and soon there were about eighty of us squeezing into the building.

"That's a good problem," my new friend Brenda told me. "It means people are hungry to know Jesus."

On a day when I missed the appointed hour with my walking group, I went out alone. I took a back road and passed a handful of modest homes in the woods where several black families lived. Dad had taken me over there once to meet toothless Eveline, who had sold Dad a rooster. The other households I didn't know. At one house, a heavy-set teenaged girl sat on the front stoop looking dejected. It wasn't my business, so I kept going, thinking there was a big gap between my life at "Watsons' Landing" and whatever life she knew. On the way back, there she still was, her head held low. This time, she had a baby in her lap.

I couldn't resist the chance to admire her baby, so I approached her. "Can I see your baby?" I asked.

"Yeah. Of course," she answered in a tired voice. She held the baby in my direction and seemed to perk up a bit. "I know you're gonna say she's purty, 'cause I think so too." She looked straight at me.

"You seem kind of sad," I said to her.

"Yeah. I am." She sighed and paused, like she wasn't sure whether to go on. But she did. "The baby and me, we got no place to stay. This house is my uncle's and he don't want me here. I have till the weekend to get out."

She went on to tell me that the baby's father had dumped them there. Her name was Dellie. My heart went out to her. With the compassion of

Jesus, I set about to know Dellie and her family and explore all her options for finding a stable living situation. She had no money and needed work.

For a full semester, I drove her thirty-five miles to attend a course leading to a CNA (Certified Nursing Assistant) diploma, which required waiting for class to be over to take her back. It didn't work out, however, because Dellie failed the final exam. It wasn't easy for anyone. Helping her resulted in a winding road that took me to places like meeting her white mother, who had problems of her own, and to the aloof father of her older son. Then I sidestepped from Dellie for awhile when she decided to live with a middle-aged druggie, and got pregnant again.

My friend from church, Michele, took an interest in helping Dellie just when I was ready to give up. We took her to church but what she really needed was a place to live. Together, we found a homeless shelter in Richmond for her that led to an urban housing arrangement that appeared to be the right solution for the time being.

At this point, I moved on to a new interest.

*W*hile reflecting on my twenty years of life, after my twenty-eight-year Navy career, I felt that I had adequately continued to serve the Navy with the founding of Naval Submarine League and other contributions I had affected for the Navy and country. I was single and had finished the final tasks of a years-long restoration of my sixteen-room, 1865-era Chesapeake Bay home, named "Pine Hall," which I then sold. It was a unique and well-known relic of Mathews County, Virginia. I bought another large home on the water in the same county and called it "Clifton." I decided to retire my consulting career at the end of 1999, some six months away, and so informed Applied Physics Laboratory and American Systems Corporation, and others, of my intentions.

A new unplanned routine developed after a day's work on Saturdays. I would retire to the TV room, watch several hours of entertainment, then fall asleep in my recliner.

One Sunday morning, I awoke to hear a new TV voice, that of Pastor Courtney McBath, a graduate of Harvard and skilled preacher of the Bible. His church was located in Virginia Beach, Virginia, just two hours south of Mathews. Suffice it to say, I had never heard the Gospel of Jesus Christ so forcefully and sincerely elucidated. I wanted to hear Courtney again, and so made the watching of his Sunday morning sermon a regular date.

It got to the point that I needed to know more about what the Scripture said and not wait a week between teachings. I searched the house for a Bible and there was not one to be had. Two employees at a 24-hour Walmart, who had been bored, found it a great thrill to get down on their hands and knees with me to page through each Bible and come up with the one that a sixty-nine-year-old newly-energized believer should purchase.

Part 7

Becoming the Admiral's Wife

Starting a Singles Group

Needing recreation, I found out about and joined a women's line dance class being held at a local consignment shop after work hours in Kilmarnock, the next town over. The teacher, Barbara, owner of the shop, welcomed me to the class. She and her husband had pushed the racks of clothes aside to create a dance floor for the five women who showed up. Her CD player sat on a high shelf. The husband, who was tall and slim and wore regionally atypical cowboy boots, stood on his toes to reach the player and start the music. He turned the volume way up.

I was introduced to a new sound, 90s country music, a beat that wanted to make a dancer out of me. I could hardly stand still.

Barbara patiently demonstrated the steps to "Achy Breaky Heart." We were all supposed to learn a pattern of right foot to the right, left foot behind, right foot to the right, left heel scuff to the left side of your right foot, walk forward, walk backward, wiggle your hips, do quarter turn and repeat. *My that's hard!* My body just wanted to bounce to the catchy rhythm and forget the instruction. And, whenever I turned to another wall, I forgot the first thing to do. By the end of the song, I may have completed the pattern correctly once. Then she would move onto "Boot Scootin' Boogie." The same thing happened. And the beat picked up with "Way Down Yonder on the Chattahoochee."

Forget it! I told myself. I was absolutely enamored with the music, but just couldn't catch on to the choreography. And I wasn't compatible with the girls. I missed the type of fellowship I had at church with

Christian friends. But still, it was sort of fun and something to do, so I continued going.

In the meantime, the Lord gave me an idea. I should locate single Christian adults and start a fellowship group, like the one in Pennsylvania. Surely there were others plagued by the fifth wheel syndrome in social situations who would appreciate a chance to make new friends. The challenge was to find them since they were geographically scattered. White Stone and Kilmarnock were only two of many small towns in Virginia's Northern Neck peninsula, each with their several churches. Just across the Rappahannock River bridge was the Middle Peninsula with more rural towns and churches.

I met a young man who said he would help me. He was native to the area, in his thirties and quite affable. He, too, was single and a motivated Christian. His name was Allen and he worked in the local feed store. As we talked, I shared my thoughts for a singles fellowship and he immediately caught the vision with a caveat, "I'll go as long as my mother and her friends don't show up!" Together, we found a pastor who supported our plan. We contacted many churches and explained what we wanted to do, and they freely gave us the names and addresses of all their single adults.

As I compiled the list, I wondered what benefit the proposed singles group would have beyond socializing. The Lord led me to a verse in the Bible. I found it in the New International Version, in the book called Hebrews, in chapter ten, verse twenty-four:

"And let us consider how we may spur one another on toward love and good deeds."

That was it! God gave me the perfect verse to describe the greater purpose and reason for getting together. We would spread God's love to one another and those around us. We would do good deeds for one another and those beyond ourselves.

The Lord then gave me the name of the group–"SPUR"–from the Bible verse. Then I said to the Lord, "But it needs to be an acronym." The Lord then popped this into my head, *Single People Under the Righteous-One.* "Oh, Lord, You are good!" I told Him.

I went to my computer to create an introductory letter in the form of a newsletter. When I started to type, the Lord had me call the newsletter "The S.P.U.R. of the Moment." All of this came about in one afternoon. I knew it was a calling from God, and that it would be blessed.

Allen and I created a schedule of activities, places and times to meet. Sometimes we had a potluck lunch at the Nazarene Church. Single moms brought little children. Older women came (but, thankfully, not Allen's mother!).

Bit-by-bit with different activities we got to know each other. We had a BBQ on the deck of "Watsons' Landing." A single neighbor up the creek brought his runabout motorboat and gave us joy rides. We met at restaurants and took day trips. I truly enjoyed putting all of that together and kept it going for a couple of years.

It started to fizzle, though. Allen dropped out when there weren't any eligible girlfriends showing up. I, myself, lost interest when the regulars dwindled to several dating couples. I sat in the restaurant as the fifth wheel, once again. *I'm organizing their social life!* I suddenly realized. The group also had forgotten our Christian aspect. No one wanted to talk about Jesus, much less do ministry projects.

I sent out the final issue of "The S.P.U.R. of the Moment" newsletter to thank everyone for participating.

All was not lost, however. I had made contact through S.P.U.R. with a woman named Esther, who was to play a role in my becoming the Admiral's wife.

*A*bout August 1999, a friend informed me that the Stepping Stones Square Dance Club was ready to hold their annual session of beginners' classes starting on 20 September, and that I should attend. He had recommended this activity for several of this club's previous autumn starting dates, and I always had a legitimate excuse not to attend. He and I both knew that this was now not the case.

On 20 September, I arrived promptly at the local Community Center at 1900 hours. One of the new students caught my eye. She was quite attractive and looked like a happy person. She appeared to be escorted by an energetic young man. They were together during pauses in the music and instruction. I soon learned that the club assigned an experienced square dancer called an "angel" to each new student, and they were to partner during the initial month of weekly instruction. My angel partner was a warm and knowledgeable elderly lady, who taught me the basic square dance steps.

I found out that the name of the lady I was attracted to was Cecily Watson. Much to my glee, her angel partner did not show up for the third weekly session. I maneuvered in position to be her partner, especially for the basic review sessions. She was a smiling, confident person, and cheerful to be around. My heart leaped when I found out that she, too, was a Christian. She said she lived with her mother in the town of White Stone, across the Rappahannock River. She described the unmarked dirt lanes and fields and barns that led to her house on the creek but, hard as I tried one afternoon to get a glimpse of where she lived, I couldn't find her.

Later, I invited her and her mother, Dorothy, to a community theater show and to my house "Clifton" afterwards for dessert. I put a white-laced tablecloth and candles on the table and served us all some Jell-o, my specialty, in my best plates.

Soon we were dating and dancing often. Cecily's worrisome issue, that I was thirteen years her senior, was mitigated after she chatted with some senior women and received their advice, "GO FOR IT!"

We were married a year later on 13 January 2001. We started to attend the same church and our Pastor was very helpful with his counsel. God had blessed us. We were to be lifelong partners.

May I Have this Dance?

It was 1999. A buzz was in the air that we could all be in catastrophic trouble when the clock struck midnight on December 31st. The fear was that all computer programs would fail to recognize the year 2000. Banks, hospitals, airlines and all systems that relied on precision data would be thrown into turmoil, affecting all of us. It became known as Y2K, or Year Two-Thousand. Not only would our computers crash but, according to the Mayan calendar, the world would end on December 12, 2012, only twelve years off. I was feeling alarmed by these predictions.

At that time, an unusual high tide caused the Antipoison Creek to rise up and flood over the banks toward our house. The previous two days of rain added to the swell. Mom said she had never seen this happen in all her twenty-three years at "Watsons' Landing." The water began to trickle, then swirl under the house, which was built on pilings two feet off the ground.

"What should we do?" I asked Mom anxiously. "Should we go upstairs to the loft?"

"Oh. Let's not worry about it, Dear. It'll soon be gone." Mom meant what she said. She lay down on the sofa, covered herself with a blanket and fell fast asleep. Meanwhile, I paced back and forth from the glass doors to the windows to check on the status of our safety. The water rose up the steps to our porch, inching its way towards the entrance to the living room and Mom's sofa.

Just as I was ready to evacuate both of us, the tide changed. The water began to subside. Mom was right. We were safe. Life resumed. I went to line dance lessons.

But still, Y2K was approaching, just like that tide. I couldn't tell Mom about it. She didn't understand computers. And, after I saw her nap during an emergency, what solace or help would she be?

I started to feel vulnerable for both of us. There was no one at church or work or elsewhere to talk to about my apprehensions. So as I was taught, I went to scripture to gain strength. Isaiah 41:10 in the King James Version was perfect. "So do not fear, for I am with you; do not be dismayed, for I am your God. I will strengthen you and **help** you." I emphasized the help part.

I was taught at Church of the Saviour to approach God's throne of grace with confidence during a time of need. That meant bold prayer. So I went to the Lord with what some would say was a command. I told the Lord that I needed Him to send me someone to help me feel more secure— at least until 2012 or whenever the world ended.

I wasn't thinking of a husband! But, God had that in mind for me.

The phone rang. It was Barbara from line dancing. She said, "I'm really sorry but I have to stop the classes. I've got gout in my right foot. It's too painful for me to teach anymore." Though unfamiliar with gout, I told her I was sorry. But the truth was that I was more sorry to lose that social outlet.

Lo, and behold, the next day I received an intriguing letter in the mail. It was an invitation to join the annual beginners class of the Stepping Stones Square Dance Club. Their secretary, Esther, had jotted a hand-written comment saying she knew me from S.P.U.R., and that she hoped I would join the Club. I had square danced once at camp decades earlier. As I recalled, there was a lot of hand holding and linking of arms. I decided to go. I needed that physical touch. And besides, the other dancers could keep me in place, unlike line dancing where I was left to mess up on my own.

The classes started in September on Thursday nights. I was advised not to miss any, because the success of the club depended on all the dancers learning the new steps each week that were taught by the live caller. The letter said I would be guaranteed an "angel," or seasoned square dancer, as my partner for the first few weeks. It sounded like such fun! I told Esther I would be there. I couldn't wait.

Syringa, Virginia, was merely a dot on the map. Somehow I found the non-town on a back country road across the river. It consisted of a post office, an Indian Chief gas store, and an old white school house, long converted to a community center, which was my destination. I drove down a dirt lane to the grass area in the back and chose an open spot among the several cars, which were parked country style, that is, every which way. But, inside there was order, not chaos.

From the moment I walked in, I was greeted by friendly, smiling people. Obviously, the regulars looked forward to the annual new crop of students to swell their ranks. The various "angels" took their partners to the dance floor to form squares of four couples facing in. My "angel" was a nice-looking man, about ten years younger, who told me he also lived across the river on the Northern Neck. We were given our first directive which was to hold hands. His hands were stiff and sweaty. I figured he was just nervous. He knew the steps well and led me through the next calls with a precise, almost too firm approach.

As the weeks went on, my smile didn't quit. I enjoyed the music, the lively interaction, and the easy camaraderie. After every two songs, called a "tip," the eight people in each square joined hands, stepped to the center, and with raised arms let out a triumphant whoop. Then everybody hugged each other before taking a break. It was wonderful. It reminded me of how we had ended the Cozy Club meetings so many years earlier. I had found a safe place with no drinking, smoking or cussing, just good clean fun and human touch.

On the fourth week, my "angel" didn't show up. He had explained that he was a staunch Episcopalian with responsibilities and busy with other commitments. So I wasn't surprised when he actually stopped coming altogether. By that time, we beginners were permitted to dance with other newcomers like ourselves.

I found myself in a square with an older man as my partner. He had asked me to dance. His name tag was hard to read. The first name "AL" was easy but the last name looked like it was missing a vowel. "KELLN" it read.

The music started. He reached for my hand. In spite of his age, I felt like I had just met my best friend.

Overcoming Reticence

Al apparently was eager to know me. We danced together often and for two beginners we were doing pretty well. There were always other partners, so I circulated happily. Mom and Marion, who was visiting from Philadelphia, came to watch. They wanted to see the spectacle of the Stepping Stones Square Dance Club in action. I sat with them during breaks in the music, and Al surprised me by coming over to meet them.

Later that evening, he asked if I would agree to be his partner for every tip. I was taken aback by his question. Part of the fun of Club dancing was the variety of partners and how they led me through the calls, which were becoming more complicated with each lesson. All of a sudden, a man I didn't know was taking an interest in me. Not only that, he wanted to pin me down.

Thoughts rushed through my head like: *Does he want to be my boyfriend!? He's too old for me. I'm not seeking a relationship with a man. Who is he anyway? No thanks. He might hurt me. I've had my three strikes. I'm out. This can't be real. Just stick to a Club dance partner thing.*

"Will you agree to dance with me every tip?" He asked so nicely. I didn't want to hurt his feelings. But didn't want to say yes either. Besides, he was a beginner like me, and was struggling, and needed my help to catch on to the new dance steps. I preferred to be led.

I had to answer his question. What came out was sudden, sincere, intimate, confessional, and somewhat of an ultimatum. But its effect drew us instantly into a supernatural union.

I looked right into his green eyes (he was just a bit taller than I) and said, "I'm a woman who's had lots of hurt in my life. I've had bad relationships and failed marriages. I'm in a happy place now. Please don't mess with me. And besides, I have to tell you that I love God more than anything in the world."

There! I thought to myself. *That will turn him off. He will go on his merry way. I can keep on being me.*

Though I couldn't know it at the time, my words struck Al to his very core. He was almost speechless. He identified with everything I had said. What I saw was a man who tenderheartedly told me he had also been divorced and that he loved God too. I decided that we could, maybe *should* be friends.

I told him, "Okay. How about this? I'll dance the first and last tips with you."

A couple of weeks later, Esther noticed that Al and I were acting chummy together. She pulled me aside during a break and asked if we were seeing each other. I told her we would be going out for Sunday dinner at the new restaurant d'Medici in Kilmarnock that weekend. It would be our first time to talk.

"Cecily, do you know anything about him?" she asked. "Did you know he's a retired Navy Admiral?"

No. I hadn't heard that. I tried to take it in. What an honor to be dancing with an Admiral! What was he doing in a country dance hall? I had thought he was just some average nice guy from Mathews on the Middle Peninsula who seemed to like me. Here I had been kind of bossy leading him through the myriad calls, fairly pulling him right and pushing him left.

I watched him more carefully the rest of the evening. He still appeared to carry himself as an average nice guy. I liked him, especially the way he held my hand. I didn't let on what I knew about his identity. It reminded me of Mom's true story about when she was eighteen, in 1930, on a transatlantic ship steaming towards Paris. She had a debonair man take an interest in her, who she discovered was the Count of Flanders, Prince Charles of Belgium. He was traveling incognito under the pseudonym "Bill." Mom played along as if she didn't who he was. She got a big kick out of treating "Bill" as a commoner, and "Bill" seemed to enjoy this new kind of attention. She taught him how to do the Charleston and the foxtrot. They walked the decks and laughed as they talked, and soon realized they were growing fond of one another. Finally, she revealed to him that she knew he was Prince Charles. He said he would invite her to the palace for tea.

The upshot was that the invitation never came. But that was for the better. Mom ended up marrying my father, Robert Watson, a humble vacuum cleaner salesman during the Depression, who was a colorful person, and whose grandfather, William Platt Pepper, was a founder and director of the Philadelphia Museum of Art.

At the Sunday afternoon d'Medici dinner table, I told Al that Esther had revealed to me that he was an Admiral. "How long were you in the Navy?" I asked him. He told me thirty-two years, if you included the four years at the Naval Academy. I clutched, thinking *That's about the extent of my knowledge on that subject! I don't know what to say next!*

But Al bailed me out. He was an engaging man, full of questions about me—where did I live; what brought me to Virginia; had I ever been fishing; did I know what a gill net was? I watched with fascination how patient he was with me whenever he did talk about the Navy. It didn't bother him that he needed to start from the beginning and just share tidbits with me. He was a gentle person.

The restaurant "date" went well, except I found out that he was thirteen years older than I. He was sixty-nine. I was fifty-six. He had white hair. Mine was dyed brown. I wasn't sure if my hair had turned white or grey underneath but, for now, I probably looked like his daughter. The age difference didn't sit well with me. *He's too old for me,* I told myself. *If I fell for him, he would die before me, and I would be abandoned once again and have to mourn the loss of a man.* Besides, I was not looking for another mate. I checked my heart and applied a skid to it.

Al then invited me and Mom to a live theater performance in Mathews. We accepted. He asked for specific directions to our house, admitting that already that week he had tried but failed to find it.

He showed up with a yellow long-stem rose and presented it to me.

We lived twenty-five miles apart. That evening meant a hundred miles of driving for Al. He came all the way to pick us up in his white SUV, took us

352

all the way back to Mathews to see the musical, "Little Mary Sunshine" by the Court House Players, then had to drive us back to White Stone.

We had accepted his offer of dessert at his house after the play. *Was I being invited to the palace?*

Al's long driveway led not to a palace, but to a sprawling French chateau he called "Clifton." It sat by a creek which Mom and I couldn't see in the dark. Al ushered us to his dining room table which he had preset with white placemats, silver candlesticks, linen napkins, and a spoon on each napkin. He seated us. Then, after a little fuss in the kitchen, he came out holding a glass bowl of Jell-o in each hand. It wasn't just any Jell-o. It was two-toned, orange and red.

"My specialty," he said proudly. Mom and I oohed and aahed over his endeavor. It was apparent he wanted to impress us. And he did. As we left his home, I saw that this bachelor's abode needed a woman's touch. He later revealed to me that he had called a neighbor woman to ask how to set a table. And she had lent him the linen napkins.

Another month went by and Al brought me two long-stem yellow roses.

Pretty soon, we were seeing each other more often. Besides square dancing, we took walks on the beach, holding hands, laughing and enjoying each other's company. They were short walks because Al had a bad hip. He visited the Nazarene Church with me. People seemed to enjoy being with us as a couple. We were making mutual friends. I still thought he was too old for me to consider seriously.

There was resistance elsewhere, too. My daughters were not happy that I was dating someone, nor Marion. Bob said on the phone from California, "He's probably not even an Admiral. Be careful. How do you know he's not really a bank robber?" People who cared about me felt protective of me and suspicious of Al. They were still reeling from my Dennis experience which had ended seven years earlier. They knew I had already been divorced three times. They saw that I was now at peace. They didn't want me to be hurt once again. I appreciated their concern and kept my heart in check.

At the third month, Al brought me three long-stem yellow roses. He took me to Donk's Li'l Ole Opry for live country music which was great fun. This man was serious about courting me. He was starting to touch my heart.

I didn't trust my discernment. *Was this love?* I sought Jesus for wisdom and clarity. I even suggested that we separate—to allow time to prove that we were on the right track. But that was hard since we liked to dance together Thursday nights and we really enjoyed each other's company.

We went to Pastor Jimmy at church for counsel. At the session, Al actually cried at the thought that he might lose me. This was the only time I ever saw him cry. Pastor Jimmy recognized our sincerity. He agreed to assure my daughters that we were under his counsel and that he would look after the well-being of their mother since they lived so far away.

Mom and Pastor Jimmy were both growing fond of Al. They were our biggest supporters. The Stepping Stones members were too. They helped chip away at my own reticence. Besides, I began to understand that age difference should not be the factor to prevent a relationship. Some couples were the same age but had strain in their marriage due to sickness, like a couple we knew at square dancing. And who was to say that Al would die first? I got a call from Sunshine to give me news. Her husband Richard's widowed grandfather had married a woman fifteen years younger. She had suddenly died from leukemia, only two years after their wedding. Life had no guarantees. Age should not be a deciding factor.

At the fourth month, Al brought me four long-stem yellow roses.

Al belonged to a health club in Gloucester where he followed an aerobic water routine to keep himself limber. He wore a float belt around his chest that kept him buoyant while he exercised. I went along to swim laps on the other side of the pool. We then soaked in a swirling, jetted hot tub. Al commented on how fun it was to have my company. He had been going to the pool alone for years.

Afterwards, I was putting my sneakers on in the ladies' locker room. Jesus surprised me with a personal encounter.

Out of the blue, a voice, a thought, so clear, not audible but not mine, said, "*I want you to love and care for this man. He needs you. You need each other. You have my go ahead. Don't hold yourself back.*"

That surely was a voice from above, because my own mind did not come up with such a clear resolve. After all, I was living out my singleness wholeheartedly. This had been a directive that was beyond me. It had to have been from God. The year 2000 had come without calamity. So Al must have been God's answer to my prayer for someone to help me and Mom get safely through to the Mayan's "end of the world" prophecy.

I decided this was a confirmation from the Lord that Al was to be my man. An undeniable love was growing between us. Even so, I still thought, *He's thirteen years older.*

I finished tying my shoes.

I had one more holdout question. It had to do with intimacy. There was a woman named Danetta who was staying in her RV in the driveway of her son and daughter-in law in White Stone. She and her husband traveled around the country to their various children's homes and stayed for a few months to join in with their children's and grandchildren's lives. She was like a mother hen to the women in our church, encouraging us in the Lord and giving us truths from the Bible. She even paid for us women to go hear a Christian speaker named Joyce Meyer in Virginia Beach.

Not knowing about older years, my quest was to find out what one could expect. I knocked on Danetta's RV door and, fortunately, she was there alone. She welcomed me in. I sat down at her little dining table and said, "Danetta, I have met a man who is thirteen years older. He's 69. I'm falling in love with him. And I wonder..."

She interrupted me to say, "Are you wondering if there's any sex life at that age?" She knew what I was there for. She said, "Yes, there is. I'm seventy and my husband is seventy-one and our sexual life is better than it's ever been." They had been married since they were young.

So that clinched it for me. I had no more reason to hold back. For years I had asked the Lord to take away my sexual drive so that I would not be frustrated as a single person. There was no telling what would transpire between Al and me but I needed to give myself the go-ahead if we were going to be more than just buddies.

It was the fifth month. Al faithfully brought me five long-stem yellow roses.

From Courtship to Ministry

Al and I continued working our jobs. Although he had retired from the Navy some twenty years earlier, his expertise as a consultant was sought after and well compensated. Often, he was away for days in the DC area working on special assignments. Bit by bit, I learned about his Navy career and my respect for him grew exponentially. The more I got to know Al and his capabilities, the more awed I was that he chose me. God had given me an important assignment. I wondered if I could live up to the call.

Al told me about building submarines, and details of nuclear propulsion, and his close working relationship with the famous, irascible, Admiral Rickover. Al had exciting adventures on the sea on both surface and submarine ships. He went twice to the North Pole in the nuclear submarine USS *SKATE*. I found out that Al was the first, and probably only, man to have stood on, flown over, and gone under the North Pole. He showed me the *National Geographic* article from 1959 that described those Navy exploratory Arctic journeys and the book written by his skipper, James Calvert, called *Surface at the Pole*.

"You ought to write a book," I told him. I was into books, because I was working with a publisher and got to meet and work with some of the authors. They were just ordinary people who had something to say. One, Mary Archer St. Clair, had a book published at age ninety-two.

Al and I started going to White Stone Nazarene Church regularly. Besides the Sunday School, we joined a group that had begun a Food Bank there. On Saturdays, people in great need lined up to receive bags of groceries that our church had purchased at a food supply outlet in Richmond.

Our job was to help load the bags and make sure the elderly got safely to their cars.

Times were tough for many people, especially for the Bay watermen who were laid off. The menhaden fish supply was in decline, so fewer boats were active. Likewise, the oyster population had suffered a disease, and the industry was halted while the reefs were being restored. There were others needing food who just didn't have jobs, or who were generationally poor.

One day, I was riding around with Al and he stopped at a thrift store. I found out that he enjoyed finding bargains at second-hand shops. It could be a model ship kit for a grandson, or a bobblehead for a neighbor's child, or a thermometer for his workshop—whatever suited his fancy. This time, though, he had an idea he wasn't sharing with me. I saw him talking to the owner, who was smiling. Al always made store clerks smile. Before I knew it, he was carrying two black trash bags of used clothes out the door.

"What are you doing?" I asked him. "You didn't need to pay? She just gave them to you? What do you want them for?"

"She was planning to throw them away," he said. "I'm going to open a clothes bank at church and give them to the poor."

I couldn't imagine how he could pull that off. The church was already crowded. I put the idea out of my mind, until he came over one day all enthusiastic and told me he had gotten Pastor Jimmy's permission to use the empty rooms on the third floor of the church for the clothes bank.

"C'mon and see," he urged me. I didn't want to be bothered with the dusty dregs from the back rooms of a thrift shop. But I climbed the stairs just to please Al and was surprised to see three ample rooms. Al had strung ropes horizontally from nails he drove in the rafters. He had collected a pile of wire hangers. The church had given him an old Sunday school table for sorting, and the Tuckers from church had donated a window air conditioner. Bags of clothes sat on the floor.

"Here you go, Honey," he said, as he handed me a hanger. He reached into the bag and brought out the sweetest pink baby's onesie. "Hang this up right here." He pointed to the rope. I did what he suggested. At that very moment, I was "hooked" myself. I couldn't wait to get the clothes hung up and sorted into categories. Pretty soon we had women's, men's, children's and babies' outfits all organized and labeled in the three rooms. Donated clothes poured in.

Al amazed me. He was showing me that if you wanted to get something done, you just did it!

We opened the Clothes Bank every Saturday. People knew they could come to our church and get free food and clothes on the same day. We were doing the Lord's work, and it felt good. Also, it was a good way for Al and me to spend time together and minister as a team.

There was a third person who joined us. Mary came regularly to haul bags of clothes home to her family and neighbors. Weeks later, she came not to take but to help.

"I sho' miss shuckin' them oysters," she said in a moment of melancholy. But the light-heartedness of our third floor interaction lifted her spirits. She noticed when Al and I were flirtatious. "Oooh! You two be in love," she teased.

Then one day she followed me to the back room. Her matted black hair was wrapped in a kerchief. Her miniature black body reached only to my chin but her voice was full, like out of Porgy and Bess. She declared to me, "Um-um-um-um, umm. Girl! What did yo' mother feed you when you was growin' up? She done good! If I had a bum like yours, I'd *flaunk* it everywhere I went!"

The first year of courtship brought me such joy. I bought a pair of water boots and learned to be a Chesapeake fisher girl. Al took me out in his runabout motor boat to explore the creeks and even parts of the expansive Bay.

He introduced me to gill netting. I steered the boat at slow speed while he let out the long gill net. It looked like the net on a tennis court but with a smaller mesh. Each end had a tall pole with a triangular red flag atop and an anchor on the bottom. Once the net was stretched out in the water, all one could see were the tops of the two poles with their flags bobbing far apart from one another. Boaters knew not to steer their boats between the two flags and snag their propellers.

We left the net rig there for a change of tide. Then we returned to haul it back into the boat by layering it in a large trash can. Al extricated all the caught fish. We threw the inedible bunkers back into the water, but kept the croakers, stripers and blues.

Al cleaned them when we got back to Mom's dock. Some he filleted. He cut off the heads and tails of the smaller ones and gutted them. I steamed them whole. We had plenty of fresh fish dinners and lots more in the freezer. We caught crabs and bought fresh oysters too.

Al had not always been a fisherman. In fact, he grew up far from water, near the panhandle of Oklahoma in a little town called Shattuck. He was a first generation American. His parents spoke German, so he did too, until he started school. They had come from the Volga River basin in Russia, where German families had farmed the lush soil according to a one-hundred-dred year arrangement made by German-born Czarina Catherine.

Another czar came along and reclaimed the land. During the subsequent time of upheaval, the Germans fled to many countries. Al's parents chose the United States. His mother, Eva, who was seventeen years younger than his dad, spent her teen years living in a dugout house in Oklahoma. She never attended school, either in Russia or the U.S. Al's father finished second grade in Russia.

As we sat in various restaurants, I learned how Al's father, David, a soft-spoken man, was a cowboy on the central western range before he married his first wife, Amelia, who died of the great flu. He later met Eva, bought land, and raised cattle. Al was the youngest of seven children, the two oldest of whom were his half-siblings. His sister Wilma always stayed in his hometown of Shattuck. His sister Cecilia lived in Brighton, Colorado. His brother, Dave, who had also settled in Colorado, had died of a sickness. Tragically, his sister, Olivia, only two years older than Al, died as a young bride from a gas explosion in her Ellis County, Oklahoma, kitchen. All of his Oklahoma family would eventually be buried in the Shattuck area cemeteries. Dave and Cecilia were buried in Olathe and Brighton cemeteries in Colorado.

Al was a good story teller and, bit by bit, I was getting a picture of his childhood and how he ended up at the U.S. Naval Academy. He lived simply and dressed the same. He didn't smoke or drink, and he loved the

Lord, so there wasn't anything pompous about him. It was easy to make him my best friend.

As a teen, Al spent his summers and weekends working on his sister Wilma's farm, running the tractor across the arable land with the dust swirling around his head. There were no cabs on the tractors, nor radios. He told me that during night shifts, as he traversed endlessly back and forth on a section of land, he would sing tunes he had heard on the radio and make up words to them. But as hard as he tried to entertain himself, the monotony was real.

One day, as a discouraged teen, he sat on a downtown curb, praying to God and thinking to himself that there had to be something greater for him in the big world out there. Then, through his father's association with a congressman, Al received an unexpected appointment to the Naval Academy.

"And that's how my Navy career began," Al explained. "It was a blessing."

When I met Al, I had told him that, besides having Jesus foremost in my heart, I was committed to looking after Mom in her senior years. That was no problem for Al, as he and Mom got along famously. She loved to cook for him too.

But she slowed down gradually when hip pain deterred her from walking to the kitchen. I took her to an orthopedic surgeon, who confirmed that she needed a hip replacement. He said that her age of eighty-seven should not be a problem. So my siblings and I all agreed that Mom should go ahead with the hip surgery. The surgery was completed and Mom recovered surprisingly well; however she seemed more passive after all the care-taking she received.

The door to Mom's room was down a long carpeted hall. When she returned home from the rehab center using a walker, I noticed that there was a concave dip in the hall floor to her room. Al saw it too and was alarmed.

"That's pretty serious," Al said.

"I'll call someone to take a look under there," I decided. I could just imagine what a tight, dirty squeeze it would be for someone to venture under a house that had once been flooded underneath. The next thing I knew, Al himself crawled under the porch, opened the trap door on the foundation, and disappeared. He was gone with his flashlight and measuring tape for what seemed like an hour.

He emerged with a grim report. The house had several flaws. The floor sagged because a joist had not been nailed into place; an air duct had become disconnected, meaning that we had been heating and cooling the world; Mom's shower water was draining onto the dirt; and, if that wasn't enough, the insulation under the floor boards of the middle room had disintegrated due to the intrusion of creek water.

Mom and I thanked Al for his sacrificial inspection. We talked it over. Al made a plan for repairs. He would recruit people to help, including Bruce and his son Jeff, who were expected for a visit, and Associate Pastor Jeff from church, who was a builder and would have house jacks.

Shortly after Al left in his muddy clothes to return to "Clifton," I heard a cat meowing. It was Purry, who had followed Al under the house and gotten himself closed in.

"Oh no!" I said to Mom. I hated to bother Al, who had already gone beyond the call of duty. But I didn't have a choice unless I crawled under the deck and over the muck to open the trap door myself. I pictured slimy eels, sharp clam shells, raccoon feces, the smell of dead fish and the like. So I called Al on his new cellular phone, and he came back and freed Purry.

"No problem," he said as I thanked him. "I'm honored you asked me. And I'm glad to see you again." He did all of this with no complaint. He showed me an aspect of his character that I admired. He was truly a willing servant.

I was getting more fond of him as I got to know him. We interacted and chatted together as peers and not like we were thirteen years apart. I had come to view myself as a new person, not one who was scarred or battered by life, but one who was fresh and ready to begin a whole new way of being. Al's positive interest in me helped greatly. I could see I was a good influence on him too.

The next time we met, Al was all cleaned up and bearing six yellow long-stem roses for me. I knew we both had fallen in love.

The months flew by. The roses continued to come—faithfully on the same day of the month. Al's constancy and admiration gave me a sense of security I had not known. He really cared about me and my well-being, about my health, and my spiritual growth. In fact, he had loved me unconditionally since the day we met. Nothing I told him concerning my past would turn him away. Even the fact that I had been a consort to rebellion against our government, while he had been devoting his life to our national defense, was not something he held against me.

Al understood that he, too, had need of forgiveness. Together we recognized that we were washed clean of our sin in the eyes of God. Just as Jesus had forgiven us, we forgave each other. It had to be God's love, compassion, and even His sense of humor that put together a former pot-smoking hippy with a patriotic hero.

Three milestones marked the end of the year 2000: we graduated from the beginners class of the Stepping Stones Square Dance Club; Al presented me with a fragrant bouquet of twelve long-stem yellow roses; and we made the decision to become officially engaged.

Yellow roses of faithfulness.

A Dazzling Proposal

Mom's sister-in-law, my Aunt Vidal Clay, unexpectedly showed up for lunch on the day Al and I had chosen to officially get engaged. She and her son George periodically stopped by when they flew from Connecticut to North Carolina in his Piper Cub. Normally, Mom would pick them up at the nearby Topping Airport but Mom had relinquished her car key to me. She had confessed that she was often getting lost when driving, even going against the traffic on a familiar one-way street into White Stone. Mom was also losing her touch in the kitchen. She would need my help to prepare a nice luncheon for her visitors.

Already I had seen signs of Mom having dementia. One icy day, she suddenly darted out of the house, without a jacket, and got in her car. Nobody dared go out on the roads that day.

I ran out and stopped her before the key was in the ignition. "Mom! Where are you going?" I asked her, out of breath.

She looked at me and announced, "We're out of cat food. I'm going out to get some."

"No, Mom. No. You can't. The roads are icy and slick. No one's going out today." She looked at me like I was scolding her as a child. In a way, I was. I added, "Besides, Mom, you don't even have a jacket on. Come back in the house with me. We'll open a can of tuna for Purry and Cerry. We can get cat food tomorrow." Mom reluctantly got out of her car and followed me into the house.

It was hard for Mom to see herself failing. When she couldn't write clearly in her checkbook or do the math, I offered to help her. She soon let me keep the register.

On another day, I came home from work and Mom complained of chest pain. "I felt it the whole time we were playing bridge," she told me. She explained that while she was looking out the window for her friend Priscilla to pick her up as arranged, she had clutched at the thought that she was delaying the start of the game. To save time, she began to walk as fast as she could down the long dirt lane to meet the car closer to the paved road. By the time Priscilla arrived, Mom had gotten all the way to the mail-boxes, "almost jogging," she said. Her chest hurt. She had not mentioned her pain to her friends.

I took her to the emergency room. They then transported her by ambulance to a hospital in Richmond, where it was determined that Mom had had a cardiac episode, not a heart attack. Thankfully, there was no damage to her heart. Her family doctor did an overall evaluation and confirmed that her impaired reasoning was being caused by dementia.

Al was fully aware of "Dottie's" changes in behavior. He had seen first hand how she was struggling with daily living. "You know Mom's not going to be able to live by herself," I told him. "Are you sure you want to marry me? Mom goes where I go."

"I'm right there with you," Al reassured me. "I respect your commitment to your mother. We'll take care of her together."

So, with Aunt Vidal's arrival by airplane, Al and I postponed our daylight engagement ceremony until that evening. Weeks earlier, we had picked out a diamond-studded band which would also serve as my wedding ring. It had arrived at "Watsons' Landing" by post in a small box. I wanted so much to peek at it but restrained myself. Al had been away in DC on a consulting job and was leaving again, so we had chosen that day for the engagement. We would motor down the creek in Al's boat, the *Krista Krat,* which was named after the first of his nine grandchildren.

By the time Aunt Vidal left, it was already quite dark. We decided to go out in the boat anyway. With no flashlights and no motor, we pushed off from the dock and paddled out. It was very quiet on the black water.

It felt like a holy moment. All the water creatures were still and we were there, just the two of us.

Al got down on one knee in the front of the boat. He reached in his pocket and pulled out the little velvet box. Just as he opened it, a startling searchlight flashed onto the ring. The diamonds sparkled with a super-natural dazzle. We both looked up to see who was spying on us, only to see a gigantic orange harvest moon rising over the trees. We both gasped, then laughed. God was so good. He loved us so much. He arranged it all.

Al spoke a proposal that truly touched my heart. Here was a thoughtful, sincere Christian man who really loved me and was asking me to share my life with his. Back in the house stood a tall vase with a dozen yellow roses, a token of Al's intention to always look out for the best for me.

He actually asked, "Cecily, will you marry me?"

My love for him had grown to where I couldn't imagine life without him. Of course, I said, "Yes."

The First Four Years

Marriage plans involved the usual practical matters like where we would live. We decided to sell Al's house "Clifton" and find a place closer to Mom, one that would also accommodate her when needed. We found a spacious, stretched out waterfront house on Indian Creek in Kilmarnock. We named it "Pebble Run" because of its long gravel driveway. It had a large workshop to accommodate Al's decades-old collection of tools, nuts and bolts. I saw early on that, happily, Al was handy, like Dad. He even shared the same birthday, December 17th.

Unlike Dad, who began by tinkering on old cars, Al's skills were developed as a boy when he worked on his sister Wilma's farm near Shattuck, Oklahoma. He was born in 1929 during the Depression. Times were tough, and then the family had to make a temporary move to Missouri to escape the dust storms. All his life, he learned to fix machinery, build things and make do. Even on submarines in the Navy, he had to be resourceful. There were no hardware stores to run to.

Al's ingenuity showed itself over and over as we created our new homestead. Into the years ahead, he continued to be clever and inventive, often having the satisfaction of using one of his boards or a piece of metal he had saved for such an occasion.

Both of us stopped working at our jobs in order to renovate and furnish "Pebble Run," sell "Clifton," and plan our wedding. At the age of seventy, Al was ready to take down his consultant shingle and enjoy full retirement with a new bride.

Combined, we had seven children. Not all of them were sharing our joy. I tried to see it from their perspective. *"Not again,"* they must have thought. I felt compassion for them. No matter how many years had passed since the family they'd known and loved had broken apart, the painful ripples of divorce continued to flow. I could see how it would hurt to see their Mom or Dad move on again and seemingly leave them in the wake. No wonder scripture said that God hated divorce. Divorce not only affected children, but our siblings, neighbors, friends, the whole extended family. It affected Al and me too and our ex-spouses.

No one plans to get a divorce. The key to recovery for me was to extend forgiveness and receive it, especially towards myself. Jesus set the example and I loved Him for that.

Al and I had both worked through our disappointments and wrong choices. We took a lot of solace from scripture. I was taught at COS to personalize verses from the Bible; to place my name in the context and see how that helped to apply God's Word to my life. As Al and I put together our wedding service, God gave me a personalized version of Isaiah 61. I typed it out and shared it with Al. It went like this:

Isaiah 61 for Al and Cecily at their Wedding – January 13, 2001

The Lord has come and anointed us.
He has brought good news to these [two] afflicted ones.
He has revived our broken hearts, and liberated us in His forgiveness.
He has comforted us in our individual mournings.
Now He is giving us a garland instead of ashes,
An oil of gladness and joy instead of mourning,
A mantle of **PRAISE** instead of a spirit of fainting.
We will be called **oaks of righteousness**, planted by the Lord,
that HE may be glorified.
The Lord is at work in our lives to rebuild the ancient ruins,

To raise up and repair former devastations and the deso-
lations of our past,
Even of many generations.
With His love, we will reach out to strangers and
loved ones,
And God will use us to show His mercy and love.
Instead of shame and humiliation,
God has promised us a double portion of His joy,
Both here on this side of Heaven,
And unto our everlasting life with Him.
We will rejoice greatly in the Lord,
Our souls will exult in our God;
For, as a bridegroom decks himself with a garland
And his bride adorns herself with her jewels,
He has clothed us with garments of salvation
And wrapped us with a robe of righteousness.
And so-
As the earth brings forth its sprouts
And as a garden causes the things sown in it to spring up,
So the Lord God will cause **righteousness** and **PRAISE**
to spring up
[In this couple] before all peoples. **AMEN**

Becoming the Admiral's Wife.

We received this word as a prophecy for our lives. It gave us hope and vision and challenge. It expressed the unity I had felt the first time I held hands with Al at the Stepping Stones class. We recognized the importance of keeping God in our relationship. Big things were ahead but we didn't know what. We began holding hands every time we prayed as a reminder that Jesus was right there with us. He promised that when two or three were gathered together, He was in their midst. And we always prayed in Jesus' Name.

Pastor Jimmy officiated our wedding ceremony, which included the lighting of three candles, two to represent the light in each of us and the third tall candle to symbolize unity with the Lord, who was the light over us both.

We decided to make our wedding fun by having a square dance reception after the ceremony. We had use of the entire hall at the Topping Airport. The owner of the Pilot House Restaurant next door took care of all the food and details. Al wore a western shirt and I had found a floor length copper-toned sateen dress topped by a matching fringed bolero jacket. Children, grandchildren, nieces, nephews, siblings, and friends, most of them from the northeast, all pieced together their best interpretation of western wear. The live caller from Stepping Stones taught everyone how to Alemande Left, Dosado and Promenade. In short order, he had all of our wedding guests configured into squares of four couples each, whirling, whooping and hollering in easy square dance moves as the dance floor came to life.

The whole wedding day was down-home and simple. There was no alcohol, just good clean fun. It set the tone for our preferred lifestyle.

We were unsure Mom should be left alone in her house. But providentially, Bob was going through a separation and divorce from his wife in California and had decided to return to the east coast to live. It worked out perfectly for him to stay with Mom during the months he was transitioning to settle back in New Hampshire, where he had raised his two boys. He was a great caretaker and companion. He played familiar music which she loved. He read to her and they worked on jigsaw puzzles. The time was therapeutic for both of them.

As spring arrived, the neighbors across the cove uncovered their tall-masted sailing boats. The brightly painted red and blue hulls immediately caught my eye. They stood out against the dark water. Weathered wood docks and spring green trees completed the colorful scene, which was reflected in the still creek.

I called Al over to the kitchen window. "Take a look," I said. "We have a true-to-life calendar view right from our own kitchen sink! How blessed we are to live here!"

Before long, "Pebble Run" became like a little farm. Miss Vickie the cat joined us. Al put up a clothesline for drying our clothes. We bought chickens and enjoyed fresh eggs for breakfast. He built us a raised garden shaped like a boat and grew tomatoes, squash, cucumbers and a variety of goodies for our meals. He established a berry patch too. He even "dug" a garden watering well by pounding a pipe deep into the ground.

Al incubated quail eggs, then released the covey into the surrounding woods and fields when they were full grown. In time, their plaintive bob-white call could be heard across the cove until it disappeared. Canada geese and wild ducks came to eat corn at our feeder. A white swan carrying babies between her upheld wings swam close-by for a visit. We saw deer in the fields and horses in a neighbor's pasture.

Our waterfront had a sturdy dock and a boat lift. Besides the runabout *Krista Krat*, we kept a larger motor boat called the *Ella B* for exploring the greater reaches of the Chesapeake Bay. We loved following the channel markers, where we saw osprey on huge stick nests. This inspired Al to get a permit to install a tall osprey pole off our bulkhead. We hoped that a pair of these large seabirds would venture up the creek to nest, so we could watch them raise a family. Sadly, they never came.

However, since gill netting was still our hobby, Al devised a way to catch fish without using a boat. He stretched the net under water from our dock to the osprey pole, attaching it with a rope and a pulley, like a city clothesline. It worked beautifully. Our freezer was always full of delicious fish. Instead of frying them in oil, I microwaved them in a special steamer.

Al was fun to cook for. He was complimentary and appreciative but he asked that I not use butter. "When I was a child, my Mom and Dad operated a cattle feed sales store in Shattuck that also purchased and tested cream from the farmers before delivering it to the creamery where it would be made into butter," Al explained. "The cream came from the dairies in metal cans that sat in a dark room. We didn't have refrigeration. Too often, I saw rodents and bugs floating in the cans and I smelled sour cream." He didn't need to say more. I understood and respected his aversion to butter.

One thing I lacked was regular exercise. Our new home in Kilmarnock was too far from White Stone for me to meet the Little Bay walking group. So I walked the wooded country roads by myself. Later, I joined a Curves women's fitness center that opened nearby. But I missed my walking friends.

Soon enough, though, we made friends. We met Ellen, the one with horses, and her husband Jim. Also, the Nazarene Church grew and we made several other close Christian friends, like Brenda and Buddy, who ate breakfast every morning at Lee's Restaurant in Kilmarnock. New friend Zena suggested, "Why don't we get a group together to join them?"

Thus began an ongoing Lee's Breakfast Group on Tuesday mornings. Each time we met at the long table, Jo and Ken reined us in from our lively chatter and laughter (which was usually sparked by Al) to ask if anyone had a need for prayer. We then began our breakfast time with prayer. I was glad they did that, because it kept us "ever mindful of the needs of others," as my family used to say during grace at Cackleberry meals.

The church outgrew the three story house and moved temporarily to the abandoned White Stone elementary school building. After a brainstorm session, our breakfast group came up with a plan to raise money for a church building fund. We would hold yard sales at the church. Zena and Ed, Brenda and Buddy, Ralph and Neelie, Al and I, and other retiree members held yard sales regularly. There was no problem getting items to sell. There were left-overs from yard sales and what we gleaned from vacated houses after families had taken everything they wanted. We displayed the sale items on tables comprised of plywood boards on saw-horses. We marked the items on each table at just one price to make it easier for us and the customers.

We each had our self-appointed tasks. Zena washed any dirty objects. Al and Ed oversaw the set-up, flow, and ultimate removal or storage of our inventory. Buddy and Ralph helped carry heavy objects to cars. Neelie was great at sorting and displaying books and linens. Brenda and I wore carpenter's aprons and took money from customers. Others came to help. We were a busy, happy, tired bunch. And we were successful to contribute money towards a new church facility.

Ed, who was an accomplished architectural interior designer of famous people's DC homes, and Buddy went on to be key builders of the big, beautiful new church. Al and I were happy to see that the Clothes Bank ministry not only continued there with a team of volunteers, but even had its own outdoor entrance.

Another way Al and I enjoyed Christian fellowship was through weekly Bible study groups. I joined a morning women's group. Al went to one for men. Their group even went on a four day retreat to Windy Gap, Virginia, which was a meaningful experience for Al. He said they had focused on forgiveness and prayer.

We held couples studies in each other's homes. Together, we opened our Bibles to read and discuss scripture, trying our best to understand how to be good disciples of Jesus. Sometimes we disagreed on interpretation but we worked through it amicably, particularly with the help of one member who was good at leading the group and teaching. After study we had homemade snacks. We ended promptly so that we didn't burden the host.

At one house, I heard Shell address her husband as "Sweetie." *That's so nice*, I thought to myself. *I wonder if I can bring myself to call Al "Sweetie"?* He already called me "Honey" and "Baby." It came naturally to him. It must have been part of his German heritage. His oldest sister, Cecilia, who lived in Colorado, called him and me "Honey" over the phone and in person when we went to see her. It made me feel good. But it wasn't natural for me to use affectionate nicknames. Mom often used "Dear" to Dad or for me, and I heard her use it over the phone. To her best friend, Catherine Stradley, she'd say something like, "Okay, Dear. I'll give it to you at Prayer Group on Wednesday."

I decided I could do it. So I began calling Al "Sweetie" that very night. The first time, it sounded like I was just quoting Shell but soon after, it became spontaneous. I was glad to break through whatever puritan heritage was holding me back. Al sure was a sweetie, and I didn't mind affirming him that way.

After Bob left White Stone, Mom wanted to continue living in her home. I hired a college student to give Mom protection, cook dinner, and do light housework, in exchange for free room and board. It worked out for awhile. But I could see changes in Mom.

One day, I stopped over at lunchtime. Mom was standing at the sink, voraciously gobbling down cottage cheese from its container. Gone was the etiquette of sitting down before a placemat, bowl, and plate, and I saw no customary favorite half green pepper. Her blouse was misbuttoned and half untucked. I talked to the student, who agreed she would leave a plated lunch for Mom in the refrigerator whenever she was away at school.

Another time, I called Mom on the phone. She had such a bad cold she could hardly talk.

"Mom, you're sick!" I exclaimed. "Why didn't you call me? I'm coming right over."

I got there to find out that Mom had not even had breakfast. The student had gone out to a babysitting job until late the night before and was still asleep. Mom, indeed, was sick and in need of food and a nap.

This was the deciding moment. Our roles had reversed. I gave her tissues to blow her nose. "Mom, come with me. Have some lunch and take a nice nap at my house," I suggested to her.

"All right, Dear," she said. There was no hesitation. I gathered a bag of essentials for Mom and took her to "Pebble Run," where she ate lunch, then slept soundly all afternoon in her new room.

She never returned to "Watsons' Landing" again. She also immediately forgot what it looked like and soon even forgot that it existed. Dementia had set in for real. I let go of the student's help. Mom was now one hundred per cent my responsibility. All of my siblings put their trust in me and expressed their gratitude that I was willing to take on that challenge.

Al and I decided to build an addition onto the "Pebble Run" house to include an office and an extra guest bedroom and bathroom. We built a large deck off the kitchen overlooking the water. Everything we did was with the hope of entertaining our children and grandchildren. Al put up swings and a jungle gym. We had fishing gear, life jackets, water skis, high chairs, por-to-cribs and all sorts of table games and even coin collecting starter books. Al prepared work projects in his shop to enjoy spending Grandpa time with the older ones. He wanted to take them out in the boats and teach them how to drive. He pictured himself imparting sea stories about his own Navy adventures and anecdotes about the Great Depression of 1929 when he was born, and how the Dust Storms rolled into Shattuck and drove his family to a tomato farm in Missouri for two years until the dust settled. He was an exemplary grandfather, which I never had because of their early deaths.

Al had a great imagination and a cleverness when it came to talking with children. I watched him with fascination. He could draw them out of shyness or spark them into giggles. He got the older ones thinking and inspired them to plan purposefully for their lives. He practiced more often with local children, however. His grandchildren and their parents were obligated to complex schedules of sports, youth activities, work and other commitments. And some lived far away. So the visits seldom happened.

Slowly, we adjusted to the prohibiting factors of time and distance. For my children there was the added limitation of funds. Under it all, was the consequential ogre called divorce, and then the annoying addition of a step-parent, both of which probably affected motivation to visit. Al and I recalled our own families' closeness; how I visited Mom and Dad as a single parent twice a year; and he took two weeks' vacation every year with his wife and four children to drive cross country for a week to visit his parents. But our parents weren't divorced.

When it came to the two of us being a sought-after pair of grandparents for regular visits, we were living a pipe dream. Through disappointment over the way things were, we held onto our hope. We tried to figure it out. Maybe we should have lived closer to them but they were scattered all over. Maybe we should go see them instead of wishing they would come see us. After all, we were more mobile. It was still early in our marriage, and, someday, there would be better communication and new traditions established, we reassured ourselves. I consoled Al that probably half the grandparents across the world were also facing a meager role. It was all part of the hustle and bustle of the current age.

Whenever we did get together, we relished the beauty and blessing of family. In 2002, Mom turned ninety. We held a huge Watson family party for her at "Pebble Run." The turnout included my children and grands and all four of my siblings and most of their children and grandchildren. We lined up for a family photo wearing custom Watson Family T-shirts designed by a niece. Bob and his two sons used their professional restaurant cooking skills to feed everyone. We formed a bell choir and the young ones played songs for their Great Grandmummy.

Al had hidden a "buried treasure"—a nest with chocolate coins in gold foil and shiny Mardi Gras bead necklaces. He led the children through the woods on a fanciful hunt to steal Pirate Pink Beard's booty. I followed along as if I were one of the children, fully entering into Al's marvelous imagination. Life with Al enriched my days with fancy, faith and fun.

"Be watchful," he told them. "Pirate Pink Beard has been seen lurking about and could pop out at any moment!" The children loved it.

In 2003, I turned sixty. Sunshine surprised me by showing up with her little girl and baby boy. I had no clue they were coming. Oh, what a joy! Then, Al added more to the fun. On the pretense that he was taking all of us out to dinner, including Mom, we made an unplanned stop at the church, which was dark. But he had the key because of the Clothes Bank. For some unknown reason, he suggested that we all get out of the car and go in with him. When we got to the front porch, the lights flicked on. I saw a room full of happy friends and heard shouts of "Surprise!" and "Happy Birthday!" They had prepared a table of food, a personalized birthday cake, and decorations. During the party, Sunshine pointed out that we had four Watson generations present, and that each of us—Mom, me, Sunshine, and her baby boy—were all thirty years apart.

On another unique occasion, after his oldest granddaughter's wedding, all four of Al's children and eight of his grandchildren came to "Pebble Run." Some of them were meeting me for the first time. What a beautiful family. We ate dinner in a restaurant overlooking the Rappahannock River. The children slept at our house. They formed a large slumber party on the living room floor. It was great fun for them to be together with their cousins.

Stepping on the "Go-Getter"

A l and I continued to open the Clothes Bank on Saturdays until a new crew from church took it over. One day after we returned home, we heard a knock on our front door, a rare sound for our deep woods location on a cul-de-sac.

It was Eileen, our friend from couples Bible Study. Because she and her husband had opted to start attending a different church across the river, we hadn't seen her in awhile. On their final time with our group, Eileen had told us that the new church met twice a week—Sunday mornings and Wednesday evenings.

"Twice a week?" I asked her with an incredulous tone. "Who would want to go to church more than once a week?"

"We do," she answered. She and her husband, Larry, both seemed excited about their new discovery. "We just can't get enough of God's Word."

"We're learning so much," Larry had said. Then he added, "You're welcome to visit the church and see for yourselves."

Good for Eileen and Larry, I had thought. *Better them than me!* I just couldn't imagine what could make anyone be so enthusiastic about two worship services a week.

So there was Eileen at our door on this Saturday afternoon, having come from across the river for a visit. We invited her in. The three of us sat at the kitchen table. She began by saying that God had prompted her to come speak to us, and that she had resisted but God kept putting our names in her heart so that she knew she needed to obey.

"I feel a little uncomfortable, because I don't know how you will receive what I have to say," she confessed. Basically, Eileen described how she and Larry had had an increased hunger to know God more. When they went to the other church, they received what people called the baptism in the Holy Spirit.

That was a new term for me. It had been new for them too.

"It's different from the water baptism," she explained, "which celebrates the new, forgiven life in Jesus. You and Al know about that. You both know that you are saved and will go to heaven to live an eternal life with Jesus. You placed your faith in Jesus, you received God's salvation, and the Holy Spirit has been at work in you."

We both agreed that we had assurance of that. Eileen went on with the reason for her visit.

"The baptism in the Holy Spirit is a separate work which we read about in the Book of Acts, where Jesus told the disciples to wait in the upper room for Him to send power from on high, and the Holy Spirit would come upon them. It did, in the form of tongues of fire. The disciples were then emboldened to teach and preach and heal in the Name of Jesus. Remember when Peter denied Jesus three times?"

We told her we remembered.

"Well, after he received the Holy Spirit, Peter went out in the market-place and boldly preached to the crowds about Jesus. We can have that boldness too."

I heard Eileen's words. I had read them many times in the Bible. But what did that have to do with me, I wondered. *She's describing Holy Roller stuff*, I said to myself. It didn't fit in with my upbringing or any of the other churches I had gone to. In fact, the Nazarene church we attended had booklets describing doctrine against a second type of baptism.

I did remember, however, the Catholic charismatic group I had visited so many years earlier, the one where I had had to smoke a joint before attending because the nuns and the others appeared unusually animated about Jesus and I had wanted to be like them. Maybe they had experienced this baptism Eileen was talking about.

But, I wasn't ready to hear any more, and Eileen sensed both Al and I had deaf ears to her message. Her eyes teared up as she got up to leave.

Her parting words were said lovingly. "Just know that you can have the Holy Spirit come upon you to empower your Christian walk. It's good for you, for others and for His heavenly Kingdom. But you need to want the baptism to receive it. I encourage you both to want it."

Eileen left.

Al and I sensed this had been a momentous visit, and we both developed a curiosity about receiving the charismatic gifts of the Spirit. But time moved on and the thoughts faded. Until one day, we were leaving a dinner gathering at another friend's house. As we backed out of her driveway, Cass ran after us, hailing for us to stop. I opened my window and she handed me a cassette tape, explaining that it was a recording of a Christian teacher who had come to a camp meeting, and that she thought we would like to hear his Bible lesson on that tape.

It turned out to be a teacher named Andrew Wommack from Colorado Springs. His lesson happened to be on the baptism of the Holy Spirit. As we listened to it in the car, it made such good sense—that Christians needed to receive all that God offered spiritually. Al decided to visit Eileen's church but I wasn't ready. I asked him to go and report back to me.

In the meantime, Al and I had volunteered to represent our church at the Nazarene District Laymen's Retreat a couple hours away. It was a rousing weekend because the lay speaker, Dan Bohi, was a huge, emotional, energetic man who stirred up the couple hundred people there as though he had a big stick to get us out of complacency. The music was extraordinarily moving because some of the worship team musicians had come from Nashville to join the others in a kind of reunion.

During a time of music and worship, I was moved to go up front and kneel by the stage. I started to pray audibly but the music was so loud I could barely hear myself. The next thing I knew, I was praying in another tongue, a new language that I had never known.

Wow! I thought to myself. *I'm speaking in tongues! I must have received the baptism in the Holy Spirit!*

I was so excited, but also confused. How could that happen in a room of people who believe that speaking in tongues is not for today, as the booklet for sale in the back purported? Speaker Dan was sitting in the third row aisle seat. I went up to him and told him what just happened. He had not mentioned the Holy Spirit all weekend but I sensed he himself was filled with the Spirit just by his passion.

"Am I wrong to speak in tongues?" I asked him.

"Do you feel like you have sinned?" he asked me back.

"No," I answered. He just nodded his head. I thought he smiled too. I figured he was Spirit-filled and knew it, but just couldn't teach on that subject with this congregation.

After this weekend experience, Al and I began to attend Eileen's church, Cornerstone Fellowship. She was there in the front pews, raising her hands and jumping up and down in excited worship whenever the music began. My style was more like a sedate Episcopalian on the outside but inside I was whooping and hollering! It felt like I had just stepped on a spiritual "Go-Getter." Like Dad's International Harvester, I had suddenly received more power to go out in the Christian harvest.

One Wednesday evening service at our new church, we had a visiting preacher, Billye Brim, and her son Chip. They gave a lesson on healing prayer; how, in His earthly ministry, Jesus healed everyone who was sick. A small team of prayer leaders stood up front and many people lined up to receive healing prayer.

There was a man in a wheelchair who lingered near the front. I felt a strong anointing to lay healing hands on him but I was unsure of what to say or if I truly believed God would use me as a conduit of His healing power. The Spirit was so heavy upon me but I stayed in my seat, almost paralyzed, like the man in the chair. It was the beginning, however, of a future healing ministry for me.

Al was touched too. That evening, he and many others were baptized in the Holy Spirit. Not only that, but Al received healing prayer for his chronic hip pain. He didn't even realize he was healed until the next morning when he got out of bed and started shaving. He looked in the mirror and thought to himself that something was different. The difference was that he had slept all night and walked to the bathroom with absolutely no pain!

The two of us recognized that we were being called to do mighty works for Jesus. We were more than ever hand-in-hand in our faith walk, and deeply in love.

As a consequence, we started going to church happily two times a week!

In September of 2003, Hurricane Isabel tore through Virginia on its way to the north. It knocked out all the power for days, including the assisted care center where Mom was living to recover from a severe bout of pneumonia. Al and I were leaving for a Watson Cousins Reunion at my cousin Ross's house near Cackleberry, so we decided to rescue Mom from the power outage and take her with us. We had to dodge downed wires and trees, but made it safely to Pennsylvania.

While there, Mom stayed with Dita. The arrangement worked so well that Dita offered to keep Mom for a spell. Her house had a first floor bedroom and walk-in shower that was perfect for Mom.

During the week when Dita's day program for children was in operation, hired caretakers came in shifts to oversee Mom. It became a family affair. Marion lived nearby and took Mom to the hairdresser or the doctor. Bruce read books to her and made sure she went to church and out on lunch dates. The day care children showed her their toys and called her Grandmummy. As a result, Mom stayed happily with Dita for several years.

Without Mom, we were freed up to enjoy life on the Chesapeake Bay in a new way, with our friends, our gill net, and local involvements. We discovered the joys of road trips too. We had grown to love the recorded teachings of Andrew Wommack. In fact he was our Bible teacher of choice. We became partners with his ministry to help defray his cost of materials. We listened to his CDs while driving for thousands of sight-seeing miles—to Shattuck family reunions, to see Al's sister Cecilia in Colorado, who was also Spirit-filled, and as we circulated through mid-Atlantic and mid-western states. We drove to Niagara Falls and enjoyed the greenery of upstate New York and spent a week with my children at "Clay Cottage."

Anna and I later explored historic Williamsburg, Virginia, with her totally cute three-year-old son. I went there another time with Sunshine and we had a memorable lunch in an outdoor cafe where our waiter was movie-star handsome dressed in his colonial vest and white puffed sleeves.

Al's daughter suggested we take a Caribbean cruise, and we did. She lived on the Gulf in Mississippi, so was able to chauffeur us to the cruise line terminal in New Orleans. On that cruise, Al and I had our first argument. It had to do with which excursions we would sign up for at Cozumel. He deemed my choice too expensive. But I won. Ironically, it was to submerge in a glass-sided submarine. We saw the colorful wonder of the coral reef life. For the first time, I could understand why people liked to deep sea dive. It was a whole other world down there. We both acknowledged the experience was worth the price. However, neither of us was tempted to try deep sea diving.

During this time, my siblings and I agreed it was prudent to sell Mom's "Watsons' Landing" house. It sold without a problem to a young architect from Richmond. The funds were added to her trust which paid for her elder care. We had her antiques appraised and the five of us divided them up between us in an admirably congenial manner. Bob and I were the successor trustees of her trust with power of attorney. It was our job to assure her savings would provide for her lifetime needs. We worked together amicably as we considered these important decisions and disbursements.

In her early years of dementia, Mom had to be reassured that she didn't need to carry a pocketbook nor worry about bills. For awhile I gave her a purse with some spending money in it. Eventually, she let go of that feeling of responsibility. Finally she reached the stage where the thoughts of expenses no longer entered her mind.

One grey, dreary day in the spring of 2005, Al was sitting alone in the screened porch looking out at Indian Creek, dreaming about the fish that would soon be up at our end of the creek and available for fishing. The Holy Spirit startled him with a sudden directive.

Sell this house, the inner voice said.

Sell "Pebble Run"? Al asked. *And go where?*

Go there, was all he heard in his spirit.

Al said later that he identified with Elijah in the story in 1 Kings 17 where God told Elijah to go to a place by a brook and He would provide for him "there."

"I don't understand why," Al told me, "but it was a clear instruction to sell this property."

Surprisingly, I was not adverse to the idea. I trusted Al's leading, especially when it was a direction given by God. I loved the house by the water. Nevertheless, my attachment wasn't so great that I couldn't let it go. We spent days praying about how to proceed and where we should live.

We came up with an exciting temporary idea. We would buy an RV and live like Danetta and her husband. We would travel around the USA to spend time with our children and grandchildren, who were at that time living in Mississippi, Texas, California, Toronto, Maryland, and Virginia. We could be nearby without being underfoot. Things moved fast. The house sold. We bought a thirty-four foot trailer and a beautiful white diesel Ford Excursion to pull it.

Our first stop was just a four hour drive to be near Sunshine and Richard for the pleasure of caring for their two children while Sunshine gave birth to their third child, a beautiful boy, in June. We returned to Kilmarnock to close on the sale of "Pebble Run," scheduled for August twenty-eight.

In the meantime, Al's daughter in Mississippi showed us Diamondhead, the golf course community where they lived. Her husband, who was Rear Admiral of the Naval Oceanography and Meteorology Command, had his headquarters at nearby Stennis Space Center. When we saw the reasonable prices of the houses there, we grabbed one to make it our home base during the upcoming vagabond years. It had the advantage of being near family, including two beloved grandsons.

The closing on "Pebble Run" went smoothly.

However, on the next day, August twenty-nine, Hurricane Katrina, an angry category five, made a bullseye landfall at Diamondhead, Mississippi, where our new house was. Al's daughter and family took shelter in a bunker at Stennis.

Our realtor there wrote a desperate email to us in Kilmarnock saying, "I know you two are praying people. Please pray for my three homes in Diamondhead. One of the homes belongs to my parents. I am evacuating now. Pray for our safety too."

We did pray, specifically for the nine homes whose owners we knew. We prayed a bold declaration, like from Psalm Ninety-one, that "no harm will befall these homes, no disaster will come near their tents. God will command His angels to guard them, in Jesus' Name!" It was a personalized Go-Getter prayer, fueled by the Holy Spirit.

We waited in our home-on-wheels for a week before we received the good report that, indeed, God had protected our family and friends. What's more, all nine homes escaped the flooding and rampant wind destruction from the felled pine trees and wires.

We all were humbled by the goodness of God and how He answered our prayers of faith.

It was immediately clear that our home in Diamondhead was spared for the needs of the local community. With no lost time, a two-generation family of educators snatched up our offer to sell at cost. We were glad to have an intact house to pass on to them. They had much work to do to clean up and restore their homes and get the school into makeshift portable buildings.

We went to see Diamondhead two weeks later. Most of the damaged roofs were covered with blue tarps. Moldy drywall and family belongings lay in disheveled heaps along the once-pruned roads. This region had to take a break from status quo to focus on the extensive recovery. There were no longer any grocery stores, village amenities, restaurants, motels, gift shops, yacht club, bridges or Gulfside beaches. Newcomer retired folks like us were not needed.

We figured we had best get out of the way in Diamondhead and move onward to "There."

Texas

Kilmarnock friends showered us with send-off parties, cards, prayers, and good wishes as we prepared to leave Virginia. One family even decorated a sheet cake with an icing rendition of our traveling rig. Miss Vicki the cat got a new home with a single dad who answered our ad.

Off we went, a twosome newly unencumbered by any semblance of land ownership. Al drove the Excursion comfortably like a weathered sea captain. He just needed a pipe! I put my total trust in his capability. Since we were leaving the eastern coast, it was natural for us to head west. My job was to pore over maps to guide us.

Our first stop was with Al's longtime friends, Bill and Bracken, in Danville, Virginia. They lived down a narrow road in a wooded ravine behind a country club, and had pre-arranged for us to park the rig in the club's lot, which worked very well. Feeling a kind of euphoria, we all but skipped down the lane to their big white house. We had no address. We were in the world, but not of the world. Our future and direction were truly in God's hands and we felt at peace.

We decided to spend a week in Branson, Missouri, to enjoy light entertainment with the shows there. It turned out to be another kind of light, God's glory, that is. Evangelist Billye Brim was holding a prayer conference at the famous Chateau on the Lake, and we were not too late to attend, along with hundreds of people from all over the world. The excitement was electric. I was loving our exposure to people who were Spirit-filled Christians. Other leaders took the stage to sing and pray and speak, like Billye's lively family, her son Chip and daughter Shelli Brim, both of whom had their own ministry focus and strengths. Kenneth and Gloria Copeland appeared too. Also, Lynne Hammond from the Living Word Christian Center in Minnesota. She and Billye prayed together with such power. What impressed me the most was a woman named Marlene Klepees who spoke about her miracle healing. She had been blind and paralyzed with cerebral palsy from birth. Now she was able to speak, to see, and to pace across a huge stage as a living testimony to the power of healing prayer that is offered in faith in Jesus' Name. We were both moved by the dynamism of Holy Spirit power. I left there wanting more.

The next day, it was pouring rain. We boarded a bus to take us to Billye Brim's Prayer Mountain south of Branson for a tent service. Volunteers met us with umbrellas to escort us from the bus to the open flap doors of the mammoth canvas structure, where, inside, there was a sea of people seated in folding wooden chairs. Thankfully, the chairs had wooden rungs on which to perch our feet, because, as the storm increased, water ran in rivulets under the section where we were sitting. Kenneth Copeland got up to speak. His theme was how God is the light. In Him is no darkness. Light is the nature and character of God. God merely had to speak light into being. Copeland's verses came from Genesis and 1 John. Ironically, the tent darkened as the clouds thickened. But during his bold closing prayer, the tent suddenly turned bright yellow and glowed for thirty seconds. A momentary, perfectly-timed clearing in the storm allowed the sun to reveal God's glory over the tent filled with faithful believers. God showed Himself at that moment and I loved Him even more.

On Sunday, we visited the huge Faith Life Church in Branson to hear Pastor Keith Moore. He spoke about being in submission within God's army of believers, according to His ranking and order. I wasn't too clear on that message but I figured it was something like the ranking and order in the Navy that helped Al's ships and sailors stay safe.

Once again, we readied the RV to continue traveling. Pretty soon, we barreled into Broken Arrow, Oklahoma, to meet up with our Virginia friend Betti's step-brother, Jerry Spurrell, who had left Virginia to work with Pastor Mark Brazee at World Outreach Church. We arrived too late to make the church service but took Jerry and his wife out to lunch.

One thing led to another, and we ended up at the Rhema Bible Training College. We walked into a large classroom just in time to hear Lynette Hagin herself wrapping up a class in their Healing School. That evening, Terry MacAlmon, the worship leader from New Glory International in Dallas, Texas, just happened to be on campus as part of a world tour. Al and I attended. We were among hundreds of hungry Christians who were singing their hearts out to the Lord, their hands high in the air like they wanted to reach the very throne of God. Terry played the keyboard and sang his original worship songs. The words were displayed on large screens so we could sing along. I happily raised my hands too. I don't know when I have felt so in love with Jesus.

Al and I were being blessed as the Holy Spirit led us from one gathering to another. It "happened" that Rhema College was holding their annual "Call to Arms" Men's Conference for the next three days. Al and I looked at each other and said, "Why not?" So Al signed up and I had a lovely respite at the RV park in our trailer to reflect on all that we had encountered since leaving Virginia.

Hurricane Katrina had propelled us into Oklahoma and would soon blow us straight south into Tomball, Texas, north of Houston. We found Corral RV Park in Tomball, a friendly place to establish our home base while we awaited the birth of my fifth grandchild. He wasn't due until February 2006. We had arrived early, which gave us three months to enjoy Anna and her husband, Gregor, and their delightful first son who was three-and-a-half. Gregor's work with the government had recently taken them from Pennsylvania to Texas. They helped us acclimate to this huge, strange, proud former republic called Texas, where there was no state income tax. The people we met were so very friendly. A boot-stomping, cowboy culture blended its machismo with the ladies' bling and they met in the dance halls and cowboy churches.

We traveled to several surrounding towns, made friends with local business people, and started a breakfast club with our RV neighbors. I had lunch with Anna, visited her church, and got to know her friends. Her son loved to be read to and to go on adventures with Grandpa Al. We took him to swimming lessons and sometimes brought him for overnight visits.

On his first lesson, he refused to go into the water. He stood at the edge of the pool, folded his little arms over his puffed up chest, and told his teacher, "I'm not ready to learn how to swim. I'll be ready when I am five." There were no tears, no flailing of arms in fear, just a calm declaration that wooed the teacher to say, "Okay. You just stand there and watch. I think you'll be ready before you turn five." She was right. He was in the water before the lesson was over.

As weeks went on, we grew to love Texas. And I could hardly believe I was near my daughter and grandchild. We began to lose our wanderlust. For fun, we started looking for real estate. There was one house in particular that caught our eye. It even had two ponds and a large workshop. The prices were much more reasonable than in Virginia.

"Al," I said. "Why don't we sell the RV trailer and stay here. It's bulky to drive and I think the thrill is gone for both of us." We were on the same wave length. We ended up doing just that. We sold the trailer and the Excursion and bought the house with two ponds on Cherokee Lane in Magnolia. We even adopted a tri-colored calico kitten named Autumn.

The baby was delivered. When I held the beautiful new baby boy, I melted with love and awe. Lo and behold, I was a local grandmother for the first time. It was a fulfillment of a longtime desire. There was no need to pack a suitcase and travel to see these grandchildren or clean a guest room in anticipation of their visit. All I had to do was drive twenty minutes to be with my daughter, cuddle a baby, and have the baby's special older brother call me "Grandmommy." We dyed Easter eggs together and hunted for them on Easter Sunday. Al and I designed and created a carpeted playroom out of our two-car garage. We bought shelves and toys and a set of bunkbeds in anticipation of overnights for the boys. We even acquired the neighbor's blue heeler dog named Zipper. Out in San Francisco, Ezra and Lisa added to the grandchildren bundle by the arrival of their first child, a little girl. They brought her to meet us later that year in 2006. It was a whole new era, and we were loving it.

Al and I found a small church with a pastor who was a graduate of Rhema Bible Training Center. His sermons were his strong point. He obviously put lots of study into his preparation and delivered the message eloquently and with such a positive attitude, as though there were hundreds of people in the room, when in fact there was only a handful of us. I found out that he posted his sermons online using something called a podcast. This must have been a new direction for pastors. It seemed he didn't care if the church grew in numbers. They held a newcomers luncheon, which we went to. We sat at one table and the pastor and his faithful followers sat at another table, all but ignoring us and the other visitors. Perhaps they forgot the purpose of the occasion?

After awhile, Al and I looked for a church with the excitement and stimulus of a larger congregation, which we found almost across the street from where we had been going. It was a growing church with lots of young families. Al approached the pastor about starting a bookstore in the church since there was no local Christian source of books. I watched Al with fascination as he set up shelves and tables in the lobby, established an account with a discounted vendor, and stocked the little store with a variety of children's and adult inspirational books and Bibles. He opened it every Sunday. People stopped by to pick up the pastor's sermon CDs too. It was a great hit.

Healing Rooms

Ever since the day back in Virginia when I sensed a calling to lay hands of healing on people in need, I had many opportunities to offer a healing touch. Once, a Bible study friend in Virginia, Annette, had showed up at the Nazarene church after several weeks' absence. During the meet and greet time, I sat beside her to find out what had kept her away. She explained it was a stiff and painful neck. She couldn't even move it. I put my hand on the back of her neck and felt a huge lump there. I asked her if I could pray for her neck to be healed. Even though she had not been taught that healing was for today, she said, "Yes. Please do." I placed my hand on the lump and commanded it to "leave her body, in Jesus' Name." I kept my hand there and quietly spoke peace to her muscles. I rebuked inflammation, just like Jesus rebuked the wind in a storm. The pastor began to speak. I kept my hand there. It was not my imagination. The lump disappeared.

Annette looked at me and smiled. With tears in her eyes, she said, "The pain is gone. I can turn my head!"

And I whispered to her, "The lump is gone too." She felt the back of her neck and found out for herself. "Praise God!" we both said quietly, so as not to interrupt the service. We grabbed each other's hands and shook them with joy.

There were other people healed on our travels when I reached out to them, like a cashier with a bad back and a young mother with a migraine headache. I always first asked if they wanted prayer and if I could lay my hands on them.

One day, Al said to me that there ought to be a place where people could go to receive healing prayer, like a room set apart for that purpose. He went to his computer and looked up the words "Healing Room." Sure enough, we found an organization called International Association of Healing Rooms. We contacted them and found out that there were several active locations in east Texas for us to visit. We got in the car and drove to Healing Rooms in Houston, Corpus Christi, Brownsville, and McAllen. They varied in their accommodations, from a converted children's Sunday School room, to a hotel lobby, to a full brick house. One church in Brownsville had a healing team that ministered at the Farmers Market on Saturday mornings, then reported to the congregation on Sundays about the healings that had taken place.

Al and I liked what we saw. The main thing we learned was that starting a healing center was very doable. We wouldn't need anything fancy, but just a place to focus on the Lord's work and use whatever facility came our way. Thankfully, our pastor at Christ Fellowship Church was in agreement. We could use the church lobby and the rooms to each side of the stage. So we set the wheels in motion to become an official IAHR Healing Rooms location. We signed up, bought the training materials, went to the Fort Worth headquarters for training, found three pastors to affirm us, and received the stamp of approval to open the doors.

We called ourselves the Pinehurst Regional Healing Rooms. Al and I were Directors along with another couple from church. I was in charge of training and within a few weeks had twelve prayer team members ready to work in teams of four twice a week for three hours. They came from various churches. We established a close fellowship and had lots of joy in this ministry.

No matter what the person had going on when they entered our Healing Rooms, they always left with a touch of God's healing love. Sometimes, just the fact that other people cared about their woes and would listen and pray for them was all they needed in order to feel better.

Often we found that people carried aches, pains, and sickness in their bodies because they held unforgiveness over some grievance in their lives. The other party or circumstance may well have moved on but the person holding the resentment developed stress or bitterness, which the Bible calls "wormwood." The unforgiveness was eating at their insides. They needed to forgive in order to move on with their lives.

Al and I and some of our team went to a healing class given at Lakewood Church in Houston. The teacher was Joan Hunter who taught us how to minister to a spirit of unforgiveness. I used her method successfully many times. Curiously, it used a box of tissues as a prop. The box represented the offending person or situation. The tissue represented the sin or offense. I asked the person who was struggling with unforgiveness to pull out a tissue. They were now holding the sin of another. We recognized what a painful impact that offensive sin had caused. I asked them if they were ready to stop holding onto that offense. When they said yes, I held out my cupped hand, which I said represented the Cross of Jesus. I asked the person to repeat after me a prayer declaring that they were now giving that burden of another's sin to Jesus as they placed the tissue in my hand. No longer were they the keeper of another person's sin.

We usually ended up laughing in joy at the release that just took place. Physical healing was then closer at hand. Sometimes the healings were instantaneous, and other times they were gradual or not at all.

Our ministry grew and we moved our spot to a storefront in a small shopping center in Tomball. We did see some miracles take place, even ones that happened over weeks. One man, for instance, came in with a life-threatening blood disease. He had been discharged from his post office job because of absenteeism caused by his many hospitalizations. He was discouraged and distraught. We quickly discovered that he had a serious grudge towards his brother that had gone on for years. He agreed to let us pray with him weekly in order to bring peace to his body, mind, and spirit. Over those weeks, he forgave his brother. He began going to church again, and his wife did too. He got filled with the Holy Spirit. We declared healing to his red and white blood cells. We taught him to see himself as healed, because Jesus had taken that blood disease on His own body when He died on the Cross. At the fifth visit, he flung open the door of our center, held up a piece of paper which was his weekly lab report. Smiling, he declared, "This is the first time I have had a normal blood count in eight years! I am healed!" He went on to appeal to the post office to take him back.

There were many other happy testimonies of healing. One woman's left leg grew two inches so that she no longer needed her shoe insert orthotic. Another woman overcame a crippling shyness and learned to interact with others. We saw a widow suffering from loneliness and self-pity set free when she forgave her husband for dying.

I even found I could minister healing prayer over the phone. It didn't depend on our healing hands. A bedridden woman in Massachusetts found our number on the IAHR website. She wanted to talk to a person of faith in the "Bible Belt," she said. She had been unable to find any prayer warriors in her town. She said she was living in the loft of a garage in such filth that her own mother could not even approach her bed, but chose rather to climb the ladder and slide a meal on the floor in her direction. The young woman had an uncontrollable intestinal problem and told me, "My room is waist deep in used paper towels." My heart went out to her. She was not insane, but lucid and completely helpless. I told her I would gladly be her prayer partner and that she could call me anytime. I also called a Spirit-filled church in her town to see if they could look in on her and help. They knew this woman. But, they said, she would not cooperate with their suggestions, so they had given up ministering to her.

I wasn't sure of the outcome myself. I sent her Joan Hunter's book on healing and some others. For a year I heard from her periodically. She was starting to sound better. Then, one day she called me to say, "Guess where I'm calling you from. The mall! My gut is healed. I have cleaned up my loft. I'm out shopping for decent clothes so I can get on with my life!"

My response to her came from 2 Corinthians 1 (I found out later), "Hallelujah! What a God we serve! His promises are Yes and Amen! When we place our faith in Jesus, he uses us for His glory. Now, it's time for you to be bold and minister to others."

Al and I were paying $600 monthly for the storefront, which we considered as part of our tithes and offerings. Since the Healing Rooms were open only two to three times a week, we decided to call the place The Christian Center and open it up for groups to use free of charge. A church gave us thirty comfortable meeting chairs. We put in a coffee center and eating tables. Local employees came in to relax and eat during their lunch breaks. Bible study groups met there, including one focused on Andrew Wommack's teachings that Al and I attended. A Baptist church held a monthly hymn sing, and a woman ran a summertime children's puppetry camp. A pastor even used the building to get his start-up church going. It all seemed to work smoothly. We felt truly blessed.

Not all people were happy about Christians offering healing prayer. Although mainline churches taught about how Jesus, at the will of His Father, went about healing everyone during His three years of earthly ministry, they relegated that role to Jesus for back then, not to the contemporary church. In fact, we had serious disagreement within my family on that subject. Ezra, who always kept open phone communication with me and Al, asked me, "So Mom, tell me about this new religion of yours." Marion and Sunshine kept their distance.

Anna and Gregor, whose Bible mentors spoke against the charismatic movement, were counseled to not have anything to do with us. We were forbidden to see the children. I was crushed at their decision. It was like they thought we were doing the devil's work, instead of heeding the words of Jesus Himself. I was being obedient to His words in Mark 16:17-18, where Jesus said, "These signs shall follow them that believe; in My name... they shall lay hands on the sick, and they shall recover." For me, since I was a believer, to NOT lay hands on the sick would have been disobedient to the will of the Father. I had this high calling and it would have been wrong of me to turn my back on it. I decided not to be distracted by the resistance. I wasn't the only one with an anointing. Throughout the world, evangelists were healing people by the hundreds as they shared God's word.

Once again, it was time to endure a period of persecution for my personal walk with Jesus. Ironically, I was giving mother's hugs to hurting women in the Healing Rooms, when I couldn't even hug my own daughter or grandchildren. I thought, if we all died tonight we would all be in Heaven and we could talk this over with the Lord so He could mediate. Thankfully, before my earthly heart broke any further, Al and I met together with Anna and Gregor by Easter of 2008 and agreed to be reconciled. I had brought Mom, age 96, from Dita's in Pennsylvania to a nursing home in Tomball by then. We all enjoyed a short time of family interaction. Then, just months later, Anna and Gregor transferred to Virginia.

Back when our Healing Rooms staff had gone to a healing class at Lakewood Church taught by Joan Hunter, Al and I had met her husband at their book table. He told us Joan was looking for property in Magnolia (where we lived) as her ministry's new headquarters. We got to know her and her team and welcomed their presence, being glad that a vibrant healing center had come to town. Al even helped walk and assess prospective properties with her and her advisors. Their arrival was perfect timing for us, because God was moving us from Healing Rooms to something different, though I still had many occasions to offer healing prayer to people who expressed a desire for it.

Tomball Pregnancy Center

Al read in the newspaper about the construction in Houston of a high-rise Planned Parenthood building. It was to be the largest in the country. The top floors were to be dedicated to women who wanted to kill their babies by an abortion procedure. Al wondered where a woman would go for the alternative, that being to give life to her baby. He discovered that there was no place in the fast growing Tomball area. The closest pro-life pregnancy center was in Houston.

"What would it take to get one started?" Al mused with me one day when we were eating our favorite loaded potato soup at a lunch booth in Tomball. *Uh-oh* I thought. *This might turn out to be something big.*

And, indeed it did. We took our usual exploratory day trip to three different pregnancy centers in Houston. They were all based on Christian values of life. Women with unplanned pregnancies met with volunteer advisors who explained the three options available to them. In the first two options, she would carry the baby to term and give birth. She could either keep and raise her own child, perhaps with help from the father or her family, or she could allow another family to keep and raise the child through adoption. The third option was abortion. It was not advised. However, so that she and the baby's father could make an informed decision, the woman watched a film on what abortion entailed. The centers did not perform abortions nor refer the client to an abortion facility.

We liked what we saw. It happened that the manager in the Katy Pregnancy Center, who had shown us around, was moving near Tomball and would be willing to help us get started. We decided to proceed with the big project. We let go of The Christian Center lease where we held the Healing Rooms and leased a larger space a few doors down from the same landlord, who gave us a good monthly price break.

Al and I set about the task of requesting seed money and ongoing support from the area churches. Very few of them were of the mindset or budget ability to help us out. Three small churches did become regular money donors. Thankfully, our breakthrough came from Salem Lutheran Church, whose pastor, Wayne Graumann, shared our vision for what would later be known as Tomball Pregnancy Center. Salem Church offered fundraising, leadership, professional expertise and godly enthusiasm to help us get established.

In three full, hardworking months, on December 1, 2008, the Pregnancy Education and Resource Center (PERC) opened its doors. We had a full staff who had arranged and decorated the rooms to look both welcoming and professional. We also had an excellent Board of Directors who established form to the vision. They also helped with fundraising ideas. I volunteered to be the secretary of the Board. It was my first time being on a Board of Directors and I learned a lot. Al, who was Chairman of the Board, did everything, from carpentry and acquisition, to hiring staff, to leadership oversight. His mind was always thinking ahead to what the next step should be. I could see his Navy officer skills at work. He had to be the alert Skipper of the "vessel" called PERC.

All of the client meetings were behind closed doors and confidential, so we relied on statistics to know how many babies were saved. The Center offered continued help to the new mothers for their babies' first year. They could earn "Baby Bucks" by attending classes on pregnancy, infant care, parenting, and household management, etc. With the coupons, they could "buy" baby clothes that volunteers had organized in a separate room. Church groups held baby showers to help supply the clothing room. Other churches held baby bottle drives where people would fill bottles with cash to donate to the Center.

One day, I did get to go behind the closed door of a confidential session with a client. I happened to be the only person nearby who could speak Spanish, so they asked me to translate. The woman had been brought to the Center by her estranged husband, who was living an hour away. I saw him outside in the parking lot standing by his truck with his hand on the open door and one foot resting on the sill. The woman explained that he wanted her to get an abortion. They both thought PERC could supply that procedure. She was distraught, and I kept having to translate the volunteer consultant's reassuring words, "Don't be afraid. We are here to help you."

Through tears, she explained that she and her husband had four children—eight, nine, fourteen and sixteen. They had been separated for a year. She didn't believe it was right according to her Catholic faith to abort the baby. But, on the other hand, she didn't want her children to find out that she was sleeping with their dad. So she was willing to consider aborting.

The happy ending of this family's story is that, after hearing all their options, the parents both decided not only to keep the baby, but to get back together and resume their marriage. I praised God for His goodness, His mercy, and love.

Al and I retired from the Board. Our new good friends, Brad Bartlett and Pastor Tim Niekerk from Salem, both of whom had worked closely with Al from the beginning, took over the leadership. The Tomball Pregnancy Center continued to grow and get funding. It moved to larger quarters and became an established institution to celebrate life for hundreds of families.

The whole project came into being because of Al's creative mind, his vision and motivation, and his faith that God would not only provide what was needed, but lead the way to see it through. I couldn't help but love and admire my husband even more. He modeled ingenuity and godly leadership for me. And he encouraged me to take an active role in both the Healing Rooms and the Pregnancy Center. I thanked God for His blessing to bring Al into my life and to "assign" me as his helpmate.

Founders of the Tomball Pregnancy Center.

Over a period of years, Al and I underwent medical conditions off and on that required surgeries and recovery time. For me, there was a fairly non-routine abdominal surgery, a torn rotator cuff repair, plus a foot surgery. For Al, there were some close calls.

One was intestinal hemorrhaging that put him in the hospital's Intensive Care Unit for days. I prayed for him and believed in faith that the bleeding would stop or the doctors would find the source and be able to seal it. They kept replenishing his blood with transfusions. One night, he flat-lined. They called me at two in the morning to come in. The Lord had given me a peace that it was not Al's time to die.

Sure enough, by the time I got into the hospital, he had come back to life and his heart was beating again. The same faith was required when he had triple bypass and heart valve replacement surgery. Al bounced back beautifully, praise God. Our belief in healing prayer did not preclude the medical know-how and expert skills of doctors. We were appreciative of all they and their medical equipment did to determine cause and to repair our earthly bodies.

Al was now in his eighties and still active in the yard outside our house on Cherokee Lane in Magnolia. He raised a flock of chickens and supplied us with fresh eggs. I kept the flower beds but he tended the raised gardens that produced such vegetables as tomatoes, zucchini, onions, carrots, cucumbers, kale, and lettuces. I learned how to can, freeze, and dehydrate the abundance of what we harvested. He started a citrus grove of lemon and orange trees, which had to be covered against freeze in the winter. We bought a golf cart that helped him get around the two acres. Our dog Zipper either rode with him in the front or trotted behind. Zipper was Al's faithful sidekick. In 2008, furious Hurricane Ike had knocked down numerous tall trees which Al later cut up and burned. The resulting benefit of that catastrophe was more sunshine for better crops.

Life was good. We missed Anna and the boys but we kept in touch with them and all our children by mail, email and cell phone. I visited my girls and their families when I could. Sometimes they came to visit, especially one of Al's daughters, who began to call and visit him regularly. Ezra and Lisa had another girl and then a boy to bring my share of grandchildren up to eight. I made trips to San Francisco whenever I could. One time, Al and I drove all the way to California on a memorable trip. Ezra was busy building a beautiful deck, so Al pitched in and helped him. I had the privilege of spray painting their back fence.

Mom had moved to a special home in Magnolia called Stagecoach Senior Living, run by a Christian Romanian family. Mom's love of music stayed with her. She could remember words of songs better than conversational sentences. I held a singalong at the senior home every Wednesday evening. I used a DVD of a family group singing old familiar songs, like "Down By the Old Mill Stream" and "You Are My Sunshine." There were song sheets too. Mom and the residents loved our musical sessions.

Llano, Texas

The Houston humidity was getting the best of Al. Every summer, he suffered from low energy. The Tomball traffic was increasing with new flyovers and toll road ramps. It became difficult to maneuver the maze of highways to get to my supermarket. Both of us decided to look for a smaller town that would be less crowded and less humid. For a year, we took exploratory day trips. We wanted to stay in Texas. We found some interesting places but all of East Texas was fraught with humidity.

Finally, in 2011, we headed west into the Hill Country of Central Texas. It had been a year of great drought, so all the ranch lands were brown. But to me they were still beautiful. Curved and spiked cactus plants abounded in the uncleared spaces. Around every bend or over every rise was another view of distant hills that were dotted with mesquite and oak trees. We were fascinated.

By noon, we pulled into a town on our map called Llano. It sat by itself in the surrounding highlands. When I saw it from afar, I thought to myself, *Oh! It's the little town of Bethlehem!* The population sign said 3,330. It was too far from Austin for a reasonable commute, which meant small town peace to us. We expected to roll right through it. But then the charm of the town hit both of us. We saw the court house with a clock tower surrounded by shade trees, the old-time western storefronts, and the multi-arched bridge crossing the rocky Llano River. There were active shops on both sides of the river. "Let's cross the bridge again," I said. We turned around to cross the water again, this time noticing the lake to the west and its sloping lawn with boulders called Badu Park.

The coup-de-gras that made us stop and get out was a sign on Main Street pointing to Fuel Coffee House. Al was not a coffee drinker but I was ready for a noontime fivesies. We opened the 1800s antique door. The wide-planked wooden floors creaked when we walked on them. Inside, there were sofas, clusters of tables, a wifi counter, high ceilings, 150-year-old exposed brick walls, a music stage with a piano, and a friendly barista at the coffee bar. I tried to take it all in. Then I saw a cross on the wall. We found out that they were a community-supported, non-profit coffee shop, founded by a pastor, and they had a Christian heart to their existence and mission.

We needed to look no further. Both of us knew that Llano was our new hometown.

A realtor found us five acres outside the city limits, three miles to the west on a hillside with a view. Ironically, the house was an old double-wide mobile home—what we used to joke about owning. But, it had irresistible appeal—an open floor plan with a huge master bedroom and walk-in closet, two guest rooms, a stone fireplace, and lots of built-in shelving for our many books and memorabilia. Out back was Al's dream–a huge workshop and storage room. To the south were four raised gardens that were surrounded by a high deer-proof fence. Best of all, there was a community water supply from established wells. In spite of any of our previous snobby opinions, the fact was that we loved the house, the shop, the grounds, and the price. So we bought it.

Before long, both the sale of the Cherokee Lane house in Magnolia and the arduous move involving many trailer loads of belongings were behind us. We were settled in Llano. Al built a dog fence in the back yard so that Zipper could safely go outdoors and not run off to chase deer or kill a neighbor's baby goats, though he did do that once. We did keep him safely contained but he succumbed to Cushing's disease in 2014. Autumn, by then a full-grown ornery lap cat, continued to have free rein to explore the surrounding fields.

Mom was still at Stagecoach Senior Living in Magnolia at the time. A new friend named Roberta drove with me to pick her up. I wanted Mom near me so I could see her every day. I visited Mom almost daily for years. Many times, Mom was sleeping in her chair or just quiet. One day, she asked me if she was going to live there the rest of her life. Because of her dementia,

I wasn't sure if Mom remembered that one lives an earthly life then dies. I told her yes, she probably would stay there.

Then I asked her, "After you die, do you know where you will be?"

Mom answered, "Heaven only knows!"

With humor in my voice, I replied, "You're right, Mom. Heaven only knows!" We both recognized our faith meant eternal life with God and celebrated the thought with a good, joyful laugh together. These moments became rare as Mom slipped away to where she didn't know if I was her mother or she was mine. Later, she didn't even understand the concept of the mother and daughter relationship. She just knew I was somebody special who lighted up her day. She told me often that she loved me. But it became harder for her to speak a full sentence.

One day I saw Mom slumped over in her wheelchair, dozing. She was a hundred years old. We had recently celebrated her birthday with a pizza party for the whole nursing home staff.

I asked her, "How are you doing, Mom?"

She looked up at me in a lucid moment and said, "I find myself exactly in love with the whole world."

I shared this inspiring comment with all our family and the staff at the home. It made us feel her love all the more. Over the years, we had each been recipients of the precious ways she had reached out to us individually. She spent the next three years in a Llano nursing home, until that final night in 2014 when she quietly slipped away in her sleep. Bruce had her inspired quote printed on refrigerator magnets. Everyone got one of these magnets at her funeral after she died at age 101.

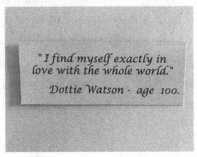

Mom stayed sweet and loving to the end of her life.

Although Mom could no longer express her love for Jesus, God reaffirmed His love for her in a supernatural way. At her funeral service, He floated a startling white cloud, shaped like a giant Holy Spirit dove, high in the blue sky over the church's steeple. We all beheld it in awe as we left the service and walked across the driveway to the reception. Mom was buried next to Dad in the cemetery behind Grace Episcopal Church in Kilmarnock, Virginia. She died on January 24, 2014.

The Holy Spirit, like a dove, escorted Mom's spirit to heaven.

It didn't take but a few months for Al to convert our home to a ranch. Or was it a farm? Whatever it was, we called it "Flag Creek Ranch." He visualized how to parcel the land into pastures and had fences built to provide three acres for animals to graze. Soon there were goats, later sheep. Al built a spacious chicken coop with an adjoining rabbit house, and we raised both chickens and rabbits. They had their own cage houses. Al decided to raise quail again too, like he did in Virginia. We got the quail eggs from a friend and incubated them to start the covey. When they were old enough, we released them. For a couple of weeks, they stuck around and I would see them on my back door steps and hear their plaintive bobwhite calls.

By a fluke, we met a woman who had two spotted miniature donkeys for sale. They were a brother and sister, one year apart. Their names were P. Newman and Missy Lou Cupcake. We bought them and they entertained us mightily with their startling hee-haws and comical antics. We gave them a half-deflated rubber ball, which they loved to pick up and toss to compete in tug-of-war with each other. Not only were they a pair of handsome, black-and-white kinetic yard art, they also qualified as livestock for us to begin the five year wait to get a county agricultural tax exemption on the three acres. Our children visited and loved the donkeys and all the farm animals.

One day we heard men's voices in the right-of-way dirt lane at the back of our property. The sounds came from near the shut-off valve for our water line. Apparently, these men oversaw the water supply and were fixing a leak. Al went out to meet them. One smiling man introduced himself. His name was Merle. Al immediately recognized him as a brother in the Lord. He even invited us to church and we went, not realizing that Merle would become our Sunday School teacher. And he was a jack of all trades. He and Al soon became bosom buddies.

Merle took an interest in helping us develop and maintain our little ranch. Over the years to come, Merle and Al proved themselves to be a synchronized construction team. If Al conceived a carport and drew it on a napkin, Merle worked up the materials and cost, and *bam!*, we had a beautiful carport. The two of them continued their enthusiasm and expertise to build a tractor barn, hay barn, aquaponics greenhouse, and a storm shelter. He and Al went to auctions and bought a livestock trailer together and shared ownership in cattle.

They interacted with a humor that helped them work through the knotty conundrums that invariably surfaced with every project. Merle loved to rib the Admiral, and I could see that the Admiral loved the attention and knew how to tease him right back. Mostly, they flung jokes about cheating each other, like, "You fed my cow the old hay and gave yours the new batch," which was all the funnier because they each owned a half a cow. Or, "I see you have a new electric drill. It looks just like mine that I left here last week." It was curious to me, because these were two of the most honest, guileless men I knew.

In spite of the community water supply, we endeavored to get our own water well for security sake. Al found a dousing witcher—a man with a huge belly and a forked stick—to walk the property and try to locate sources of underground water. He identified four spots. So we hired a well drilling company that offered a free second drilling if the first attempt came up dry. It was very exciting having the huge, noisy rig throw up white granite dust on our front yard.

We lived on what was known as the Llano Uplift, only sixteen miles north of the famed Enchanted Rock, where one can climb up the exposed granite dome of a sixty-two-square-mile underground batholift. With all that rock in the area, it seemed unlikely to me that we would access water. There were no known aquifers, and any water would have to seep from between layers of rock. Sure enough, four holes were dry. The company put cement plugs in the openings and apologized to Al as he handed them a check for two wells.

The water well saga was not over, however. Six months later, Merle and Al, my hero "can do" team, set out to determine if the drillers were mistaken. One by one, they pulled the plugs then lowered a 200-foot rope weighted down by an iron wrench until it rested on the bottom of the hole. On the first three holes, the recovered wrench was dry. But on the fourth well hole, which was nearest to the dry Flag Creek, they both heard the wrench splash only twenty feet down! Eureka! Water had trickled its way through the rock crevices and collected in the hole. The guys felt victorious. The ranch now had a well to provide water via a solar pump to the livestock drinking tubs. I marveled at the brilliance and skill of these two men. And what faith they had to undertake a grueling, speculative task, especially this one with such a dubious outcome.

The Lodge at Flag Creek

The surprises kept coming. Two big transformational additions to the ranch involved the harnessing of nature's resources. They were the amazing installation of solar power, and then the intricate gutter, pipe, and tank arrangements for rain water collection.

To my delight, Al came up with the idea to build us a Guest Lodge on the southwest corner of the property. He and I sketched an architectural concept on the proverbial napkin over lunch at a booth in the Llano restaurant that kept changing its name. We designed it with three bedrooms and two baths, a large open area to include the kitchen and community rooms, a big covered porch, and a storage shed in back. Of course, Merle was hired to bring it into being.

Merle was known to be a Christian mentor to his workers. When he finished, he proudly announced that there had not been one cigarette smoked, not one can of beer opened, nor one cuss word spoken during the entire construction phase. We were blessed. The final result was a stunning addition to our ranch. The Lodge interior was all lined with horizontal eight-inch pine boards. We outfitted it with beds, furniture, kitchen supplies, artwork and even a TV.

The Lord had given me a vision of a traffic light at the Lodge driveway which would help direct all the traffic that would be coming and going. And we did have a variety of people. The first overnight guests were Al's oldest daughter and husband, their daughter, and her three children, all from Richmond, Virginia. They logged their fun visit in a guest book, which we kept for all the subsequent visitors.

Future guests included family and friends from far and wide. There were such visitors as a distraught mother needing a private week with her wayward teenaged daughter; a couple of Nashville singers in for a gig; a Texas Supreme Court Judge and his family; a woman on a prayerful getaway from her husband; a preacher in town to preach; and the overflow family of some friends who were having a family reunion. In 2013, all three of my children each brought one of their children to stay in the Lodge and help me celebrate my seventieth birthday. In 2014, they came again, and this time brought their spouses and all eight of my grandchildren. The adults stayed in the Lodge and the children slept up the hill with us at our home compound, which they affectionately called "Cousin Town." The highlight of that visit was a climb up the Enchanted Rock.

The Lodge also served as a perfect venue for group studies. Al had been a perennial student of the Bible. He also collected DVDs of Andrew Wommack's Bible teachings. We invited interested Christians to meet at the Lodge to hear these lessons together on a weekly basis. We met as a group for a few years and formed a close bond.

Andrew was the first Bible teacher who pointed out to me and all of us that, when Jesus took our sin on the Cross, He also took our diseases and infirmities. "With His stripes we are healed," it says in Isaiah 53 verse 5 and 1 Peter 2:24. God had already provided through Jesus' death all the things we tended to pray for. All we had to do was believe the Scripture then receive and declare the manifested results. Once we delved into the scripture verses to back this up, it seemed so obvious. I had been busy asking God to do something when He had already done it. My prayers changed from a series of petitions to an outpouring of declarations and gratitude. "Thank You, God, that I am healed, whole, prosperous and blessed. Thank You God that, in Jesus, You have provided this wholeness for everybody."

As we phased out that particular Bible study, Al began sharing his other passion, which was understanding God's plan for biblical end times. He had another large collection of books and DVDs on the subject. He put together an End Times course of study which took seventeen weeks to complete. Again, we invited interested students to come to the Lodge. It was a popular subject because world events were pointing more and more toward the fulfillment of God's prophetic wisdom as revealed in Scripture.

We were a group that wanted knowledge and understanding of our place in the Church Age. Many of us had avoided the last book of the Bible, Revelation. We also glossed over other prophetic writings in such books of the Bible as Isaiah, Ezekiel, Daniel, Matthew, II Peter and II Thessalonians. Whenever I had read them, I considered that all the prophesies were to be the fate of future generations; they were certainly not scenarios pertaining to me. I remembered taking my girls to a scary movie that showed graphic examples of martyrdom. It had turned them and me off from the study of prophecy. The churches Al and I had attended had not taught us to pay attention to these signs, nor that we should be alert and wise to the Second Coming of Jesus.

However, in this collection of prophecy DVDs, teachers like Irvin Baxter and John Ankerberg presented the material with great hope and faith. They helped open my mind to the mystery and understanding of God's big picture. Especially helpful was Tim LaHaye's book "Charting the End Times." We discovered that we may be the generation that experiences what is called the Rapture, or snatching away, where Jesus comes in the clouds to catch us up to heaven to be with Him. The Bible says it (the rapture) happens in the "twinkling of an eye" (1 Corinthians 15:52). We are given a new, glorified body. Even the dead in Christ (like Mom—or Dad?) will be raised from their graves to be with Jesus in heaven.

There are some who believe this catching away will happen before the seven-year period in the Bible that is known as the Tribulation but others interpret that the Rapture will occur either "mid-Trib" or "post-Trib." Al made it clear at the beginning of the study that we each needed to follow what our hearts' understanding of scripture told us. The Holy Spirit would guide us, he said.

The End Times class was sought after, so Al repeated the whole series four times in different venues. We experienced first hand the words of Revelation 1:3, "Blessed is he who reads and those who hear the words of this prophecy."

Al and Cecily at home in Texas.

Fuel Coffee House

E
ven before we had fully unpacked at our new ranch house, I started
going to Fuel Coffee House for morning coffee. Al joined me,
though for a soda, not for coffee. (Years earlier while on active duty in
the Navy, he had developed a sudden allergic reaction to caffeine.) Fuel
Coffee House became our place to meet people in the community.

Whenever one walked into Fuel, more than likely there would be
something different going on; like a knitters group gathering, or a fid-
dlers class in session, or a jazz group playing. On some evenings, there
was live bluegrass or country music being performed on their stage. On
Sunday evenings, free hamburger suppers were offered to anyone. It was
part of Fuel's ministry.

In 2012, Fuel Coffee House almost disappeared. The volunteer couple
who managed the venue announced that they were closing the doors with
lock and key in two weeks. Besides being burnt out, they were not making
it work financially, even with the help of monthly donations by philan-
thropic people. My heart was heavy at the thought of losing Fuel. We had
already become monthly donors. Fuel was my special place for fivesies.

Thankfully, a school teacher named John, who depended on Fuel for
his daily coffee on his way to work, decided to call for an urgent meeting
at Fuel to discuss options for keeping it open. He even offered to pay all
expenses–rent, salaries, supplies, insurance–for two weeks. Al and I were
two of several interested people who showed up. We discussed our levels of
commitment and voted ourselves to be the new Board of Directors and to

accept John's offer. We agreed on the original intent by the founding pastor that Fuel Coffee House should continue to be a Christian-based entity.

Having the recent experience as Board Secretary for the Pregnancy Center in Tomball, I volunteered for that role. I began documenting secretarial minutes at that very first meeting and continued in that role happily for the next four years. Most of the Board members knew each other, and it was natural for them to select a capable man named Shane to be the President. With Shane's leadership, and even his generous financial gift to cover an outstanding debt, we began increasing our income by serving lunch and pastries at a suggested donated price. We set up a kitchen that met food safety standards and hired an experienced cook, Charlotte, to oversee it. In spite of the new Federal administration's bias against awarding non-profit status to new Christian organizations, our Fuel Board pushed through the bureaucratic hurdles, and, with hired help from an agency, we achieved our Non-Profit 501(c)3 legal status. Fuel Coffee House continued to be a way station to weary travelers and locals alike, who sought moments of community interaction or merely a shot of caffeine to keep them going.

For two summers, Al taught an inspirational and challenging class for young students at Fuel. Besides Navy sea stories, he covered a variety of topics, like principles of physics and nuclear power, or thermodynamics, and even how to be obedient to parents. The six-week course was aptly named "Sea Adventures and Knowledge Grabbers With Admiral Al." These classes were recorded and transcribed. They were published as an Appendix to Al's book, "Living the MIRACLES."

One hot day in July of 2014, I sauntered into Fuel and bought an iced coffee. A blonde-haired woman was busily working on the jigsaw puzzle on a table under the stairway. She took a break and sat on the sofa next to me. We started to talk and immediately hit it off. Both of us had experienced divorce and were in fresh start relationships. She was about ten years younger and had lived in Austin before Llano. She shared a short account of her past.

Then I shared some of mine. Shirley was amazed. "Oh, Cecily," she declared. "You should write a book! You've had such a varied, interesting life! I've read hundreds of books, and yours would be something different."

I laughed and told Shirley, "You and many others have said the same thing to me."

How often I had felt shame at my many failed marriages and poor choices. They caused such irregularity along the way. Just like Mrs. Duffy's scarf, my life had holes, dropped stitches, clashing colors, and tight and itchy sections. But then again, when I had offered my knitted work up to her, Mrs. Duffy received it so graciously that it became a thing of beauty, even in my own eyes.

Likewise, Jesus had freely offered me His grace. He received me with all my faults. He loved me unconditionally and healed my pain. He broke through the hard "NO" of my unbelief, showed me His beauty, and gave me direction for my life.

"I tell you what," Shirley started. With enthusiasm, she moved to the edge of the sofa and faced me. I could see she was going to be sincere in whatever was on her mind. Her words spilled out. "I love to hear people's stories. And I love to type." She went on. "How about if we meet at Fuel; you relate your details year by year; we record what you say; and I take the tapes home to transcribe them on my computer?"

I couldn't believe she was for real. I had thought to write about my life even before I met Al. I had stopped at Barnes and Noble and bought "how to" books on my way to live with Mom in White Stone, Virginia. That was in 1997.

"Oh, Shirley, I'd love to do that," I told her.

Over the next four months, we met faithfully twice a week, mostly at Fuel, but sometimes at the Llano Library when Fuel was too loud and busy for our sessions. Shirley was the best audience, asking me questions for clarity, or laughing out loud about scenes like Mr. Floppy Socks with his orange skin from eating only carrots, and about how Dad poked puffed wheat through the Cackleberry window frame to feed my pet chicken. Her interest spurred me on to keep going, even when the going got tough.

413

Al, himself, was always a fan as a reader. My story was not an easy one, especially in certain chapters but I tried to be truthful and fair, and shine the glory of God in all situations. I learned without a doubt that God was always there, even in the period of my life when I didn't know Him.

And, it was God's arrangement for me to become the Admiral's wife.

Epilogue

Thanks to a daughter's coaxing in 2019, Al and I designed and ordered a granite gravestone for our reserved spot at the U.S. Naval Academy Cemetery in Annapolis, Maryland.

"We kids don't know what you want inscribed on it," she had said. "Help us out, Dad, and please get it done." We heeded her good advice.

A monument company was conveniently located in downtown Llano, Texas, where we were living. On the appointed day in May of 2019, which coincided with an upcoming 1,600-mile road trip to a grandson's wedding near Annapolis, the heavy stone was lowered by crane into the bed of our '03 pick up truck.

We stopped at McDonalds for breakfast first thing before the long trip east. The monument's backside inscription showed. A wizened man peeked into the truck to read it. It said:

> KELLN, USNA 1952
> FOUNDER NAVAL SUBMARINE LEAGUE
> FIRST TO FLY OVER, STAND ON, SAIL UNDER
> ICE AT THE NORTH POLE.

On the bottom was an inscribed cross and the words,

> SERVING THE LORD TOGETHER.

When we got to the counter, the cashier announced that our breakfast had been paid for. She pointed to the shaggy man we had seen. We went over to thank him.

"I seen y'all are on a mercy mission," he said through missing teeth. "I wanted to do somethin' t'lighten your burden of sorrow."

"Oh. We're not grieving over anyone," we explained. "This is our own gravestone which we're carrying to our final resting place in Annapolis."

He looked at Al. "Are you da one dat's talked about on the stone—the Navy man who went up to da North Pole?"

"Yes. I am," Al replied. The man reached out his right hand and shook Al's firmly. Then he couldn't stop himself. He gave Al a big old hug. With tears in his eyes, he thanked Al humbly, over and over.

We thanked him again for the breakfast. He told us he was on his way to the hospital for an x-ray of his lungs. My heart was moved and I asked him if I could lay hands of healing prayer on him. He said, "Yes, Ma'am. I'd like dat." I put my hand on his shoulder. I rebuked any disease in his lungs and told it to leave him in Jesus' Name. I spoke healing and health to his body, and peace to his soul, giving thanks to God for His goodness and provision. The man thanked me again and left, saying he felt better about his trip to the hospital.

Four driving days later, we delivered the stone to a monument company in Delaware, the only monument company that had acquired the security clearance needed for working at the Naval Academy Cemetery. The next day, they installed the headstone at our site and we had the satisfaction of seeing it in place. Our mission was accomplished.

The grandson's wedding was lots of fun. Al saw two of his daughters (the third daughter was far off in South Africa), all nine of his grandchildren and his three great-granddaughters. We traveled further to visit Sunshine and her family in Maryland and Anna and her family in Pennsylvania. We also met Bruce at his cute first floor apartment and took him out to his favorite lunch restaurant. On the way back to Texas, we saw a good friend in Ohio and stopped to tour the new life-sized Noah's Ark in Kentucky.

As usual, Al did all the driving. I held my maps and my iPhone with its GPS to guide us home. I looked over at Al and reflected on how we now had a stone marker to prove we had been here on this earth. He was sipping from a can of Diet Dr. Pepper.

"Your next birthday's a big one, Sweetie. Do you feel old?" I asked him.

"No!" he answered quickly. "I'm getting younger. As soon as I get through puberty, I'll be a real stud. After all, I'll only be ninety. The next ten years are going to be even funner."

How I love that man!

About the Author

C ecily Watson Kelln's confessional memoir, *Becoming the Admiral's Wife: A Dual Memoir of a Called Pair*, is her first book.

Cecily graduated from Lake Erie College in Painesville, Ohio, with a B.A. in English Literature. Her short story, "Little Rowboat," won second place in the Juvenile Fiction Category at the Nineteenth Annual Chesapeake Writers' Conference in the year 2000. She is a member of Writers' League of Texas.

Cecily was born and raised in Bryn Mawr, Pennsylvania. She and her husband, Albert Kelln, who contributed some of his own writings in this book, enjoy travel, friends, Bible study, and their little ranch in the Hill County of Texas.

Cecily encourages readers to share the impact of her book by communicating with her. She can be reached by email at:

<u>becomingadmiralswife@gmail.com</u>.

CPSIA information can be obtained
at www.ICGtesting.com
Printed in the USA
BVHW032022181220
595528BV00007B/9